Communities in Conflict

Communities in Conflict

Evangelicals and Jews

David A. Rausch

Trinity Press International   Philadelphia

First published 1991

Trinity Press International
3725 Chestnut Street
Philadelphia, PA 19104

Cover Design: Steven Zellers

Library of Congress Cataloging-in-Publication Data

Rausch, David A.
    Communities in conflict : evangelicals and Jews / by David
A. Rausch.
        p.   cm.
    Includes bibliographical references and index.
    ISBN 1-56338-029-3
    1. Evangleicalism—Relations—Judaism. 2. Judaism—
Relations—Evangelicalism. 3. United States—Religion—1960-
I. Title.
BR1641.J83R38   1991   91-24449
261.2′6—dc20   CIP

DEDICATED TO MY FRIENDS

J. RAY AND CHRISTINE KLINGENSMITH

Contents

PREFACE

I hope that *Communities in Conflict* will provide information and clarification for the average reader and grist for discussion and further research by educators. This book seeks to fill a void in understanding the reactions and interactions of two great traditions vibrantly active on American soil today: evangelicalism and Judaism. The questions being asked are succinct in wording, but much more complicated in exposition. What is the composition and orientation of each group? How do they differ, and what are their similarities? What is the historic interaction of evangelicals and Jews, and what relationship do they maintain today? How do they view one another? What do evangelicals and Jews hold dear? Are there any signs indicating future conflicts between evangelicals and Jews? Is there hope for future cooperation between these peoplehoods?

Because both traditions have fallen victim to stereotype and caricature, *Communities in Conflict* attempts to give the reader an understanding of both of these peoplehoods in the words of their adherents, at some points liberally quoting in context the logic of each proponent when crucial issues require a more detailed understanding. Examples of such format are clearly evident in the evangelical portrayal of Jews in the Sunday school materials overviewed in chapter 2 and in the discussion on mission and witness in chapter 4 (the most verbal and visible conflict between the

Jewish and evangelical communities). Even in these sections, it is the goal of this text to provide a readable account throughout.

A number of individuals have helped to make this text relevant and accessible. Harold Rast, director of Trinity Press International, discerned the importance of this project, working diligently to make it available to the public. Laura Barrett, administrator of Trinity Press International, provided crucial technical assistance. The staff and administrators of the American Jewish Committee opened their files and collections in the early stages of this study, cheerfully providing assistance and constructive criticism at various junctures of research. A Bermann Grant from the AJC provided partial funding toward what became an expensive endeavor and time-consuming process. Faculty and staff at my liberal arts institution, Ashland University, provided encouragement and support at every stage, and I must personally thank President Joseph R. Shultz who has maintained a special interest in my publication efforts.

As a historian who writes extensively about both movements (and who's life is consumed by past and recent documents of each), I have had to convey the facts, anomalies, and conclusions as they have appeared to me. For this, I alone am responsible.

My wish is that this book will provide a balance of perspective, promote understanding and compassion, prioritize dangers that exist, and provoke further study.

1

EVANGELICALS AND JEWS

As our plane lifted off in the early morning sunlight from Ben-Gurion airport for Paris, a young American Jewish woman complained emphatically to the Israeli businessman next to her: "My brother has become so religious that I could not bear to stay with him one more day! He wanted me to stay through Yom Kippur, telling me I shouldn't fly until the Holy Days had come and gone. His family is so observant that they are driving me crazy!" The Israeli businessman replied sympathetically, "I know what you mean," and they proceeded to discuss the problem of being too religious.

I had to smile at their predicament as they discussed relatives and friends who had become too traditional in their religious practice. They related incident after incident, more or less becoming one another's counselor and confidant. The woman was an aspiring investment broker in her latter twenties, and her voice pierced the plane as she became more excited about her brother's newfound religious zeal. Actually, Yom Kippur would not officially begin for another twelve hours, and most of those on the plane had elected to leave Israel before all transportation shut down. I settled back as we climbed smoothly to 30,000 feet, the animated conversation clearly audible against the drone of the jet.

Suddenly the monotonous whine of the engine cut back dramatically, and I sensed we were in trouble. Oxygen masks dropped from the recepticles above the seats as our plane quickly plunged 15,000 feet. Ears popped and pressure built within each head. An infant screamed in pain while the shocked passengers remained strangely quiet. Visibly nervous stewardesses and the steward made certain that each passenger put on their oxygen mask properly, and quite a few of us were convinced that no oxygen was flowing from our masks.

The young Jewish woman cried out: "My brother was right! I should have listened to my brother! We should not be flying on Yom Kippur!" She talked incessantly about this even when the pilot explained that we had mysteriously lost all cabin pressure and the plane had to be taken down to a safe altitude. Although this was the first time a pressure failure had happened to him in thirty-three years of flight time, he was pleased to announce that the backup system was working properly and that we would proceed to Paris. When the pilot came back to assure the passengers and answer their questions, the young woman incredulously informed him that he "was flying on Yom Kippur" and that her brother was correct in his assessment that they should not be flying during the Holy Days.

"Do you know you are flying on Yom Kippur?" she questioned the captain in what appeared to be her newfound religious zeal. "Do you think that is wise? *My brother* says we should not be flying today."

"I certainly do know it," he bantered back. "Why do you think I am getting out of Israel—just in time!" The captain took her to the back of the plane to talk while his copilot (I assume) flew the jet. The Israeli businessman was in extreme pain from a migraine headache he had developed during the change in pressure, and the stewardess attempted to help him with capsules and cold packs.

After the vibrant Jewish investment broker returned to her seat, she assured me that she was going to call her brother as soon as she arrived home to tell him that he was right. When she discovered that I was a historian, she asked, "What is all of this business about the Third Death?" I had no idea what she was talking about, but she explained that the captain of the plane had been telling her about prophecy and something about the Third Death before the return of the Messiah. "Are you sure he did not say Third Temple?"

I asked. "Yes...yes...that was it...the Third Temple!" she confirmed. I was amazed. The captain of our plane had discussed with this young Jewish woman the rebuilding of the Third Temple before the coming Armageddon and the appearance of the Messiah. His explanation seemed to convey some of the elements of fundamentalist-evangelical prophetic interpretation, although he did not appear to be particularly religious himself. Such explanation was a foreign world to the young woman who just had had a momentous "religious" encounter and, at least for the moment, had developed a newfound respect for her brother's traditional Jewish faith. The captain probably never suspected that she did not comprehend much of what he was saying. She ducked him for the rest of the flight, although he came back once again trying to find her.

In my mind, this incident underscores how historical circumstance, religious background, and human personality interact to produce individual religious attitudes and responses. When one views the complex factors that encompass *one* religious life and multiply them by millions to portray a religious movement, such as Judaism or evangelicalism, the potential diversity within a religion is mind-boggling.

ANALYZING ATTITUDES

Ironically, most evangelicals view the Jewish community as monolithic in belief and practice, while most Jews view all fundamentalists and evangelicals as basically the same. Both the evangelical and Jewish movements, however, are diverse in their individual makeup and, as this study will show, both movements today face a crisis of identity and self-definition. To the outside observer these two groups, in every single viable position, should be in conflict and collision; yet there is less friction than one would reasonably imagine. In fact, although communication between evangelicals and Jews has historically been strained, friendships between individual members of each movement have occurred and are occurring. Evangelicals and Jews are increasingly coming into encounters in politics, domestic policy, and foreign policy that necessitate a clearer understanding of one another. This study intends to analyze the positions of each movement and attitudes of each toward the other in an effort to facilitate that development. As will be shown, current evangelical and Jewish attitudes toward one another trace back at least to the nineteenth century. Modern conflicts and concerns, such as Bible reading and prayer in public schools, "fanaticism," missionary activity and revivalism ("evangelism"), and issues concerning a "Christian state" are deeply embedded in the past and can give insight into the current struggles. This study will show that evangelicalism's most dangerous stereotypes and caricatures of Jews and Judaism lie in the theological sphere—the constant denigration of Pharisees and misunderstanding of Judaism. Jewish stereotypes and caricatures abound in the belief that evangelicals are (or tend to be) anti-Semitic, that evangelicals are a threat to democracy, that evangelicals want to force their beliefs, and that evangelicals are lurking around every corner to convert Jews.

This study will also confirm that, in the areas of "conservativism" and "liberalism," the evangelical and Jewish communities generally differ. For the most part, evangelicals view themselves as moderates or conservatives. In contrast, Jews often prefer to characterize themselves as "liberals" or liberally oriented. To most Jews, liberalism in political, economic, and social issues is the key to what it means to be a Jew. Even Orthodox Jews view Jewish values as basically liberal values, and although their views on some issues are decidedly more conservative than their non-Orthodox brethren, Orthodox Jews identify with Democrats and liberals about as much as the non-Orthodox do. No significant change in these labels and identifications is foreseen either on the political or the social scene.

While becoming more politically astute, the broad evangelical movement continues to be plagued by right-wing opportunists. As shall be seen, the small but growing Christian reconstructionist organizations with their "dominion" theology should be a concern for evangelicals and Jews alike. The "Christian state" mentality, while opposed by the large majority of evangelicals, is still too tempting an alternative for naive and uninformed Christians. The evangelical movement must draw strength for the current era from its historic social concern in the nineteenth century. This study will also seek to explain that some evangelical positions are directly related to the historic Christian faith and that this complex movement must be understood within the Christian context.

Complicating Jewish-evangelical relationships is the fact that the large majority of Jews do not trust "conservatives." No group has been more loyal to the Democratic Party for more than half a century than the Jewish community. The shift of Jewish votes from the Republican to the Democratic Party began during the presidential candidancy of the Catholic Democrat, Alfred E. Smith, in 1928. Jews decisively shifted their allegiance during the subsequent candidacy of Franklin Delano Roosevelt in 1932. While F.D.R. received approximately 58 percent of the popular vote, Jewish voters gave him a phenomenal 86 percent average. By 1966, George Gallup's polls revealed that only 25 percent of American Jews voted Republican in contrast to 55 percent of American Protestants. In spite of resounding Republican presidential victories in the last three elections (1980, 1984, 1988), Jews have consistently backed the Democratic candidate by approximately a two to three margin. As a group they have defied the national average by landslide proportions.

Although some Jewish neoconservatives had maintained during the 1988 campaign that the Democratic Party was not conducive to Jewish needs, self-interests, social status, attitudes, etc., and that election day would "inaugurate a new political era for Jews in the United States,"[1] the loyalty continued. The Jewish support for the more liberal candidate, Michael Dukakis, over the more conservative candidate, George Bush, was indicated by every poll.[2] Once again, the Jewish community's vote for president was out of step with the rest of the nation.

Steven M. Cohen's *The Political Attitudes of American Jews, 1988: A National Survey in Comparative Perspective* insisted that Jews had interests and values that determined their presidential vote—interests and values that did not depend on economic position and self-interest alone. "In the most simple of terms," Dr. Cohen wrote, "the principal reason underlying Jews' Democratic allegiance is that they remain politically liberal, or more precisely, more liberal

and less conservative than the rest of America." Cohen perceptively realized, however, that the term "liberal," like the term
"conservative," was vague and imprecise.

Among Professor Cohen's major findings were few surprises.
Statistics showed that compared with non-Jewish whites, a higher
proportion of Jews identify as liberals and fewer identify as conservatives. His survey showed that while most Americans were
about equally divided between Democrats and Republicans, in the
Jewish community only one in four identified themselves as a
Republican. More than white gentiles, Jews had positive impressions of political agencies associated with the liberal camp and
were supportive of social spending as well as cuts in the defense
budget. Cohen's study found that Jews oppose prayer in schools
and the display of religious symbols on public property far more
than other Americans, white or black. Jewish respondents to his
survey, however, were more anxious about American anti-
Semitism than were those in previous surveys of American Jews
conducted from 1983 to 1986.[3]

Israel

Jews and evangelicals appear to have more in common when it
comes to support of the state of Israel. Since the nineteenth century,
the fundamentalist-evangelical movement's penchant for
prophecy and biblical literalism has led it to support the right of
the Jewish people to have their own state in Eretz Yisrael. Early
members of this movement included Christian Zionist William E.
Blackstone, whose Blackstone Memorial of 1891 urged the president of the United States, Benjamin Harrison, to give Palestine back
to the Jews. A fundamentalist-evangelical to the core, Blackstone
never abandoned the fight for a Jewish state. He presented a similar
petition to President Woodrow Wilson in 1918 and addressed
Zionist conferences as well as Christian audiences in the early
twentieth century on the importance of a Jewish state in Palestine
and the right of the Jewish people to have their ancient homeland
back.

In fact, the view that God promised to return his "chosen
people" to the land and that Jesus would return someday and

reveal himself to his Jewish people in that very land, is a key component of the premillennial eschatology. As our study will show, this fundamentalist-evangelical view of the future permeated evangelicalism during the twentieth century, and important modern figures within the movement—from the moderate Billy Graham to the right-wing Jerry Falwell—hold to its tenets. Furthermore, there is a strong parallel movement within evangelicalism that insists that God's biblical promises to the Jewish people are not usurped by the Christian church and that God has a continuing relationship with his chosen people, the Jews. Surprisingly, these movements have sought to counter much of Christendom's historic triumphalism, a triumphalism that inferred that there was no future for the Jewish people and that the biblical promises were now being fulfilled in the church.

Jews and other Christians often have not understood such "premillennial" prophetic analyses and have been skeptical and critical of the motives behind them. Increasingly attacked by evangelical academics and missionary movements, the premillennial prophetic view of the future and its dominance within such organizations as the National Association of Evangelicals has begun to slip. While support for Israel continues to remain strong among the grassroots evangelical movement, a change of eschatology (view of the future) within evangelicalism could signal a radical reevaluation in the next few decades. The penchant of most evangelicals to listen to the Jewish side first would be decisively compromised.

Evangelical support for Israel and the theological base of such a view was clearly evident in the Nationwide Attitudes Survey of evangelicals conducted for the Anti-Defamation League of B'nai B'rith in September 1986. Over 56 percent of the evangelicals surveyed in that study had favorable views of Israel; only 10 percent reported unfavorable views. "Much of the positive sentiment toward Israel is apparently based on the country's religious connection to Christianity," the researchers reported. "Negative attitudes appear to be based mostly on secular factors, rather than religiously-based views."[4] That the survey included a large percentage of mainline Protestant evangelicals who were part of organizations that opposed Israel, or denominations that had little official regard for Israel or the fundamentalist-evangelical prophetic interpretation, only underscores the depth of evangelical support for Israel.

If supporters for the Jewish state among evangelicals had to combat a triumphalistic Christianity in the latter decades of the nineteenth century, American Jews certainly faced a similar, formidable opposition in their own religious tradition. At the Pittsburgh Conference of American Rabbis in 1885, the Union of American Hebrew Congregations (founded in 1873 by Rabbi Isaac Mayer Wise) adopted an eight-point program that would guide Reform Judaism for the next half century. Article 5 of the Pittsburgh Platform of 1885 read: "We are no longer a nation, but a 'religious community,' and we no longer expect to return to Palestine or a Jewish state or offer sacrifices in a Temple." *The American Israelite* consistently ridiculed Jewish Zionists as well as the growing Christian Zionist movement. This national periodical, for example, declared in its September 10, 1891 issue that "national enthusiasm among Jews is merely romantic without any practical idea at the bottom." And in a following issue, Rabbi Isaac M. Wise mocked the great Orthodox Zionist leader, Dr. H. Pereira Mendes.[5]

Rabbi Emil G. Hirsh shocked Rev. William E. Blackstone in 1890 by asserting for himself and his colleagues: "We modern Jews do not wish to be restored to Palestine...the country wherein we live is our Palestine...We will not go back...to form again a nationality of our own." In spite of these words, the fundamentalist-evangelical Blackstone continued with his Zionist efforts. Even during the Holocaust, the academics, rabbis, socialites, businesspersons, and media and political personalities of the American Council for Judaism spread anti-Zionism throughout the Jewish and Christian world with great effect, and the influence of this organization and its offshoots was felt long after Israel had become a nation. When Golda Meir (Meyerson) came to the United States to raise funds for arms at the end of January 1948, the executive director of the United Jewish Appeal, Henry Montor, told her that there was no need for her to travel to the Council of Jewish Federations meeting in

Chicago because this council of the leaders of organized Jewry in the United States was anti-Zionist.

Yet American Jewish support for Israel increased and strengthened even more phenomenally than the evangelical support for Israel that had blossomed during the twentieth century. In Steven Cohen's *Ties and Tensions: The 1986 Survey of American Jewish Attitudes Toward Israel and Israelis,* the American Jewish community's ongoing passionate commitment to Israel was demonstrated, with large numbers proclaiming deep sentimental attachment to Israel and a concern for Israel's survival. Ironically, Cohen found that "most American Jews displayed a surprising ignorance about the fundamentals of Israeli society and politics." This study concluded that "the actions of Israel and its policymakers can play a crucial role in deepening or diminishing the attachment and involvement of specific elements of American Jewry with the Jewish state."[6] In Cohen's national survey on *The Political Attitudes of American Jews, 1988,* 76 percent of the Jews surveyed asserted that "caring about Israel is a very important part of my being a Jew." Only 15 percent disagreed with this statement, while 9 percent were not sure.

DEFINING COMMUNITIES

Both Jews and evangelicals are extremely diverse groups of people. Nevertheless, their definitions of what constitutes a member of their persuasion helps one to understand the differing perspectives that often separate Jews and evangelicals. In answering the question, What is a Jew? Jews often emphasize the concepts of birth, community, and peoplehood. When answering the question, What is an evangelical? evangelicals often emphasize personal conversion, faith, and doctrinal beliefs. Chapter 3, "Perspectives: Two Different Worlds," will deal in greater depth with the issues surrounding these differences and how interaction between Jews and evangelicals is affected by these factors and a number of others. Nevertheless, it is constructive to understand at the outset how Jews and evangelicals define themselves.

Jews and Judaism

"In truth, even Jews themselves have difficulty agreeing on the question of who is a Jew and how to define Jewishness," Rabbi Yechiel Eckstein explained to Christians with evangelical inclinations in *What Christians Should Know About Jews and Judaism.* "Judaism comprises more than the sum total of its parts," he asserted. "Indeed, the ties that bond Jews throughout the world are intangible, transcending their bonds of faith."[7] Because Rabbi Eckstein is one of the few Orthodox rabbis working in the area of Jewish-evangelical dialogue, his analysis of how complicated it is for the average Jewish person to define "a Jew" is revealing.

Halakhah (literally "the way one goes") is the collected legal rulings of the scribes who clarified and amplified the written Torah so that its precepts could be fully lived out by Jews. More than rules of conduct, halakhah can be described as the traditional "Jewish way of life." In halakhah a child born of a Jewish mother or a convert to the Jewish faith is considered a Jew. If a child is born into a family in which one parent is a Jew and the other is a gentile, the Talmud states that the status of the child follows the status of the mother.[8] In traditional Jewish thought, one who is born of Jewish parents or one who is a convert to Judaism becomes a part of the "holy nation" and the "kingdom of priests" described in such biblical passages as Exodus 19:6. This chosenness carried the obligation to obey God's commandments and to live responsibly upon the earth. Thus the bonds of heritage and responsibility linked Jews of diverse backgrounds into a worldwide peoplehood even in traditional definition.

The teaching has existed in some Jewish circles that all Jewish souls (including those living now and those to be born in the future) were present when the Torah was given at Sinai. In his recent book, *Where Are We?: The Inner Life of America's Jews,* Leonard Fein (who is not a traditional Jew) tells the story of a young friend of his who, while wandering the port area of Haifa smiled genially at a hasid walking toward him "in full hasidic regalia." As the traditional and non-traditional Jews met, the hasid squinted and asked, "Do I know you?" "Yes, of course," Fein's friend responded, "We met at Sinai." The hasid slapped his forehead and exclaimed,

"Oh dear, you must forgive me. It was so hot and crowded that day. How have you been?" To nontraditional Leonard Fein, this sense of faithfulness to community and the responsibility to humankind that accompanies such exercise of Jewish community is much more important to Jewish definition than faith itself. "Now, the question of whether or not there was a revelation at Sinai seems to me considerably less important than the question of whether or not I was there," Fein wrote about the Haifa incident. "The first question requires of me a faith I do not have, cannot invent, and regard (perhaps for that reason) as irrelevant; the second requires of me a faithfulness that is mine to offer."[9]

To many Jewish interpreters of the past and the present it is the exercise of community that helps a Jew to know what community is. Conversely, without community, a Jew cannot truly know holiness. Even Rabbi Eckstein continued to explain to his evangelical readers that "despite their many ethnic, cultural, religious, racial (there are black Jews, too), and socio-economic differences, Jews are one organic unit, linked together by their mutual faith, heritage, and responsibility to serve as their brothers' keepers." "Just as the domains of the sacred and the profane are inextricably intertwined in Judaism," the Orthodox rabbi told evangelicals, "so the secular Jew who acts on behalf of Jewish causes actually engages in the religious act of sanctifying life." "As difficult as it may be for Christians to comprehend (and for many Jews to accept)," Rabbi Yechiel Eckstein concluded, "a Jew can be deeply devoted to his Jewishness while actually being devoid of any religious faith."[10]

Three centuries earlier, the Jewish community of Baruch Spinoza (1632-1677) was not so charitable. In the case of this Dutch philosopher, the question arose, What if a child is Jewish (even by talmudic standards) and is secularist in both belief and practice? His community concluded that he could be "cut off from the nation of Israel." Born in Amsterdam to Sephardi parents, Spinoza had begun to question whether Adam was the first man, debated whether Moses wrote the Pentateuch, and argued that natural law took precedence over Torah.

In later writings he would replace religious tradition completely with rationalism and scientific reasoning. For Spinoza there was no possibility of prophecy or miracles; the Bible was neither mysterious nor divine. God is nature, nature is God, with no purpose or goals for humankind. By that time Spinoza had been excommunicated by leaders of his Jewish community who had tried to dissuade him from his "evil ways." The rabbinical pronouncement declared on July 27, 1656, that all the evidence "having been examined in the presence of the rabbis, the council decided, with the advice of the rabbis, that the said [Baruch de] Spinoza should be excommunicated and cut off from the nation of Israel." Spinoza was twenty-four years of age.

In a conference on secularism and pluralism sponsored by the Spinoza Institute in Israel in 1987, scholars debated the possibility of a secular Judaism. Some Jewish scholars believed that Judaism that called itself "secular" was in trouble, often replaced with decadence and anarchy. Others explained that secularism original-ly penetrated Judaism as a foreign influence and was intrinsically linked with assimilation. Nonetheless, fears were expressed by a number of Jewish scholars that Orthodoxy led to a "barbaric" exclusive form of Judaism, contrary to a pluralistic Jewish state.

Under a portrait of Baruch Spinoza, Professor Yirmiyahu Yovei gave the closing remarks to the participants and audience. He declared:

> Secularism is a value system competitive to religion. It's neither nihilistic nor transcendental. It is superior to religion and harder to live by, because it insists on individual responsibility. Spinoza tried to be secular and to stay a Jew. He wasn't allowed to do it. But times have changed. I and we can do it. We must struggle to keep the possibility alive for ourselves and others.

Professor Yovei made it evident to all involved that the secularist Jew had no intention of going away.

Today few Jews consider themselves purely secularist, "non-believers," or "non-Jewish Jews." In the 1960s it was not uncommon for Jewish young people in college to claim to be "agnostics," but there has been considerable return to Jewish prac-tice and belief since that turbulent decade. Only a small percentage of Jews would describe themselves as atheists (deniers of God) or would even question the existence of God. For example, more than 80 percent of American Jews define themselves in religious terms or as a part of a religious movement. Yet Judaism as a "way of life," the importance of mitzvot, and the sanctifying nature of participation in Jewish causes and organizations further complicate the issue of definition for the present-day Jewish community. In Judaism, the concept of activism is basic. Furthermore, the diversity of belief and practice within established American Jewish movements leads to a variety of definitions about what characterizes a "good Jew."

In *The Chosen People in America: A Study in Jewish Religious Ideology*, Arnold M. Eisen declared at the outset that "chosenness, the traditional vehicle for self-definition among Jews, became in America the single concept most often 'blurred' and denied 'real referents.'" Although central, Eisen viewed chosenness as historically an "unformulated dogma" related to the concepts of covenant and exile in guiding Jewish self-understanding. "Chosenness marks the point at which the three lines of relation which define Jews—those binding them to God, to their fellowmen, and to each other—of necessity intersect," Professor Eisen wrote. He reminded his readers that the views of rabbis and theologians "are not representative of American Jewry as a whole." Nevertheless, the Columbia University professor concluded that "chosenness 'succeeded' when other ideas 'failed' because it possessed both coherence and relevance to American Jews."[11]

In an analysis of the 1988 national survey, Steven Cohen pointed out that "the Jewish religion is less important to (Jews) than Christianity is to American Christians." His survey showed that almost one-half of the non-Jews polled declared that religion was "very important" in their own lives, while only one-quarter of the Jews polled made a similar claim. Weekly churchgoers were three times more frequent than weekly synagoguegoers. The survey showed that most Jews only attended synagogue four times a year or less. Yet "being Jewish" was very important to the same Jewish sampling. When asked about the importance of "being Jewish...in your own life," almost half of the Jews surveyed declared that being

Jewish was "very important" to them—twice as many as those who were willing to say that religion was "very important" to them. Forty-two percent of the Jews polled answered that they felt "very close" to other Jews, and an additional 47 percent answered that they felt "fairly close" to other Jews. "We can interpret these results very broadly (and loosely)," Professor Cohen wrote, "to suggest that, for many, Jewishness takes precedence over Judaism." He also interpreted:

> Being Jewish embraces not only (and not always) commitment to a Jewish faith, but involvement with the Jewish group. The peoplehood and the religious dimensions reinforce one another. But many Jews sustain a commitment to peoplehood without an equally high commitment to religious faith (assuming, of course, that one can speak fruitfully of such comparisons).[12]

"Religion, in a sense, occupies a smaller segment of Jewish identity than it does of Christian identity," Cohen concluded.

The 1988 survey also revealed that 81 percent of the Jewish community believed in God, 66 percent believed that God gave the Torah to the Jewish people at Mount Sinai (only 11 percent disagreed while 23 percent were not sure), and 79 percent attended a Passover Seder that year. Of the Jews polled, however, 69 percent disagreed with the statement—"The Exodus from Egypt and the giving of the Torah to the Jewish people mean more to me as a Jew than do the Holocaust and the founding of the state of Israel." Only 14 percent agreed with this statement.[13]

Crisis of Identity with Judaism

A crisis of identity faces American Jews today, and a debate is ensuing about Judaism, Jewish values, and Jewish institutions in the face of assimilation, intermarriage, and the attempt to expunge the sacred from public institutions and personal practice. Even the television producer Norman Lear—a self-styled civil libertarian, a firm believer in the separation of church and state, a man who helped to found People for the American Way in 1980, and a vociferous opponent of the conservative religious right—has voiced concern that "the aversion toward discussing moral values, let alone religion, can reach absurd extremes."

In November 1989, a chagrined Lear addressed the American Academy of Religion in Anaheim, California, shocking most of the scholars present by declaring that he had "parted company" with those who are so secularist that they "would purge any reference to God or religion from the public schools." "While we civil libertarians have been triumphant in most of our legal and constitutional battles," Lear asserted, "I am troubled that so many of us remain blocked or blind to the spiritual emptiness in our culture which the televangelists exploited so successfully." Although opposing prayers in public schools and textbooks that conform to creationist theology, Norman Lear credited "the rank and file of the religious right for helping to focus a spotlight on the spiritual yearnings of our people." He suggested that schools teach about the role of religion in history and "nurture spiritual imagination." He also criticized textbooks that had removed references to religion in an effort to avoid offending anyone and discredited a high school guidance counselor who refused to tell students whether they would be morally obliged to return a wallet with one thousand dollars in it because "he didn't want to impose his values on his students."

The same month Norman Lear spoke to the Academy, the president of a small Reform synagogue pleaded in the Temple newsletter with his fellow Jews for help in maintaining their synagogue. His letter conveys the exasperation felt by many modern Jewish leaders. "A short while ago I was asked, Why does a small group within the congregation work so hard to try and revive interest in the Temple, when the majority of our congregation is apathetic?" He noted that their Reform Temple was "not unique in its declining attendance" and that "this malaise has invaded most Temples." "But why?" he questioned. "What are we doing wrong? Everyone has a pearl of wisdom, but none offer a panacea."

"There has to be a better reason why people stay away than that we are a more affluent society than were our parents," the distraught congregational president wrote. "I can't accept that explanation. There are too many highly educated and intelligent people in the world, our world, who see a value in believing." "Do we need 'Born-again Jews'?" he asked. "I certainly hope not. To me, if I understand correctly such people, and I certainly do not want to offend that American phenomenon, they tend to overreact and have little patience or understanding of those who are still searching." In desperation, then, this president turned his column over to those who received the monthly mailing in the hope that they might offer some explanation as to why they had stopped attending, what they were looking for in a Temple, what they were looking for in a religion, and what could be done to persuade them actively to participate.

Both Norman Lear and the Reform Temple president have acknowledged concerns that are increasingly coming to the forefront of Jewish thinking today. Since 1985, the Wexner Heritage Foundation has handpicked scores of highly intelligent and successful Jewish men and women in a number of cities in the United States to cultivate a new generation of young Jewish lay leadership steeped in Jewish values and cognizant of Judaism, its history and culture. Dennis Prager has addressed these groups (largely made up of young adults who are Jewish but uncommitted to Judaism) on "Why I Am A Jew: The Case For A Religious Life." His edited remarks, drawn from a transcript of his lecture and dialogue with the pilot group, place a new emphasis on cultivating Judaism in the young. "I want you to see life through Judaism's eyes," he began in an introduction to the group, explaining "that is what Judaism is about. It is not an ethnic society, it is not a cultural club. It is a way of looking at, and of course living, life. It is not Christian, and it is not humanist, though it is in fact closer to Christianity than to the secular humanism that most Jews hold."

Prager insisted that "Judaism is its own way of looking at the world" and declared that "if Judaism doesn't have a different and unique way of approaching life, then I submit to you there really is no very good reason for us to continue—certainly not after the Holocaust." In Prager's estimation, most Jews fifty-five years and older have a Jewish identity that "is overwhelmingly ethnic," and few in this age group have wrestled with the soul searching question, Why am I a Jew? "To most Jews of our parent's generation," Prager explained, "the question is as meaningless as an American asking Why am I an American?"[14] Born and raised in a Jewish world, from an early age expecting to remain Jewish and to marry a Jew, such parents are utterly confused when their child intermarries.

In a detailed three-point lecture and discussion, Dennis Prager underscored to the young Jewish lawyers, businesspersons, social workers, and doctors that the Jewish people have a mission, that people are not naturally good, and that Judaism makes people better. "I am a Jew first and foremost because I believe the Jewish people has a unique and God-given role to play in this world," Prager noted of the mission. "This mission, which will unfortunately not only come as news to you, but will actually oppose many of the beliefs you now hold, is to bring the world to ethical monotheism." He elaborated:

> Ethical monotheism is the doctrine that there is one God, that He is therefore the God of all people, and that God's primary demand upon people is that they live ethical (kind, good, just) lives. It sounds simple, but it is the most radical idea in human history, and it is the ultimate cause of the greatest hatred in history, antisemitism.
>
> Ethical monotheism means that we Jews should be announcing the following to the world. To the religious world we must incessantly repeat that any belief in God that does not teach that God's primary demand is that we treat our fellow human beings properly, will lead to evil....On the other hand, we Jews should also be incessantly repeating to the secular world that just as God without ethics leads to evil, ethics that eliminate God as their basis will also lead to evil. And it is in this aspect of ethical monotheism that Jews overwhelmingly fail.[15]

"Not only do most Jews not declare this to the world," Prager proclaimed, "most Jews actually believe in the opposite. Most Jews really believe that God is not necessary to ethics." Dennis Prager then elaborated on the concept of God, later asserting that ethics without religion are flowers without soil.[16]

To Dennis Prager, Judaism is important to his identity and to his definition of community—an essential ingredient to his being a Jew. After an extended treatment of the three points, he apologized to the readers of the *Ultimate Issues* transcripts that he had "included little about how much I simply love Judaism, how it serves as such a source of strength to me in times of crisis, how it provides the sense of community and belonging for which Judaism is uniquely known." He related in closing: "I have not spoken of the meaning of the resurrection of the Jewish state after almost two thousand years of Jewish exile, of the joy—the instant intimacy—that I have experienced with fellow Jews in Morocco, the Soviet Union, and elsewhere throughout the world." He hoped to elaborate on these personal aspects later, and welcomed reactions, questions, disagreements.

That Dennis Prager received "fan letters" from both Norman Lamm, the Orthodox president of Yeshiva University in New York City, and from Jakob J. Petuchowski, one of the great Reform rabbinic professors of Hebrew Union College-Jewish Institute of Religion in Cincinnati, indicates that he was touching a broad nerve center within contemporary American Judaism. Rabbi Petuchowski wrote: "On the air, in printed form, and on the lecture circuit, I have found new grounds for optimism regarding the Jewish future in America. For too long and by too many rabbis has Judaism been confused with humanistic secularism. How refreshing, therefore, to find you making the case for authentic religious Judaism!"[17]

Evangelical Beliefs

The word "evangelical" is derived from the Greek noun *euangelion*, originally meaning "a reward for good news," but later interpreted as "glad tidings" or "good news." In the Christian Testament, *euangelion* was directly related to Jesus Christ and came to refer specifically to God's "good news," the gospel. Thus Matthew 4:23 states that "Jesus went throughout Galilee, teaching in their synagogues, preaching the gospel (*euangelion*, "good news") of the kingdom, and healing every disease and sickness among the people."

In Romans 1:1, the great Christian missionary, Paul, asserts that he was "called to be an apostle and set apart for the gospel (*euangelion*, "good news") of God." In 1 Corinthians 15:1, Paul notes: "Now, brothers, I want to remind you of the gospel (*euangelion*) I preached to you, which you received and on which you have taken your stand." Verses 3 and 4 of this chapter became a central message of the early Christian church, that is, "that Christ died for our sins according to the Scriptures, that he was buried, that he was raised on the third day according to the Scriptures." The word *euangelion* appears in nearly every book of the Christian Testament, almost one hundred times, and from the Latin *evangelium* passed into modern languages. These early Christian emphases on personal conversion, doctrinal beliefs, and devotion to the Bible remain central to modern evangelicalism. They circumscribe the definitions that most evangelicals apply to themselves and to their community.

This is not to imply, however, that the evangelical community is monolithic in its composition. When Wheaton College Professor Robert E. Webber wrote *Common Roots: A Call To Evangelical Maturity* (1978), he divided evangelicalism into fourteen "subcultures," including fundamentalist evangelicalism, dispensational evangelicalism, conservative evangelicalism, nondenominational evangelicalism, reformed evangelicalism, Anabaptist evangelicalism, Wesleyan evangelicalism, holiness evangelicalism, pentecostal evangelicalism, charismatic evangelicalism, black evangelicalism, progressive evangelicalism, radical evangelicalism, and mainline evangelicalism. While many evangelicals would disagree with his divisions (even he admitted that "it certainly does not tell the whole story"),[18] Dr. Webber's analysis underscores the diversity and complexity within contemporary evangelicalism.

Bernard L. Ramm certainly agrees. While serving as evangelical professor of theology at the American Baptist Seminary of the West in Berkeley, California, Dr. Ramm wrote *The Evangelical Heritage* (1973), a book that is quoted or cited in nearly every book on the contemporary evangelical movement. Ramm explained that it "is impossible to give one, neat, precise definition of an evangelical," but that "evangelical Christianity refers to that version of Christianity which places the priority of the Word and Act of God over the faith, responses, or experiences of men." He contrasted this with liberalism, modernism, and other nonevangelical theologies in which "religion is primarily the religious experiences of man or

the religious potential of man or the religious a priori in man."
The use of the term evangelical will then be flexible. It will include
the obscurantistic fundamentalist and the learned Lutheran or
Reformed confessional theologian. It includes the Pentecostals who,
in spite of their emphasis on experience to the neglect of theology
and biblical interpretation, nevertheless hold to the historic
doctrines of the church. It also includes a person who might bear a
vague title as an evangelical neoorthodox.[19]

For the evangelical, the supremacy and authority of the Word of
God overrides all human philosophies or religions. God's truth
transcends all faith and experience.

Kenneth S. Kantzer, professor at Trinity Evangelical Divinity
School and former editor of *Christianity Today*, points out that for
evangelicals the "watershed" and first great unifying factor is the
authority of the Bible. This first factor is wed to the second unifying
factor of modern evangelicalism, the gospel, "the good news of
how man can be rightly related to God." To Dr. Kantzer, the virgin
birth of Jesus Christ, the death of Christ on the cross, the bodily
resurrection of a crucified Jesus, and the second coming of Jesus to
the earth at the end of the age summarize a "logical arrangement"
of twelve fundamentals of evangelicalism. In his essay, "Unity and
Diversity in Evangelical Faith," Kantzer claims that "no true evangelical would admit for a moment that anyone who clearly denied
any one of the above is evangelical in the full sense of the word."[20]

Evangelical historian, George Marsden, for many years a professor at Calvin College and recently appointed to the faculty at Duke
University, grappled with the complexity of the evangelical movement in *Evangelicalism and Modern America* (1984), a book he edited.
In an introductory essay, "The Evangelical Denomination," Dr.
Marsden admits that "the greatest conceptual challenge in a discussion of this sort is to say what evangelicalism is." He postulates
that in some ways evangelicalism is "a kind of denomination," not
as an organized religious structure, but as a religious grouping.
Borrowing an illustration from evangelical historian Timothy
Smith of Johns Hopkins University, whose students have been
doing a major study on this subject, Marsden notes that evangelicalism is a mosaic or a kaleidoscope. He asserts that most of

evangelicalism's parts "are not only disconnected, they are strikingly diverse." Yet Marsden believes that one may properly speak of evangelicalism as a denomination or single phenomenon because "today among Protestants the lines between evangelical and nonevangelical often seem more significant than do traditional denominational distinctions."[21]

Marsden emphasizes the "conceptual unity" of evangelicalism, underscoring evangelical belief in the Reformation doctrine of the final authority of Scripture, in the real historical character of God's saving work recorded in Scripture, in eternal salvation only through personal trust in Jesus Christ, and in the importance of a spiritually transformed life. These, of course, have been underscored by all of the other leaders we have quoted. But the Duke University historian also declares that "for many, evangelicalism is a *community.*" He explains:

> In this respect evangelicalism is most like a denomination. It is a religious fellowship or coalition of which people feel a part. This sense of an informed evangelical community or coalition goes back to the international Pietism of the eighteenth century. Common zeal for spreading the gospel transcended party lines. By the first half of the nineteenth century this movement had assumed something like its present shape. Evangelicalism in this more specific sense is essentially a transdenominational assemblage of independent agencies and their supporters, plus some denominationally sponsored seminaries and colleges which support such parachurch institutions.[22]

For Dr. Marsden, the decisive factor in this usage is "a degree of transdenominational orientation." This separates the "card-carrying" evangelicals from those who channel their religious outlook through the programs of their particular denomination, that is, Southern Baptists, Missouri Synod Lutherans, Wesleyan Methodists, etc. In addition, he admits that defining evangelicalism as a community is a "narrow" definition (in contrast to what we have seen in the general Jewish perception of community and peoplehood). The broader communal usage would be to view evangelicalism as a dynamic movement with common historical experiences, common tendencies, a basic identity, values, and cultural experience.

Crisis of Identity in Evangelicalism

George Marsden recognized the "crisis of identity" which faced the evangelical movement in the 1980s. Perhaps the "card-carrying" evangelical statesman, Carl F.H. Henry—a former editor of *Christianity Today*, an early supporter of the National Association of Evangelicals, a founding member of The Evangelical Theological Society, a seminary professor, writer, and in his seventies lecturer-at-large for World Vision International (an organization started by evangelicals in 1947 to foster childcare, social ministry, medical missions, and relief in the Third World)—is indicative of this struggle. By the early 1970s, the religion editor of United Press International singled out Henry as "probably the most noted evangelical theologian in the United States," and Henry's *A Plea For Evangelical Demonstration* was published in 1971. Early in the preface of that book, Carl Henry maintained:

> If Bible-believing Christians can wade against the secular stream by mass evangelistic crusades aimed to rescue otherwise doomed sinners, they can summon enough courage and concern in public—at least, I am convinced they can, and will, if fully aroused to the urgency of these times—to stand against the culture in majestic witness to the holy commandments of God.[23]

"The evangelical community has carried the burden for evangelism," Henry observed, "more surely than it has carried the burden for social justice." While recognizing that much evangelistic work "remains to be done" and pleading for "a widening and deepening of evangelistic commitments," Henry emphasized that "continuing neglect of the evangelical social witness will be a tragic and costly mistake."

Fifteen years later in *Confessions of a Theologian* (1986), his autobiography, Carl Henry lamented the inroads that secular culture, materialism, and liberalism had made into the evangelical community. He insisted that nonevangelicals were somewhat unsure of the definition of evangelicalism, because "many evangelicals now measure growth mainly in terms of numbers," diluting the doctrine and practice of the movement in a "broad welcome." Henry noted that "theological differences are minimized by evangelical publishers and publications reaching for mass circulation, by evangelicals luring capacity audiences, and even by evangelism festivals seeking the largest possible involvement." "Numerical bigness has become an infectious epidemic," Dr. Henry commented sadly on his beloved movement.[24]

Several times in his critique, Carl Henry insisted that the evangelical movement appears stronger and more unified than it really is. He argued that evangelicals must not be overly impressed with media hype or statistical data. "Evangelicalism presumptively acts as if it were the permanently appointed preserver of 'the faith once-for-all delivered' and specially entrusted with the ecclesial keys to the Kingdom," the evangelical statesman concluded. "But no earthly movement holds the Lion of the Tribe of Judah by the tail. We may need for a season to be encaged in the Lion's den until we recover an apostolic awe of the Risen Christ, the invincible Head of a dependent body sustained by his supernatural power. Apart from life in and by the Spirit we are all pseudoevangelicals."[25]

Evangelical theologian Donald G. Bloesch of the University of Dubuque Theological Seminary, a scholar who received his doctorate from the University of Chicago and who has done postdoctoral work at the universities of Oxford, Tübingen, and Basel attempts to build bridges between the various groups of evangelicals in his two volume *Essentials of Evangelical Theology* (1979). He stresses common concepts held by evangelicals throughout Christian history. Nevertheless, Bloesch underscores the point that "one danger today is that the word *evangelical* is given too broad a connotation, with the result that the distinctive tenets that it has defended in the past are obscured or compromised." "Though evangelicalism crosses all denominational lines," he says, "it definitely excludes all religion based on the law and not on Gospel."[26] On the other hand, Dr. Bloesch emphasizes that "while the term evangelicalism is often employed to include too much, it is also used to include too little." Unlike Carl Henry, Bloesch believes that there are authentic evangelical voices in both Roman Catholicism and Eastern Orthodoxy.

Disagreeing with other evangelical interpreters, Donald Bloesch declares that "the watershed of evangelicalism is not the inerrancy of Scripture" but rather "the cross of Christ, the doctrine of salvation through the righteousness of Christ procured for us by His sacrificial life, death, and resurrection." "It is the cross of Christ that gives authority to Scripture," Dr. Bloesch explains, "and it is the cross that reveals and confirms the Messianic identity of Jesus as the Son of God." Affirming evangelicalism's devotion to the gospel, he explains: "Evangelical religion places the accent not on a universal God-consciousness which needs only to be cultivated (as in Schleiermacher), but on the 'God-created vacuum in the soul,' which can be filled only by Jesus Christ (as with Pascal)." Drawing his theological distinctions very carefully, Bloesch concludes that evangelical religion "sees the hope of man not in techniques of self-sanctification or in universal education but in the glory of the cross, for it was there that divine grace invaded human history and gave birth to a new humanity."[27]

While Carl Henry was declaring the need for narrowing the evangelical definition in the midst of an acute crisis within evangelicalism, and while Donald Bloesch was asking for more clarification before expanding the definition to include some Roman Catholics and Eastern Orthodox, the 14 million member Southern Baptist Convention was at the same time being riddled with dissension between conservatives and moderates, a confrontation bordering on civil war. While outside interpreters had often labeled Southern Baptists as *the* example of a denomination of evangelicals, some Southern Baptists were not so sure.

Two Southern Baptist seminary professors debated this issue in a 1983 book entitled *Are Southern Baptists "Evangelicals"?* James Leo Garrett, Jr., professor of historical and systematic theology at Southwestern Baptist Seminary in Fort Worth, Texas, concluded that "*Southern Baptists are denominational evangelicals.* They belong to and exemplify the great heritage of scriptural authority, christocentric doctrine, gospel proclamation, experience of grace, and evangelistic endeavor which is evangelicalism." He noted that some would "doubtless have reservations" about his conclusion.[28]

E. Glenn Hinson, at that time professor of church history at Southern Baptist Theological Seminary in Louisville, Kentucky (now at Wake Forest), not only had reservations, but totally disagreed. He declared that "Evangelicalism threatens our most central and basic concerns as Baptists." He explained: "It is quite clear that we are talking about an *essential* difference between the Baptist and the evangelical traditions. This difference boils down to an entirely different attitude toward human response to the Word of God." Dr. Hinson maintained that the difference between evangelicals and Baptists was one of forcing your beliefs on others. He declared that "for evangelicals the Word has such an objective character that human beings can impose it by force, if necessary, on other human beings. For Baptists this cannot be so." "Nothing handled by human beings can have such an objective character that we, fallible human beings, can presume to impose it on others," the Southern Baptist church historian concluded. "To be valid, our response must be voluntary. It can never be coerced. The Word itself will win us. But it will never coerce."[29]

If the Southern Baptist Convention was in turmoil over the issue, Jewish interpreters were having their own struggles as well. In the Nationwide Attitudes Survey, September 1986, conducted for the Anti-Defamation League, an evangelical was defined as "a Christian who has deeply felt Christian views, with a basic agreement on the part of that Christian that it is the requirement of the Christian to evangelize or convert others to his or her faith."[30] The survey went on to define the "fundamentalist Christian" as a group that was "usually considered to be a subset or smaller group within the evangelical Christian population" and to state that fundamentalists "generally are considered to be those who have more extremely conservative Christian views, including in particular an unwavering view of the literal or infallible nature of the Bible." Unfortunately, revolving the definition of "evangelical" around evangelism and sincerity of viewpoint skewed the study somewhat, because Mormons made up 5 percent of the "evangelical sample."

Mormons do not consider themselves part of the evangelical movement and they have been rejected by evangelicals (often labeled a "cult"). They have added the *Book of Mormon* as their holy scriptures, and they have an entirely different theology and faith principle. The lesson, of course, is that *evangelists are not necessarily evangelicals.* More important, all who sincerely hold to their Christian views and who support missionary movements are not necessarily evangelicals—throughout history, nonevangelicals have met these qualifications as well.

EVANGELICALS AND JEWS

For the most part, evangelicals are traditional Christians who emphasize the importance of the Bible, the potency of the gospel, and the necessity of personal conversion. To evangelicals, personal faith and doctrinal belief are paramount to life itself. Indeed they claim that such belief circumscribes their whole life and reason for being. They also fervently claim that there is a life after death, and their dedicated faith will be honored with a blessed eternal life from God. Today the average evangelical strives to be consumed with heavenly pursuits and reward in heaven, rather than with the temporal scene. In political, economic, and social areas, the evangelical generally is moderate to conservative in orientation.

In contrast, many Jews claim that a Jew can be deeply devoted to his or her Jewishness while being devoid of any religious faith. Personal faith and doctrinal belief do not circumscribe identity for most modern Jews. Instead, birth into a chosen community and identification with a distinct peoplehood encompass the whole life and reason for being for the average Jew. Jewishness takes precedence over Judaism. A commitment to peoplehood is generally more important in definition than a commitment to religious faith. Today the average Jew focuses on issues of social justice and temporal concern rather than abstract theological constructs and thoughts of an afterlife. In political, economic, and social areas, the Jewish community generally is liberal to moderately liberal in orientation.

Yet theology and deep religious commitment are not foreign to the Jewish experience just as social justice, community, and social concern are not foreign to evangelical history. In their modern crises of identity, both Jews and evangelicals appear to be seeking more balance in those respective areas that they have tended to minimize. Nevertheless, one can readily recognize that with such differing perspectives, evangelicals and Jews (figuratively speaking) live in two different worlds.

Today the American Jewish community of approximately 6 million has entered a period of new anxiety over the growth of an American evangelical movement numbering approximately 60 million. Concerns are expressed over the influence of evangelicalism on the social and political sphere of our great country, over mission and witness, and over the evangelical penchant for fitting Jews and Israel into a Christian theological mold. For their part, modern evangelicals are concerned that Jews are trying to eradicate or nullify Christian theology and the proclamation of the gospel message in the name of dialogue and as a prerequisite to friendship. Both groups believe that they are being misunderstood, and at worst, are being slandered. Both groups ironically are interacting with one another to a greater extent than they have ever interacted before. Both groups unfortunately have a very long way to go in understanding each other and in dealing with their concerns on a grassroots level.

This study will examine these tensions and the questions that surround them. The findings in the present chapter will be elaborated upon and clarified in the chapters that follow. In chapter 2, "Roots and Reactions," the evangelical phenomenon and Jewish observations will be traced to their roots in the nineteenth century. Attitudes and reactions in the past will be analyzed in an effort to understand current beliefs and caricatures. Chapter 3, "Perspectives: Two Different Worlds," will elaborate on some of the themes and questions we have encountered in our definitions and analysis thus far. In chapter 4, "Theologies in Conflict: Mission and Witness," the most verbal and visible conflicts between the Jewish and evangelical communities will be forthrightly discussed and evaluated. Chapter 5, "Politics in Conflict: Domestic Agendas," assesses issues of liberalism versus conservativism, Republican versus Democrat, and the rise of the political fundamentalist movement. A concluding chapter, "Toward the Twenty-first Century," solidifies the themes that have been discovered and offers suggestions for the future. In all of these chapters, positive and negative views and attitudes toward the Jewish state of Israel will be considered.

As the decade of the 1980s drew to a close, signs of conflict for both of these vibrant communities seemed to fester in the press. Bill Bright's Campus Crusade for Christ, an evangelistic organization, announced "New Life 2000." The program's focus, according to Bright, "is to help bring the wonderful news, that every person can experience new life in Christ, to every person by the end of the next decade." He pointed out that for thirty-eight years Campus Crusade had developed "a comprehensive global strategy to help accelerate the fulfillment of the Great Commission (evangelization of the world) by the end of the century" and that New Life 2000 was "a collaborative effort, designed to work with other organizations." One goal of New Life 2000 is to provide training in discipleship, evangelism, and spiritual multiplication through 5,000 New Life Training Centers. Hoping to establish 5 million New Life Groups around the world to train 200 million Christians, Bright wants to expand Campus Crusade for Christ's evangelistic ministry on 8000 additional campuses worldwide. Providing such tools for wide-ranging evangelism strategies, the program seeks to present the gospel to more than 6.5 billion people during the next ten years, hoping to covert more that 1 billion of these "to Jesus Christ as Savior and Lord."[31]

For many Jews, the hype surrounding the New Life 2000 program may well remind them of the Key '73 fiasco discussed in chapter 4. However, "The Willowbank Declaration on the Christian Gospel and the Jewish People," issued by fifteen evangelical leaders on April 29, 1989 under the auspices of the World Evangelical Fellowship, has received even more publicity and has embroiled the evangelical and Jewish leadership in a renewed conflict over calculated Christian evangelism of Jewish people. Noting that the evangelical declaration from the Willowbank, Bermuda consultation called upon Christian churches to make the evangelization of Jews a priority, Rabbi A. James Rudin, National Interreligious Affairs Director of the American Jewish Committee, insisted that "the document is shot through with the ancient Christian 'teaching of contempt' for Jews and Judaism." He affirmed that the Willowbank Declaration was "one of the most aggressive and problematical evangelical statements of recent times." Rabbi

Yechiel Eckstein was "terribly disheartened" by the declaration, returning from Israel to find letters from Jewish colleagues that stated: "We told you, Yechiel, that you were naive in believing evangelical Christians genuinely cared about Jews. In fact, they only care about converting Jews."

Both of these men had worked in the area of evangelical-Jewish relations and had developed friendships with leading evangelicals. They hoped that many Christians would speak out against the signers of the declaration. Indeed some evangelicals were quick to do so, relating the problems with such a declaration. Other developments quickly ensued. In November 1989, the National Association of Evangelicals (NAE) chose leaders to meet with Jewish leadership on the topics of relationships and the feasibility of joint enterprises between evangelicals and Jews. For the first time in its history this national evangelical organization formally discussed how evangelicals and Jews might establish a network to handle such crises as the Willowbank Declaration. Some of the NAE leaders found definite problems in the declaration and referred it to their theological committee for further discussion. In the past, they had often given blanket approval to the consultation findings of the World Evangelical Fellowship. Nevertheless, while a significant number of American Jews today encourage Israeli leaders to talk to the PLO for the sake of peace, very few American Jews would suggest that evangelicals and Jews should build bridges of understanding through expanded interaction and dialogue. This indeed is the plight evangelicals and Jews face in the decade of the 1990s.

Yet there are signs of hope in the news as well. David Waughtal, a former neo-Nazi who had terrorized the Phoenix Jewish community with anti-Semitic telephone calls, was converted to evangelical Christianity while on the run in Eugene, Oregon. Encouraged by his Baptist pastor to return to Arizona to face charges against him, the twenty-four-year-old former member of the White Aryan Resistance met personally with Joel Breshin, the director of the Anti-Defamation League's (ADL) Arizona regional office, to apologize. Convinced that the young evangelical had indeed changed through his religious experience, thirty-nine-year-old

Breshin stood by Waughtal's side as he pleaded guilty to all charges. Insisting that he did not need a lawyer, David Waughtal refused to plead "not guilty" even when a judge suggested that it was in his best interest to do so. Now a student at Southwestern Bible College in Phoenix, David Waughtal is studying for foreign missionary service. He has become good friends with Joel Breshin and speaks against anti-Semitism and racism in high schools for the ADL.

As we shall see in the next chapter, evangelicalism appeared to reach a publicity peak in the 1970s and 1980s. The real roots of the modern movement, however, are grounded in the 1800s: The Century of Evangelicalism.

2

Roots And Reactions

During the 1970s and 1980s a significant number of books and articles appeared on "evangelicals." Evangelical-Jewish dialogue began to blossom and bloom as well in the course of those decades. If the Jewish community was confused over who these evangelicals were, the evangelicals themselves seemed absorbed in self-definition, both theologically and historically. The media attention had totally surprised them. *Newsweek*, October 25, 1976, declared that this was "The Year of the Evangelical."

In the midst of the evangelicals' seeming popularity on both the political and social scene, matters appeared to be getting out of hand. The same year that Jimmy Carter was elected to the presidency and George Gallup's poll indicated that approximately 50 percent of all Protestants and 20 percent of all Catholics claimed to have had a "born-again" experience, Paul Craft recorded "Dropkick Me, Jesus" on the Black Sheep Music label. The lyrics stunned evangelicals and provided grist for critics for a decade thereafter. The chorus intoned:

> Dropkick me, Jesus, through the goalposts of life,
> end over end, neither left nor to the right.
>
> Straight through the heart of them righteous uprights.
> Dropkick me, Jesus, through the goalposts of life.

Today during college and NFL football games, a television viewer will see religious fans lift large banners with inscriptions from the

Christian Testament (such as John 3:16, John 3:3, or Hebrews 9:28) in the end zone in the hope of capturing the camera during an extra point or field goal. They usually do.[1] Newspapers wanted to record such sensations, but seemed lost in the evangelical maze. Octogenarian evangelical educator, writer and editor, Frank E. Gaebelein of Arlington, Virginia, would fume every time he opened his Washington, D.C. newspaper to find that the religion editor had once again titled the National Association of Evangelicals (NAE) as the "National Association of Evangelists." Even reliable interpreters in the academic community seemed to falter at the task of explaining the evangelical phenomenon. Some, searching for who the evangelicals were, bluntly stated that "Southern Baptist" was synonymous with "evangelical." Yet the term "evangelical" had had quite a history.

HISTORICAL EVANGELICALISM

While the term "evangelical" was used in the Roman Catholic Church, it came into prominence during the Protestant Reformation in the sixteenth century. The Protestant movement affirmed the concepts of individual conscience and freedom of religion,[2] grace and faith, the authority of the Bible, and the priesthood of all believers. Lutherans were described as "evangelicals" because of their assertion of such principles during the Reformation period, and soon the term "evangelical" was commonly applied to all German Protestants, Lutheran and Reformed (Calvinist). Today in German usage *evangelisch* is a synonym for "Protestant," and in Latin America "evangelical" invariably means "Protestant," in contrast to Roman Catholic. In England, "evangelical" refers to the Anglican "Low Church" party in contrast to "High Church" sacramentalism.

By 1600, those Protestants within the Church of England who believed that the English Reformation had not gone far enough and who insisted that the church must be further purified from Roman Catholic influence were dubbed "Puritans." As Puritanism increased in political power in England, it was destined to have an important influence also on the American colonies.

While Puritan Protestantism attempted to reform the ecclesiastical order through political means in England, the Pietist Protestant movement challenged the Protestant status quo on the European continent. Pietism emphasized an individual expression of heartfelt religion, insisting that intellect and will alone could not lead Protestants into a meaningful relationship with God. In an effort to "complete" the Protestant Reformation, Pietism taught that love and joy in an emotional commitment to God were necessary for a dedicated life in God's service.

The seeds planted by the Puritan and Pietist movements provided crosscurrents to the emerging Enlightenment. Moreover, these two movements, transplanted to America, gave an evangelical cast to American Protestantism.[3] Evangelical revivals with their emphasis on "the miracle of the new birth" broke out in Germany, Scandinavia, England, and New England in the 1700s. By 1800, "evangelical" connoted a broad, ecumenical spirit that influenced the Protestant movement in Britain and America.

THE CENTURY OF EVANGELICALISM

The nineteenth century was the century of modern evangelicalism. Protestantism was permeated by revivalism, whose adherents sought to spread the message of the gospel to every corner of the earth. In England the small minority of evangelicals had grown remarkably in spite of opposition from High Church clergy. Cambridge University became the training center for evangelical clergymen, and gradually the British middle classes were drawn to the movement. Building on the foundation provided by the Methodist revivals of John Wesley and George Whitefield, evangelicalism had become the most vital religious force in England by the nineteenth century.

English evangelicals achieved their most notable successes in philanthropic endeavors and social reform. Distinguished evangelical Anglicans, such as Lord Shaftesbury and William E. Gladstone, were leading political personalities. William Wilberforce, Tory member of Parliament, became an influential evangelical layman of the upper middle class, and relentlessly led the fight to abolish the slave trade. In 1807, Parliament issued the Abolition Bill, and Wilberforce joyfully wrote in his journal (March 22, 1807): "How wonderfully the providence of God has been manifested in the Abolition Bill!.. Oh, what thanks do I owe the Giver of all good, for bringing me in His gracious providence to this great cause, which at length after almost nineteen years' labour, is successful!"

In the United States, the mainline Protestant churches (Episcopalians, Methodists, Presbyterians, and Baptists) called themselves "evangelicals." Like the British, their enthusiasm to "spread the gospel" and "win precious souls to Christ" was fervent and aggressive. Through winning souls and through social reform, they wanted to revamp society. But American evangelicals wanted more. Indeed these optimistic Protestants intended to remake the world. Foreign missionary and Bible societies flourished in the belief that the Protestant Christian church would bring in "the millennium," a thousand-year period of peace and prosperity. Through the auspices of Protestantism, the world would be "Christianized." They believed that the world would become progressively better, and *then* Jesus Christ would return to earth. This theological view was known as *postmillennialism* ("after millennium"). Postmillennial evangelicalism dominated the culture of the nineteenth century, and it was socially acceptable to be such an evangelical.

Ecumenical Revivalism

By the early 1800s, revivals and great religious enthusiasm had not only occurred in the frontier areas from western New York to Tennessee, but had also spread to college campuses. In 1802, during a series of chapel sermons at Yale University, one-third of the student body professed conversion and dedicated their lives to serve God unreservedly. Students from the Yale Revival spread the influence of the evangelical tradition, as other campuses followed suit.

As a diverse, ecumenical movement in Britain and America, evangelicalism gave birth to a multitude of voluntary and missionary societies that drew membership from an interdenominational base. Carrying out their activities with little church or state control, these societies sought to reform society and purify the world. Their optimism abounded—the "kingdom of God was at hand!"

In 1846 the Evangelical Alliance was formed in London to provide a worldwide fellowship "on the basis of great evangelical principles" and to present a united front. While declaring that the summary of beliefs it espoused should not be "regarded in any formal or ecclesiastical sense as a creed or confession," the articles adopted by the Evangelical Alliance remain instructive as to the beliefs and mentality of the nineteenth century evangelical movement. The articles affirmed the "Divine Inspiration, Authority, and Sufficiency of the Holy Scriptures," while maintaining the right and duty of private judgment in interpreting those scriptures. They underscored the unity of the Godhead, but claimed that there was "the Trinity of Persons therein." Because of the "utter depravity" of the human nature after the fall in the Garden of Eden, the articles of the Evangelical Alliance stated that Jesus became the incarnate Son of God to atone for the sins of humankind, and that he rose again as a mediator and intercessor for those who accept him as their Savior. A century later this very same Evangelical Alliance would sponsor the evangelistic crusades in England led by Billy Graham (1954-55 and 1966-67). Graham's message, which stresses personal salvation, sounds much the same as the articles summarized above.[4]

The ecumenical spirit of early modern evangelicalism eventually waned as the century progressed, and the word "denomination" (originally an *inclusive* term) took on new connotations. Princeton Seminary's Charles Hodge, professor of theology for fifty years, wrote in 1836 that "no such thing exists on the face of the earth as Christianity in the abstract...Every man you see is either an Episcopalian or a Methodist, a Presbyterian or an Independent, Arminian or a Calvinist. No one is a Christian in general."[5] In the midst of growing rivalries, the quest "to win the world for Christ" was the primary unifier of the transatlantic, transdenominational evangelical movement.

A resurgence of revivals from 1857 to 1859 underscored the fact that the power and prestige of evangelical Protestantism dominated the culture and institutions of nineteenth-century America. Revivalism even created a political ethos for Protestantism that affected the way the American populace voted for many years. A. James Reichley has pointed out that the revivalism of the New School Presbyterians was consistent with the political approach of Thomas Jefferson and the antiestablishment Republicans. Baptists were also drawn to the Republican Party. Later, William Lloyd Garrison exerted a revivalist style that won northern evangelical Protestants to the abolitionist crusade.[6]

The nineteenth century, the century of evangelicalism, presented many challenges. Industrialization, immigration, and urbanization presented social and economic dilemmas that demanded responses, yet seemingly defied solution. A number of new religious movements (including Mormonism) first appeared in this century. Biblical criticism, fast gaining ground in Europe, and Darwin's theory of evolution required theological response. Twentieth-century fascist and communist movements would test the constructs of the century of evangelicalism, as would a rapid expansion of scientific knowledge and technology.

In America, both liberalism and fundamentalism arose within the vast theological and social sea of nineteenth-century evangelical Protestantism. As scientific, historical-critical methods of biblical interpretation began to question the authorship and dating of each book of the Bible, the biblical account of creation, miracles, and historical data in general came under attack. Englishman Charles Darwin's theory of evolution proposed a purely biological development of the species. His followers generalized his theory to include the evolution of religion itself. Evangelical Protestantism was in a quandary.

In the 1873 world gathering of the Evangelical Alliance in New York, a debate raged over the evangelical's relationship to Darwinism. Some evangelicals felt that evolution did not pose a serious threat to the Christian faith; others insisted that "man" in the Book of Genesis could not be "sprung from primeval matter." Throughout America, evangelical theologians struggled with the question of whether they could retain the Protestant emphasis on the centrality of the Bible and still be biblical scholars of integrity in the brave new world of modern scholarship. One choice worked in a liberal direction: to modify the biblical faith and adapt it to the modern world.

Liberal Evangelicalism

The most rapid movement of liberal evangelicalism against Protestant orthodoxy occurred in the last quarter of the nineteenth century. Conservative evangelicals, such as Lyman Abbot, were won to the liberal movement through reading and reconstruction. As optimistic postmillennialists, they deplored Darwin's "survival of the fittest" ethic, and so they proposed that God himself was the source of physical evolution as well as spiritual evolution, constantly involved in the upward progress of his creation. This theological reconstruction of a beneficent divine design of upward evolutionary progress caught on quickly, and although mainline evangelical denominations would initially balk at such a philosophy (attempting to dismiss seminary professors who held to it), by 1890 liberalism had made spectacular gains among the American intelligentsia. Protestant liberalism matured in the next three decades of the twentieth century. This reconstruction within the world of evangelicalism affected professors and ministerial candidates. It was not due to rationalistic or irreligious forces, but rather was the response of one segment of the evangelical movement to develop a living faith that could meet the demands of the modern, scientific world.

Seminaries such as Union, Harvard, and Yale took up the gauntlet of liberalism, while Boston University (Methodist) and Crozer (Baptist) soon followed suit. When John D. Rockefeller generously funded the University of Chicago Divinity School (Baptist), it hired an accomplished faculty, soon becoming one of the country's strongest centers of a Protestant liberalism called "modernism." Congregationalist, Episcopal, Methodist, Presbyterian, and Baptist churches were heavily affected by liberalism, and each denomination found itself in crisis over the new challenge.

As denominational seminaries graduated liberal ministers, however, the "new theology" progressively penetrated the grassroots of Protestant evangelicalism. In an 1899 meeting of several hundred New York evangelical ministers of the Methodist Church, Rev. Samuel Parkes Cadman boldly proclaimed that the "absolute inerrancy and infallibility of the Bible are no longer possible of belief among reasoning men" and that half of the pages of the "Old Testament" were of "unknown authorship" and that the "New Testament" contained "contradictions." The large majority of Methodist evangelicals present applauded Cadman's remarks.[7]

It is important to realize that these theological liberals often continued to call themselves "evangelicals." While the advocates of liberalism progressively dominated the Protestant educational and intellectual milieu in the early decades of the twentieth century, many unashamedly traced their roots to nineteenth-century evangelicalism, declaring that they were fulfilling the mandate of that great movement. Shailer Mathews, dean of the University of Chicago Divinity School, asserted in *The Faith of Modernism* (1924): "Modernists as a class are evangelical Christians. That is, they accept Jesus Christ as the revelation of a Savior God." He explained that while the "religious starting point" was inherited orthodoxy, "the use of scientific, historical, social method in understanding and applying evangelical Christianity to the needs of living persons, is Modernism." "Confessionalism is the evangelicalism of the dogmatic mind," Dr. Mathews concluded. "Modernism is the evangelicalism of the scientific mind."[8]

The diversity within the great sea of evangelical Protestantism was even evident in the family of the most important evangelist of the nineteenth century, Dwight L. Moody. Upon Moody's death in 1899, his son Paul would lean toward liberalism, while his other son, William, remained a conservative evangelical. When Paul Moody wrote in *The Christian Century* (August 2, 1923) that his father would have been "more in sympathy" with the objectives of liberalism, an article and letter war broke out between conservatives and liberals—both groups claiming that Dwight L. Moody was one of their own! This underscores for the contemporary interpreter the danger of creating a false dichotomy between the conservative and liberal movements. While extreme religious viewpoints do exist on both the right and the left, there are in actuality a spectrum of parties as well as denominational groupings within evangelicalism.

FUNDAMENTALISM

Conservative evangelicals were distessed by the rise of liberalism within evangelical ranks. As biblical criticism became more vocal in the latter nineteenth century, a number of books defending the infallibility of the Bible were published. Francois Samuel Robert Louis Gaussen's *Theopneustia: The Plenary Inspiration of the Holy Scriptures deduced from Internal Evidence, and the Testimonies of Nature, History and Science* (1841) was translated from French into English and was distributed throughout Britain and America. "Scripture is then from God; it is everywhere from God, and everywhere it is entirely from God," Gaussen asserted. He concluded that "there are in the Christian world but two schools, or two religions: that which puts the Bible above every thing, and that which puts something above the Bible."[9] Over a century later this work was reissued by American fundamentalist-evangelicals under the title *The Inspiration of the Holy Scriptures* (1949).

The great nineteenth-century English Baptist preacher and prolific writer, Charles Haddon Spurgeon, praised Gaussen's *Theopneustia* as "the turning point in the battle between those who hold 'the faith once delivered to the saints,' and their opponents." Spurgeon insisted: "If we have in the Word of God no infallible standard of truth, we are at sea without a compass, and no danger from rough weather without can be equal to this loss within."[10] American conservative evangelicals agreed.

At Princeton Theological Seminary a defense of the Bible ensued that became known as the "Princeton Theology." Charles Hodge, professor of exegetical and didactic theology, published a three-volume *Systematic Theology* (1872-73) that maintained that the Bible was "the protestant rule of faith." "All Protestants agree in teaching that 'the word of God, as contained in the Scriptures of the Old and New Testaments, is the only infallible rule of faith and practice,'" Dr. Hodge wrote.[11] He substantiated his claim by quoting

Lutheran, Reformed, and Anglican confessions of faith, and affirmed that all of the books of the Protestant canon were "fully inspired." His student, Benjamin Breckinridge Warfield, who also became a professor at Princeton Theological Seminary, would carry this interpretation into the twentieth century, spending a considerable amount of time demonstrating how discrepancies in the biblical documents could be resolved.

Evangelist Dwight L. Moody was familiar with Hodge's work and agreed with his biblical interpretation. Moody began his book, *Heaven: Where It Is, Its Inhabitants, and How to Get There* (1880), with these words:

> What the Bible says about heaven is just as true as what it says about everything else. The Bible is inspired. What we are taught about heaven could not have come to us in any other way than by inspiration. No one knew anything about it but God, and so if we want to find anything about it we have to turn to His Word. Dr. Hodge, of Princeton, says that the best evidence of the Bible being the Word of God is to be found between its own two covers. It proves itself.[12]

Four years before his death, after speaking to an estimated 100 million people, and possibly the "most-listened-to-man-in-the-world" before microphones, radios, and televisions, Dwight L. Moody complained in *Pleasure and Profit in Bible Study* (1895): "Now, if I have a right to cut out a certain portion of the Bible, I don't know why one of my friends has not the right to cut out another....You would have a queer kind of Bible if everybody cut out what he wanted."[13]

This was the message of conservative evangelicalism that dominated most of the nineteenth century. Moody differed from Hodge and Warfield, however, in his view of the future and the second coming of Jesus Christ. He was a *pre*millennialist in contrast to the *post*millennialism of most of nineteenth-century evangelicalism. Moody did not believe that cultural progress and conversion would Christianize the world and evolve into the millennium. He believed that the world was in trouble and only the return of Jesus Christ would save it and initiate the millennium (*pre*millennial, that is, before millennium). This premillennial view of the future would characterize the emerging fundamentalist-evangelical movement in the latter decades of the nineteenth century. Growing in popularity through thousands of books on prophecy, prophetic and Bible conferences, and fundamentalist teachers who crisscrossed the nation, the premillennial viewpoint would become an important grassroots theological position in the contemporary evangelical movement.

Zionism and Anti-Semitism

The fundamentalist-evangelical movement contrasted with the Puritans and many postmillennialist evangelicals in that it maintained that the Christian church had no right to usurp God's promises to the Jewish people. These premillennial fundamentalists proclaimed that God had given the Holy Land to the Jewish people. Among their number was William E. Blackstone and his Blackstone Memorial of 1891 that urged President Benjamin Harrison (and later Woodrow Wilson) to give Palestine back to the Jews (see chapter 1). Fundamentalist-evangelicals also took to task anti-Semites, underscoring that anti-Semitism and Christianity should be antithetical. Nevertheless, their heavy emphasis on spreading the gospel message among the Jewish people in the hope that they would "save some" precipitated the same deep animosities and barriers to Christian-Jewish interaction that have filtered down to our day.

Yet the fundamentalist-evangelical movement of the latter nineteenth century and early twentieth century was bold in its accusations against Christian triumphalism. Nathaniel West (1826-1906), one of the early fundamentalist-evangelical founding fathers and organizer of the First International Prophetic Conference in 1878, insisted that the "anti-Semitism of our modern times, with its hatred of the Jew, a thing disgraceful to Christendom, and so unlike the philo-Israelism of the apostolic days" was due in no small degree to "false systems of [Christian] interpretation" that had infested the century of evangelicalism. He questioned the triumphalistic interpretation of mainline postmillennial evangelicalism that attributed the biblical curses of the Bible to the Jewish people while assigning the biblical blessings of the same scriptures to the Christian church. Dr. West

believed that the pro-Jewish premillennial prophetic interpretation had been crushed by the union of church and state under
Constantine in the fourth century, and that the Roman Catholic
church then "spiritualized" all of God's promises to the Jewish
people to apply to itself. That Protestants had continued such
"vapid idealism" to claim that the Christian church was promoting the kingdom of God in an unbroken evolution toward
absolute perfection, nauseated the fundamentalist-evangelical
leader.[14]

That Christians could deny the Jewish people the right to their
Promised Land, spiritualizing away the promises of God regarding
the Holy Land, infuriated Professor West. "It is not to be denied
that a large part of the professing church, swayed by its teachers,
is indifferent to these [prophetic] themes...and regard the word of
prophecy as unprofitable, and its unfulfilled part as unintelligible,"
West asserted in *The Thousand Years in Both Testaments* (1880). He
explained that "a false spiritualizing, allegorizing, and idealizing,
interpretation has contributed to rob the predictions concerning
Israel of their realistic value," regarding the "doctrine of the premillennial coming of Israel's Messiah as a 'Jewish fable' not to be
believed."[15]

But times were changing and the fundamentalist-evangelical
prophetic interpretation (including its Christian Zionism) was
spreading throughout the United States. The Second International
Prophetic Conference was held in Farwell Hall in Chicago, November 16-21, 1886. Many eminent fundamentalist-evangelical
ministers and theologians attended. Dwight L. Moody was unable
to be present because of "binding engagements," but like a few
others he sent a letter expressing "for the purpose of the conference
the greatest sympathy." George C. Needham, organizer and
secretary of the conference, stated that one of the major reasons for
holding the conference was "that unfulfilled prophecy has, for
centuries, been relegated to the theologians grave."[16]

Professor Ernst F. Stroeter, Wesleyan University, Warrenton,
Missouri, concurred in his address the first day. In "Christ's
Second Coming Premillennial," Dr. Stroeter gently castigated the
religious commentators who "are very ready to simply spiritualize

away all that is prophesied to the political Israel and to the geographical Palestine of restitution and rehabilitation...and to appropriate quietly to the Gentile church all there is predicted of BLESSING TO ISRAEL." He intimated that anti-Semitism was linked to this spiritualization of the word "Israel" in the Bible to mean the "Christian church." "Without the equally literal fulfillment of this aspect of Israel's hope—to which Jesus himself and his disciples likewise stand committed—Israel's glory among the nations is lost forever... the name of Israel will continue a reproach forever among the nations."[17]

Three days later, Dr. Nathaniel West delivered a major address on the topic "Prophecy and Israel." Concerning the Jewish people, West began by emphasizing that Israel was the focal point of God's plan. He preached: "The fortunes of the chosen people decides the fortunes of the world. History itself is Messianic." Dr. West explained that Israel was comparable to the Messiah: "Israel and Messiah, though historically separated now, are indissolvably united, as mediators and bringers of salvation to the world; the one nationally, the other personally, alike in their humiliation and glory." As Israel brought salvation to the gentiles during the "first" coming of Jesus Christ, so Israel would bring salvation at the "second" coming of Christ. Nathaniel West added that "Israel" meant the Jewish people and must not be substituted symbolically for the Christian church, as theologians had attempted over the centuries.[18]

Presbyterian theologian W.J. Erdman agreed, criticizing in his presentation the "conceit" of Christians who claim that Israel has "as a nation no future of SPECIAL BLESSING and preeminence." He noted that even John Calvin erred in this interpretation and that it was high time that such an error was brought to light. Other speakers, such as the Rev. Henry M. Parsons, openly declared that "the Jews are to be the missionaries to the nations in the opening of the next age, and have preeminence among them as God's earthly people."[19] All of these fundamentalist-evangelical speakers were clearly confident that the Jewish people would one day be restored to the Holy Land because the Bible clearly predicted it.

In addition, the emerging fundamentalist-evangelical movement held a special reverence for the Jewish people that would be
criticized by other Christians throughout the twentieth century as
extreme philo-Semitism and would be viewed by many Jews as
syrupy, sentimental, and unrealistic. Indicative of these many
statements regarding the Jewish people was that of Bishop William
R. Nicholson of the Reformed Episcopal Church in Philadelphia.
Rev. Nicholson was a fervent fundamentalist-evangelical who
delivered the principal address for the First International Prophetic
Conference, New York City, in 1878. Exclaiming that the world had
not seen anything like the miraculous preservation of the Jewish
people, Bishop Nicholson declared to the thousands of Christians
assembled:

> Can the world show anything like it? Twice 1,800 years old, they
> saw the proud Egyptian perish in the waters of the Red Sea; they
> heard the fall of great Babylon's power; they witnessed the ruins of
> the Syro-Macedonian Caesars, and outlived the dark ages. They
> have been through all civilizations, shared in all convulsions, and
> have kept pace with the entire progress of discovery and art. And
> here they [the Jewish people] stand today, as distinct as ever, occupy-
> ing no country of their own, scattered through all countries, identical
> in their immemorial physiognomy, earth's men of destiny, before
> the venerableness of whose pedigree the proudest scutcheons of
> mankind are but trifles of yesterday.[20]

Even during this early era, Bishop Nicholson and other fundamentalist-evangelicals perceived a spark of hope of restoration of the
Jewish people to Palestine through the auspices of the nation of
England. Rev. Nicholson interjected: "Even now we may almost
speak of England's protectorate of the Holy Land. God's
providence is moving apace, and evidently is rapidly nearing the
crisis of Israel's first recovery." Recalling the sufferings of the
Jewish people up to the year 1878, Nicholson pointed out that "if
so literally have been fulfilled the prophecies which foretold their
sufferings and their preservation, equally sure are the predicted
grandeurs of their future."[21]

In the Third International Prophetic Conference held in Allegheny, Pennsylvania, December 3 through 6, 1895, Dr. Ernst F.

Stroeter, who had left his teaching position to join Dr. Arno C. Gaebelein in his Hope of Israel mission in New York City, also emphasized such themes and was an example of the constant criticism of Christian anti-Semitism by the early fundamentalist-evangelical movement. Stroeter blamed Christendom for any Jewish hostility toward Jesus. "Fifteen centuries of Christian history, during which the professed followers of Jesus have shed more Jewish blood alone than Titus and Epiphanes combined, accentuate the Jew's objection," Ernst Stroeter declared, later underscoring that "it is as good as forgotten, that Christianity is the legitimate daughter of Biblical Judaism; that in all the essentials of a supernatural, revealed religion the orthodox Jew is our elder brother, not a heathen who imagines vain things and worships devils."[22]

Dr. Stroeter reminded scholars and laypersons at the conference that "Israel's history is unique. No other people on earth ever did or ever will stand as Israel does in covenant relation with the God of heaven and earth." He spoke of a basically triumphalistic Christendom that had dominated the century of evangelicalism, noting that "Greek and Roman, American and Chinaman, may in Christ Jesus, approach that same God and call Him Abba Father; but God has never undertaken to be the God of Americans or of the Chinese as He has to be the God of Israel."

Ernst F. Stroeter insisted that "anti-Semitism and Jew-hatred" was not "a thing of the past in Christendom." In addition, he believed that the Bible taught that the "greatest and most awful foe and destroyer of that wonderful people (the Jews) is still to arise." Fundamentalist-evangelicals believed that the Bible taught of a Great Tribulation period that would occur in the future and an antichrist led by Satan who would try to destroy God's chosen people, the Jews. "The time of Jacob's greatest trouble is still to come," Professor Stroeter stated. Nevertheless, he believed that the Jewish people would be delivered from such a calamity, and God would bless the nations through Israel. Stroeter was glad that some Christian believers were "awakening to a deeper sense of their obligation and responsibility toward the long despised and neglected Jew." "Talk of Egyptian Sphynxes and of Gordian knots," the former professor at Wesleyan and Denver

Universities exclaimed, "the greatest riddle, the one unsolvable mystery of all the ages, is the Jew. His very existence and preservation is an unanswerable challenge to the human mind for a rational explanation. No philosophy (is) yet equal to the task."[23]

Dr. Stroeter was German in background and was appalled at the rise of anti-Semitism in his homeland. During one of his trips overseas, in 1897, he traveled to Palestine and then to Europe, deciding to stay and fight the anti-Semitic waves there. He also campaigned to convince rationalistic Reform Jews to return to their traditional roots. He remarked in correspondence to the journal *Our Hope* about his discussions with Reform Jews: "And when I upbraided them for their 'reform,' i.e., their rationalizing and unbelieving Judaism, they took it in excellent grace, and acknowledged quite readily, that underneath the garb of assimilation and reform, the genuine, national Jew was still very much alive." Stroeter claimed that the Reform Jews of Germany "were frank enough to admit that the influence of 'reform' was, after all, not very strong over the Jewish mind and heart," and that after an initial period of shyness at his Christian Zionism, "it did not take them long to discover that they all were, in the depths of their hearts, real Zionists."[24]

Only Stroeter's word is recorded on the Reform Jewish response in Germany but, as we see in the next section, the response of American Reform leader, Rabbi Isaac Mayer Wise, would have been quite different had Stroeter spoken personally with him. On the whole, fundamentalist-evangelicals had little regard for the rationalistic Reform Judaism advocated by Isaac Mayer Wise and many of his American colleagues. For fundamentalist-evangelicals, their perception of the attitudes of traditional Judaism toward the Bible and the Holy Land were much more palatable. *Our Hope* published part of a letter Orthodox Rabbi H. Pereira Mendes wrote to the editor of the *New York Sun* which insisted that the Bible was a central key to national restoration of the Jewish people. "True Zionism is founded on the Bible," Rabbi Mendes asserted, and "any idea at variance with the teachings, direct or indirect, of the Bible, will ever be rejected by the vast majority of Hebrews as not being true Zionism." Fundamentalist-evangelicals with their prophetic mindset could only concur.

Rabbi Mendes, who was chazzan of the Congregation Shearith Israel in New York City, also declared: "If there are Jews who do not live up to high ideas, they are no more Jews than the convicts at Sing Sing are Christians." And "if there are Hebrews who reject the Bible as an authority and who oppose any idea of a Jewish state, even as a religious influence, they may be born in the race, but they are not inspired by the spirit which moved our prophets to preach, our psalmists to sing, our poets and philosophers to write, and our martyrs to die."[25] A few Reform rabbis, such as Stephen S. Wise, would also work to turn the classical Reform movement of Isaac Mayer Wise (no relation) back to Judaism's Zionist heritage.

Zionism was criticized not only in classical Reform Jewish circles, but was also castigated by most Christians in the century of evangelicalism. The nineteenth-century, prophetic-minded fundamentalist-evangelicals held to a strongly divergent biblical hermeneutic in comparison to other Christian theologians of their day. *The Princeton Review* attempted to warn Presbyterian ministers not to be swayed by premillennial doctrine, while the Dutch Reformed *Christian Intelligencer* observed that very few ministers in the Dutch Reformed Church could accept this view of the Bible. At times the *Christian Observer*, the voice of the evangelical party in the Church of England, seemed confused over the doctrine and ridiculed belief in the Jewish restoration to Palestine. The *Catholic World* was much more blunt, stressing that rather than the Jewish people being restored, the Jews would eventually accept the true faith (Catholicism) and only then could "the captivity of Judah and the captivity of Jerusalem" be ended.[26]

In contrast, not only were fundamentalist-evangelical periodicals, books, and sermons supportive of the restoration of the Jewish people to Palestine during the latter decades of the nineteenth century and the early decades of the twentieth century, but they firmly spoke out against anti-Semitism around the world and anti-Semitic acts in the United States. And early fundamentalist-evangelicals were convinced that those who persecuted the Jewish people would be punished by God, both in this life and in the next. C.I. Scofield, the famed editor of the *Scofield Reference Bible*, a standard in fundamentalist-evangelical circles during most of the twentieth century, wrote in 1902 that the promises of God to the Jewish people in Genesis 12:1-3 were as valid as the day in which they were written. He declared:

> Can you point to me a passage in this Bible which revokes that last promise ("I will bless those who bless you, and whoever curses you I will curse")? Can you bring me one single illustration from the history of a nation that has persecuted the Jew and escaped chastisement? If I had no other proof that this Bible is inspired, the literal fulfillment in human history of that last promise would be to me the convincing, unanswerable demonstration that this book is from God. Never, never, has that statement been revoked. No nation ever persecuted the Jew and escaped national retribution. Hamen is always hanged ultimately on the gallows prepared for Mordecai.[27]

Scofield added that "the Scriptures account for the Jew, and that the Jew, in turn, is the ever-lasting, everywhere-present, verification of the Scriptures."

From Fundamentalism to the NAE

Contrary to high school and college textbooks that portray American fundamentalism as a "redneck" agrarian phenomenon of the rural South and point to the 1925 Scopes Trial about teaching evolution as an example of the fundamentalist mentality, the fundamentalist-evangelical movement was in fact the product of highly educated northerners from an urban environment. Like the Puritan movement, its leadership, periodicals, and meetings are extremely visible but difficult to classify and categorize. Diverse denominational, educational, social, and vocational backgrounds of the adherents of early fundamentalism make classification along these lines impractical if not impossible. Because most of its members belonged to a major American Protestant denomination, the early fundamentalist movement developed into a church within the church.

Even the word "fundamentalist" predates the Scopes debacle. Premillennialist evangelicals were fond of expressions such as "returning to the fundamentals" and "holding forth the fundamentals of the faith" during the early decades of the twentieth century. *The Fundamentals*, a series of twelve books published from 1910 to

1915, intended to reaffirm these "fundamentals" of Christianity. Espousing inerrancy of the Bible and a premillennial view of the future, they were donated to Protestant leaders "compliments of two Christian laymen." At first, these moderate conservative evangelicals wore the new label of "fundamentalist" with pride.

The rancor of the fundamentalist-modernist controversy of the 1920s and 1930s with its accompanying splitting of denominations, churches, and seminaries, however, changed the meaning of the term for these Christians. They watched helplessly as right-wing militant Protestants in their movement seized the term "fundamentalist" as a battle cry. Mass media began to portray "fundamentalism" as narrow, divisive, bigoted, anti-intellectual, uncaring, unloving, antisocial, etc. Refusing to be caricatured in such a manner, most moderate fundamentalist-evangelicals abandoned the term by the 1940s. They simply began to call themselves "evangelicals" once again, and fundamentalist-evangelicalism took a leading role among a much larger and diverse evangelical movement. They felt more comfortable with the label "evangelical" at that time, because liberal American Protestants were no longer calling themselves "evangelicals" by the 1940s. In addition, the massive immigration from 1880 to 1925 had made the nation much more pluralistic, and the United States no longer considered itself evangelical.

Fundamentalist-evangelicals joined with other conservative evangelicals in 1942 to form The National Association of Evangelicals for United Action. The words "fundamentals" and "fundamentalist" were conspicuously missing from their policy statements, but their doctrinal statement was quite traditional as they claimed "to facilitate action among the various evangelical groups" and promised "to seek the advancement of the cause of Christ." Heavily premillennial among its diverse founding constituency (much more so than today), the NAE adopted a doctrinal basis that required their members to believe that the Bible is the inspired, authoritative word of God, that God eternally existed in three persons, and that Christ was born of a virgin, atoning in his death and resurrection for the sins of the world.[28] In an effort to bury the hatchet of doctrinal animosity over the "gifts of the Spirit," the fundamentalist-evangelical majority permitted Holiness and Pentecostal groups to become charter members of the National Association of Evangelicals. The first president of the NAE was Dr. Harold J. Ockenga, a fundamentalist-evangelical. Today one of the leading evangelicals in Christian-Jewish relations is Dr. Marvin R. Wilson, Harold J. Ockenga Professor of Biblical Studies at Gordon College in Wenham, Massachusetts. In addition, evangelicals associated with the NAE helped prepare the 1949 Los Angeles evangelistic crusade that launched a premillennial Southern Baptist, Billy Graham, to national recognition. Graham has been an important supporter of the NAE for four decades and has reaped the assistance of the organization in return.

The broad sea that once again characterizes contemporary evangelicalism differs from its nineteenth-century ancestor in one important area: it is no longer postmillennial. Both liberal and conservative Protestantism abandoned the optimistic and imperialistic postmillennial viewpoint that through the auspices of the Protestant churches the world would become progressively better, would be "Christianized," and then Jesus Christ would return to the resultant millennium. World War I was the final shattering stumbling block to the postmillennial movement. Premillennialism and amillennialism (no millennium) replaced it on the theological scene, influencing tens of millions of Protestant Christians. Only recently has the postmillennial viewpoint resurfaced among militant, right-wing Protestants, the Christian reconstructionists, who are attempting to turn the United States into a "Christian nation." As we shall see in chapter 5, the Christian reconstructionists attempted to capture the charismatic movement in the 1980s and to channel the political aspirations of Pat Robertson as their "Christian" candidate.

JEWS AS OBSERVERS

As has been amply illustrated, the real roots of the modern evangelical movement were grounded in the 1800s, "The Century of Evangelicalism." Many of the factors that are viewed in the current evangelical movement are clearly visible by the end of the nineteenth century. In light of this history of evangelicalism, with its belief system, social status, views of the future, attitudes toward the Jewish people, and domination of nineteenth century America, a question arises: How did the Jewish community of the nineteenth century view this dominant Christian movement? It may come as a surprise that the Jewish community was clearly cognizant of the evangelical phenomenon, and their basic attitudes differed little from those encountered today. This may be illustrated in the life of the famed rabbi, Isaac Mayer Wise, and in the pages of his English-language weekly, *The American Israelite.*

Isaac Mayer Wise (1819-1900) became an important leader in American Judaism during the latter half of the nineteenth century. Wise was a keen observer of contemporary Christianity and had much to say about evangelicals, revivalism, Christian origins, and the future of Christianity in America. A native of Steingrub, Bohemia and the son of a poverty-stricken teacher, Wise was dramatically affected by the free religious atmosphere in America after he emigrated in 1846. As rabbi of Congregation Beth El in Albany, New York, he introduced reforms such as mixed seating, a choir of men and women, elimination of Hebrew prayers that included reference to the messiah, and confirmation for Jewish young people. In 1850 the congregation split, and Wise and his supporters organized Albany's first Reform synagogue. In 1853 Rabbi Isaac Mayer Wise was hired at Cincinnati's B'nai Jeshurun, where he spent his life as leader of Reform Judaism. His goal in the beginning was to unite all American synagogues into one organization, and in 1873 he established the Union of American Hebrew Congregations, the cooperative organization of Jewish congregations.

Rabbi Isaac Mayer Wise planned that the Union of American Hebrew Congregations would be an umbrella organization for all of American Judaism, and this kept the organization from radical changes during the first decade of its existence. The Union grew from an initial twenty-eight congregations that included some traditional synagogues to almost 200 synagogues by 1880. To Wise's delight, Hebrew Union College was founded in 1875 in

Cincinnati, the first extant institution of Jewish higher learning in America. For nearly half a century, Wise edited and published *The American Israelite* (until July 3, 1874, it was called *The Israelite*), and one can gain a keen understanding of this rabbi from that periodical. More importantly, *The American Israelite* of the 1870s and early 1880s reflects the attitudes of American Jews of all persuasions toward American Protestants. Articles, excerpts, and speeches abound in a potpourri of Jewish perceptions and ideas.

In the October 24, 1873 issue of *The Israelite*, the New York correspondent contrasted the meetings of the Evangelical Alliance in New York City with meetings of the ultra-liberal Free Religious Association which soon followed in the same city. This was the very same world gathering of the Evangelical Alliance mentioned earlier in this chapter, where evangelicals debated topics such as Darwinism. *The Israelite*, however, mentions none of the debate over evolution in the Evangelical Alliance: rather, its New York correspondent appears to be uncomfortable with the religious "fanaticism" of the evangelicals. He insists that they came to New York "for the purpose of advancing the interests of Protestantism, and this was best accomplished by finding effective means to check the growing influence of science, skepticism, and Roman Catholicism—those three terrors of the evangelical Christian."[29]

In addition, what really seemed to scare the Jews of New York and, in turn, this Jewish correspondent, was the enthusiasm the evangelicals showed for their religion. "While the Alliance was in session," the correspondent related, "the halls and churches where the different branches met were always filled by people whose enthusiasm was of a fervid kind, and akin to fanaticism." This evangelical "enthusiasm" was contrasted in some detail in *The Israelite* to the liberal free thinkers in the Free Religious Association, whose goal was "the consecration of the human mind to its highest uses" and who included all men "whether they profess anything or nothing, if they are seekers after the truth they belong to the religion of humanity." It was evident that the Jewish correspondent and *The Israelite* felt much more comfortable with the Free Religious Association. Jewish readers did obtain, however, an understanding of the diversity among Protestants from the recorded speeches of the free thinkers.

In November 1873, Isaac Mayer Wise himself applauded the "liberal sentiments in religion" propounded by "the eloquent and generous President of the Free Religious Association, Rev. O.B. Frothingham." Agreeing with Rev. Frothingham that religion for the future generations of America would not be "Christian," Rabbi Wise devoted his editorial remarks to "What the Religion of America Will Be." Insisting that there "will never be a religion without a God, and the God of Israel is the loftiest conception of which the human mind is capable," Rabbi Wise concluded:

> But the world has not outgrown its prejudices against the Jew and Judaism; therefore not even Mr. Frothingham, as liberal a gentleman as there is one in this country or elsewhere, can tell us what the religion of America will be, and must stop short in telling us what it will not be. Every thinker in this country knows that the belief in the Christian story, miracles, and dogmas, evaporates rapidly; that science, philosophy, reason, and humanity demolish the bulwark of traditional faith; every rational mind can see that monarchical Christianity can not live much longer in democratic America. The unsophisticated and unprejudiced can see no less clear that the rational and humane elements of Christianity will survive the revolution; but these elements are part and parcel of rational Judaism. Therefore we know what the Religion of America will be.[30]

Because the principles of freedom, human dignity, the striving for goodness and perfection, equal opportunity, etc. were central to the Jewish faith, Rabbi Wise (after elaborating his arguments to a friendly questioner in several more issues) underscored his major thesis: "Therefore we declare Judaism, in its pure and denationalized form, as the religion of future generations—the religion of all free men."[31]

In a century that was absorbed in the upward progress of mankind, many Jews agreed with Rabbi Isaac Mayer Wise that "Christianity, in any of its known forms, can not maintain itself beyond the current phase of civilization, which is absolutistic in State and Church." Wise asserted:

> Therefore, the perpetual warfare of the Church against the onward march of progressive and irresistible liberty in all parts of the civilized world, by the Pope and his prelates on the one hand, by the established churches of England and Prussia on the other, and by

the fragments thereof in our own country. Make this country Catholic, Episcopalian, Presbyterian, or Evangelical in any sense, and free government is at an end. This is generally admitted.[32]

The pages of *The Israelite* in the 1870s abound with actions and court cases attempting to prohibit the use of the Bible in public schools. The imposition of religion on secular institutions was feared and constantly combatted by the Jewish community in the nineteenth century as well as the twentieth. In the 1800s, the Jewish community deplored what it felt to be "the repeated attempt to change the Constitution of the United States into an instrument of evangelical sectarianism."[33]

Thus the Jewish community was at odds with the influence of evangelicals in politics and education. American Jewish opposition to American evangelicals is seen in a number of other areas as well, including theological perceptions, revivalism, and mission. The sense of distaste and repugnance is clearly evident in *The Israelite*.

Theological Perceptions

From July 11 through September 5, 1873, Rabbi Isaac Mayer Wise reprinted three lectures on the origin of Christianity that he had delivered in Albany, Cincinnati, Chicago, Detroit, Memphis, Milwaukee, New York, and New Orleans. In Lecture 1, "Jesus the Pharisee," he presents to the readers of *The Israelite* a very Jewish Jesus who was "an enthusiastic Jewish patriot" hated by the Roman authorities and their collaborators in Judea. "Like many of the prophets and the psalmists, and in perfect harmony with the Essenes and the Pharisean associates," Wise explained, "Jesus was opposed to the entire Levitical laws and institutions," opposing the high priest and chief priests that had "purchased their offices for high prices, and used them to enrich themselves from the sweat and tears of the oppressed people." Jesus had "a scheme of salvation," to save his people and to restore the kingdom of heaven. Unfortunately, "there was always a Messianic mania among the Hebrew people," and Jesus' follower Peter "proclaimed Jesus the Messiah." Although Jesus protested "loudly and emphatically against this appeal to popular prejudice" to secure the confidence of the masses, the "spark had been thrown on combustibles," and

Jesus' "death was inevitable, unless his supporters had upset the Roman power." Since Jesus had not come to start a bloody revolution and he knew it could only result in calamity to his followers, "he sacrificed himself to save his own."[34]

To Rabbi Wise, Jesus was certainly Jewish, but he was not the founder of Christianity. "Had he lived in Palestine at any other time," Wise asserted, "he would have lived long enough to stand now prominently among the sages of the Talmud, and undoubtedly he would have gained a high reputation. But he was too young when he lost his life. There was no originality in his words. His disciples estranged him to the Jew. His followers made of the cross the symbol of persecution. Therefore the Jews did not think of reclaiming him, who was actually theirs." Rabbi Isaac Mayer Wise taught his readers and disciples that Jesus was not the author of Christianity, but rather became the cause of the origin of Christianity.[35]

In the second lecture, "The Apostles and the Essenes," and the third lecture, "Paul and the Mystics," Rabbi Wise elaborated in lengthy discourse how Peter and the nascent church used the allegorical method of the Essenes to unite and form the body of Christ. "What they added, viz., the dogmas of the resurrection and the second advent of the Messiah, did not alienate them from, or estrange them to, the Hebrew people, among whom all sorts of opinions and sects were tolerated."[36] In contrast, the apostle Paul was, in Wise's words, "the author of Gentile Christianity."

A "master machinist" in the world "machine-shop," Paul "conceived the idea of carrying into effect, what all the prophets, all pious Israelites of all ages hoped and expected, the denationalization of the Hebrew ideas and their promulgation in the form of universal religion, among the Gentiles, to conciliate and unite the human family under the great banner inscribed with the motto of 'One God and one code of morals to all.'" Not surprisingly, Rabbi Wise's description of the hopes and expectations of "all pious Israelites" sounds much like his own nineteenth-century liberal Jewish beliefs and ideals.

"All Jews of all ages hoped and expected that the kingdom of heaven should be extended to all nations and tongues," Wise continued, "but Paul went forth TO DO it; this is his particular greatness." Rabbi Wise taught that to bring the gospel to pagans, Paul was "obliged to paganize the gospel." Paul also was forced to proclaim "The end is nigh!" to wake up the pagans. But in his quest to convert his generation, Paul could never have foreseen how the gentile followers would turn means "adopted for momentary purposes" into rigid dogmas. Rabbi Isaac Mayer Wise declared to audience and reader alike that "the entire New Testament has no knowledge of the Trinity and the orthodox creed...if any of our modern congregations are Christian, the apostolic congregation of Jerusalem was heretic...if the orthodox creed tells what one must believe in order to be a Christian, Paul was none."[37]

To Wise, the four Christian Gospels (Matthew, Mark, Luke, and John) were written long after Peter, Paul, and the other apostles died. Rabbi Wise dates the Gospel of John as late as 160 C.E. This is in accordance with the higher-critical biblical theories of his day. The third century is of particular interest to him in respect to church history, because he views four distinct systems of Christianity visible during the that century: (1) that of Jesus with pure theocracy, (2) that of Peter with the Messiah and his second advent, (3) that of Paul with the Son of God and the approaching end of all flesh, and (4) that of John with the Logos and the self-aggrandizing demigod or man-god on earth. "The difficulties and dissensions arising from the attempts of uniting all these contradictory systems in one, ended with the Council of Nicea (325) in the beginning of the fourth century," Rabbi Isaac Mayer Wise concluded, "and the establishment of an orthodox creed, the excommunication of Jewish Christians, and the establishment of the Church as a State institution. Then the sword and the pyre established doctrines."[38]

Comparing Rabbi Wise's view of the Bible, Christian doctrine, and church history with the evangelical statements of faith in the earlier part of this chapter, one is struck by the vast theological differences that separated Wise and his followers from the evangelical milieu. It was impossible to reconcile the two world views. Furthermore, the evangelical's penchant to spread a "gospel message" that was diametrically opposed in such Jewish thought enflamed Jewish passions and Jewish fears. Revivalism, a central key to the rise of the modern evangelical movement, engendered volatile reaction from the Jewish community of the 1800s.

Revivalism

This is clearly seen in the response of the Jewish community to the most popular evangelist of the day, Dwight Lyman Moody (1837-1899). In August 1875, Moody landed in New York after a two-year evangelistic tour to the British Isles. He had left his home in Chicago in relative obscurity, but his success and fame in England and Scotland made him an instant national figure upon his return. Teamed with his ever-loyal singing associate, Ira Sankey, Moody's influence and message remind one of Billy Graham and his singing associate in the 1950s, George Beverly Shea. After a month-long evangelistic campaign at the invitation of the churches in Brooklyn, D.L. Moody campaigned from November 1875 to January 1876 in Philadelphia. Chicago and Boston, Nashville, St. Louis, and Kansas City followed. Organized through the efforts of a cross section of mainstream evangelical churches, vast audiences attended these revivalistic meetings and evangelistic enterprises. The American Jewish community was not amused.

Correspondents from the campaign cities wrote faithfully to *The American Israelite* and letters poured in. Moody's Brooklyn crusade, for example, prompted this response from Washington, D.C.:

Brooklyn, that great city of religious sensationalism, after having supplied the press and the public with the famous, or rather infamous scandal of last year (the accusation of adultery leveled on liberal minister, Henry Ward Beecher, pastor of Plymouth Congregational Church in Brooklyn) has now gone vigorously into the preaching business. The great revivalists, Moody and Sankey, are making their parades and ostentatious harangues in order to excite people to an open and public *profession*, of what is called religion. As one of the papers of the day irreverently states, Brooklyn is trying to run God Almighty in the high pressure circus style. People who remember the same sort of cant that prevailed in various parts of the United States about a year or two back, run by a moly of so-called crusaders, will recognize in the present forced excitement about the same sort of an affair. Van Pelt, the first convert of the crusaders, and their special apostle, soon fell from grace, and it may be of course expected that the new fangled patent saints that are being gathered into the folds under the rink in the city of churches, will, when the tension is withdrawn, relapse to their old ways, this is the history of all such movements, when sudden impulses are appealed to and not convictions. The proceedings become almost ridiculous at times, and quite a farce.[39]

The writer then related illustrations of "the familiar and profane manner in which sacred things are treated" in the revivalistic crusade. A section entitled "Flippant Moodyisms" followed, mocking the revivalist's statements. Moody was accused of using revivals for his own personal monetary gain, and future editions of *The American Israelite* included sections entitled "More Moodyisms." "The revival still rages and will have its run all through the country, like baseball (fanaticism)," the November 26, 1875 edition announced. A letter sent by a Jewish man two days later to *The American Israelite* from Philadelphia began: "It is Thanksgiving Eve. I sit pondering over the events of the day...What makes me so pensive? Moody and Sankey are in our city."[40]

The spectre of "Moody fanaticism" with revivals and conversions was acutely distressing to the American Jewish community. In spite of the fact that both liberal Protestants and fundamentalist Protestants would claim Dwight L. Moody as one of their own, the fear associated with revivalism never subsided. Henry Drummond had referred to Moody as "the biggest human being I have ever met." Liberal Protestant, Lyman Abbott, wrote affectionately, "The greatest evangelist of my time was Dwight L. Moody; the monuments which he built and which will long preserve his memory are the school for girls at Northfield and the school for boys at Mount Hermon." Moody's colleagues and associates consistently portrayed him as selfless, humble in spirit, charitable (he died nearly penniless and his family often complained of his always giving things away), and yet a man of conviction with a passion "to save the lost." He combined both liberals and conservatives in his crusades, and had a catholicity of spirit and love that impressed ministers of all sectors of the Protestant faith. To most Jews, however, D.L. Moody was a huckster, a villain, "an illiterate charlatan, ignorant of the Bible, not being able to distinguish logic from logwood" (as one Jewish writer insisted).

Furthermore, revivalism and Moody were linked to anti-Semitism. During the Philadelphia crusade, Moody was cited in the newspapers as having preached a "passion sermon" that declared that the Jews crucified Jesus. He was reported to have stated that a thousand Jews in Paris had recently declared that they were glad they had killed "the Christian God." Jewish letters and editorials concerning the incident poured in to *The American Israelite*. When the account of Moody's disclaimer was finally published in the March 25, 1876 issue of Wise's periodical, it was treated as another of the "pious frauds sent forth by Mr. Moody." Moody's private conversation with a young Jewish man concerning the allegations were published in newspapers around the country and appeared in *The American Israelite* as follows:

> "I do not blame the Jews, and I have never spoken against them," said Mr. Moody. "The statement in a Philadelphia newspaper, that I did is untrue. I never see a Jew but I feel like taking off my hat to him. In my opinion, your people are to be the great missionaries to convert the world to Christ. What better agency could there be? You are scattered throughout the earth, and speak all languages. I believe you will all go back to Jerusalem one day, and be restored to your old kingdom—don't you?"

> "No, I do not," was the reply. "You never could induce intelligent Jews to settle in such a miserable, sterile little patch of land as Palestine, when they can sit in luxury in their homes in London, Paris, Frankfort, and Berlin, and there control the commerce of nations and the destinies of empires. Why should they go back to Palestine? In all their ancient glory—which was not very great after all—they were never as prosperous and as powerful as they are now."

> "You will all go back to Jerusalem, and you will all be brought to Christ at last," said Mr. Moody. "I tell you, it's bound to come."[41]

Although he was not a systematic theologian, Dwight L. Moody evidences his *premillennial* view of the future—a view that gave rise to the Zionism of the fundamentalist-evangelical movement in the last quarter of the nineteenth century. As we have seen, this theology came to dominate evangelical theology in the twentieth century. Contrary to the triumphalistic postmillennial Protestant thought that dominated both liberalism and conservatism in the nineteenth century (stating that the Protestant Christian church would bring in the millennium through conversion and upward progress), this premillennial view insisted that only the return of Jesus as the delivering Messiah could straighten out the evil world. Jesus himself would convince the Jewish people that he was their Messiah. And Dwight L. Moody preached that Jesus could return at any moment.

The Jewish interviewer continued with a crucial question:

> "I have given you some reasons for not believing in Christianity, and I could give many more," said the young man. "I am open to conviction, but I cannot believe what my reason rejects. Prove to me that Christianity is purer than Judaism, and I will become a Christian."

> "It is not a matter of reason. Conversion must come from the heart, and not from the head," replied the preacher. "But it will come at last. You will all be brought to Christ."

> "By a miracle, I presume. Do you believe in modern miracles, Mr. Moody?"

> "Well, I don't know. Every conversion is a miracle, I suppose. But when I was in England, a Mr. Midwood assured me that a female relative of his had, by means of his prayers, been cured of a disease of long standing. You can write to him, if you like, and he'll tell you all about it. Address him, 'Care of the Young Men's Christian Association, Manchester.' Surely that was a miracle. Now if I should convert you, I should call it a miracle."

> "So should I," rejoined the young man.

> "Have you made any Jewish converts?" he asked, as he rose to leave.

> "Well, several have stood up and professed Christ. But," said Mr. Moody, as he took the visitor's proffered hand, "I cannot say that I put much faith in converted Jews."

"We never heard of any Jew placing much confidence in Mr. Moody, in Christian dogmatism or the revival *furor*," Rabbi Isaac Mayer Wise lashed out editorially at the end of this account. "Nor do we think the Philadelphia papers misrepresented Mr. M.'s speech. He is not responsible all the time for what he says, as the Holy Ghost sometimes makes a fool of him who speaks ungrammatical rigmarole. But we give him credit for his disclaimer. It is what might be called a backing out. Let him pass."

Mission to the Jews

If revivalism sparked such an intensity of feeling, the attempt to convert Jews and the enigma of the "Hebrew Christian" was appalling. "The fools are not all dead yet, and there are a few still living who believe in the conversion of the Jews to Christianity," a letter from New York to *The American Israelite* (dated March 31, 1876) began. "And not only do they believe this, but they are even foolish enough to subscribe money to enable the 'Society for Promoting Christianity Among the Jews' to continue its feeble existence." Mocking the 152,000 pages of tracts and the Bibles the society distributed in 1875, the writer pointed to a Christian clergyman in New York who did not know one Jew who had been converted. Of the society's claim that six adults and two children had been baptized by a former rabbi, the writer noted that Rabbi Dr. Gottheil offered "to give $25 to any Christian charity if the name of the converted man be given publicly to him, and if he can satisfy any competent man that he is a rabbi."[42] Another letter from Washington, D.C. refuted a sensational *New York Times* report that a number of Jews had been converted during Rev. Hammond's revival in the District of Columbia, declaring that "though the meetings have been held incessantly for over six weeks, and though the fanatics raved and tore, and coaxed and persuaded, and threatened and implored, they failed to secure a single Jewish apostate."

Yet *The American Israelite* and its readers spent a considerable amount of time during the 1870s exposing "Jewish apostates" and documenting these meetings. For example, Joseph Loeb from Staunton, Virginia, wrote in June 1873:

To the Editor of the Israelite:

Through your valuable paper, we have for some time been acquainted with a certain individual by the name of Abraham Jaeger, and his mission as ex-Jew Baptist.

But not for a moment had we expected that such a distinguished personage as ex-Jew Jaeger would select for his field of action such a small place as our little town of Staunton, where only a few Jewish families are living, and where there is no organized Jewish congregation; and, of course, the Baptist Jew can expect but limited success—if any.[43]

Loeb promised to report to *The Israelite* on Jaeger's meetings, "knowing your willingness and ability to defend Judaism at all times, and with your clear and forcible argument set aright such invincible creatures without doing any damage to mankind."

Another letter from Springfield, Ohio, dated August 5, 1873, indicated that while many in the town expected a former Jew to "annihilate Judaism" in his church meeting, he surprised them all:

To the Editor of The Israelite:

There exists in this world at least one man who deserves a widespread notice in your columns, and this man's name is, or was, Rev.(?) Mr. Levy, formerly, or now, of Philadelphia, Pa. This Mr. Levy was once an Israelite—certainly of no great consequence—and because we do not believe in the "Holy Jesus" he left us and joined some other religious faith, until this hour unknown to him or to the world at large. At any rate, he came here (this is a moral city), whether on charitable purposes, or business matters, we know not, but think he has some connection with some Bible house in the East. Anyhow he, by some "hocus pocus" arrangement, occupied a portion of a Christian pulpit in this city last Sunday. Think of an Israelite by birth, education, and instinct in such a position. Anyhow he drew an immense audience—no admission fee demanded—and everybody expected him to annihilate Judaism. On the contrary he did nothing of the kind, but eulogized them as a race, and praised their soundness of doctrine, and gloried in their being the chosen people; but the burden of his song and the weight of his complaint was, that the Israelites do not accept Jesus Christ. What good Israelite can? Mr. Levy's address was acceptable to the Christians, and secured for him an excellent meal at the house of a leading Christian divine of this city. The amount of the collection, if any, is not known.

The question among the Israelites is: Who is Mr. "Rev." Levy? and where does he come from? and who converted him?

I think the good people of Columbus [Ohio] are next to be "shocked" by Mr. Levy, unless a collection is made up before he reaches the city limits. Fortunately none of our Israelites made his acquaintance, as far as I can learn—not even "our own divine"—and he left.[44]

The Israelite published the letter under the heading: "Another Converted Rabbi." An earlier account in the same issue announced: "Messrs. Moody and Sankey ended their New York revival last night in 'a blaze of glory.' The Hippodrome was terribly crowded with a weeping, shouting, perspiring, and amen-crying mass of people."

Isaac Mayer Wise assured his readers in 1876 that the Hebrew Christian phenomena was only an indication that evangelicalism was dying. When a reader from Corning, New York reported in vivid detail the testimony to the Methodist Church of "Rev. Rider" (who claimed to be a former rabbi from Chicago), Editor Wise insisted:

> It appears that dogmatic Christianity is well-nigh played out. If such men like this Rider, or like Nathan, Jaeger, and Levy, must keep it up by plan and unmitigated falsehoods, it is certainly pretty well gone. The story told by Rider is rehashed, and has been rehashed a thousand times, without having since been believed by any sensible man. It is the old pattern for pious frauds. No rabbi in this country—mark it once for all—NO RABBI has turned apostate, and those Christianity peddlers who call themselves rabbis are liars, willful liars. As a usual thing, they are adventurers and beggars, who can do nothing among Jews, and go to work to impose upon credulous Christians especially in small towns and villages, who appear to put up with any sort of imposition.[45]

By 1884, however, Rabbi Wise had to confess that "the missionaries caught a big fish in Russia in the person of the Kabbalist, Joseph Rabinowitz, of Kischinew, who, in connection with his few friends, seeks to establish a Unitarian Jew-Christian congregation, i.e., as he proposes, to remain Jewish *de facto* and accept into the creed of the congregation the belief in Jesus of Nazareth as the true Messiah, and not as a son of God or a Divinity, in order to be Christian in name at least."[46]

The following year Reform Judaism and Rabbi Isaac Mayer Wise would move to a more radical position in Jewish thought and practice with the adoption of the Pittsburgh Platform of 1885. This severed Wise from Jewish traditionalists and dashed his hopes of a united

American Judaism. Joseph Rabinowitz, by contrast, moved from a rational Judaism to a mystical Jewish-Christian traditionalism, totally accepting Jesus as the promised Messiah. Rabinowitz's fame spread as his "messianic synagogue" became the darling of the Hebrew Christian missions. He was invited by Dwight L. Moody to visit Chicago and to travel throughout the United States.[47] More than anything else, the threat of being objects of conversion colored the American Jewish peoples' perception of evangelicals.

* * *

Nineteenth-century American Jews understood much more about traditional Christian belief and practice, differences and polity, than they are often given credit for discerning. Nevertheless, to Rabbi Wise and many of his readers, evangelical Christianity was "monarchical" and obsolete, "absolutistic" and unsophisticated, antidemocratic and antiprogressive. In contrast, evangelicals saw their belief as a return to an enlightened and divinely ordained first-century Christianity, the answer and salvation for all humankind. Revivalism had turned seventeenth-century American Puritanism into nineteenth-century American evangelicalism, and evangelicals testified to the abundant life, freedom, and purpose their religious beliefs had brought them. This "fanaticism" and "enthusiasm" was viewed by the Jewish community, however, as barbaric and uncivilized, a threat to pure religion and liberty. Evangelists, using the "extreme measures" the apostle Paul had "adopted" to reach the heathen Roman masses, were only a further indication to Wise and other leaders that traditional Christianity would soon be (or would have to be) demolished. For other American Jews, fear of further evangelical control and the spread of the Christian gospel message was intense.

Most of the roots and reactions of the nineteenth-century evangelical and Jewish movements in America that we have uncovered in this chapter have persisted to the present day. This analysis should help us understand the background to many of the attitudes each group holds toward the other as we approach the twenty-first century. It is no surprise that Jews and evangelicals often seem to live in two different worlds. In the next chapter, we will attempt to understand how Jews and evangelicals perceive and relate to one another in our own time.

3

PERSPECTIVES: TWO DIFFERENT WORLDS

Relationships between Jews and evangelicals have been affected by many factors, not the least of which is demography. Most Jews and evangelicals simply do not live next to one another. Approximately 40 percent of the American Jewish population today is concentrated in the New York-Northern New Jersey metropolitan area. This area is not an evangelical stronghold. In other metropolitan areas of significant Jewish population, Jews and evangelicals have had relatively little social contact. In many rural areas of the nation, evangelicals have rarely met a Jewish person. If they do meet, it is usually in a business transaction, on a university campus, or in some professional gathering.

Recent population studies have suggested, however, that the Jewish community has become increasingly spread out in the past half century. Although the Northeast continues to have a disproportionate share of the Jewish population, Jewish individuals appear to be more mobile than the general population. In search of work and promotion, Jews are more willing to travel to other smaller, basically urban centers. Therefore there are more Jewish population centers in the United States today with fewer Jews in each center.[1] The Jewish population of 6 million and the evangelical population of perhaps 60 million are coming into closer contact, at least demographically.

The intensified media attention toward the evangelical resurgence in the past fifteen years has undoubtedly stimulated interest and anxiety in the Jewish community. Whereas the large majority of Jews consider themselves left of center and liberal, the majority of evangelicals consider themselves "middle of the road" or basically conservative. While both communities, evangelical and Jewish, are complex and diverse, these cultural differences help to form each group's sense of the other.

To most Jews, evangelicals are "New Religious Right" fundamentalists who endanger free thought and social progress. Their world view contributes to anti-Semitism and anti-intellectualism. Their representatives include leaders who declare "God Almighty does not hear the prayer of a Jew"; little children who insist on screaming Bible verses outside a public school; missionaries who hawk gospel tracts on street corners to seduce Jewish young people to "accept Jesus as their Savior"; beauty queens in low-cut bathing suits who smile sweetly as they tell how much they "love Jesus"; and personalities like Jerry Falwell, Jim and Tammy Bakker, Jimmy Swaggert, and even Billy Graham.

To evangelicals, Jews and Judaism are often portrayed in ancient biblical categories that have been transformed by Christian doctrine. While actually comprehending little about the Jewish community, evangelicals often think they know more than they really do. Jews are portrayed as wealthy and talented, blessed by God. Yet the Jewish community is viewed as "rejecting God's special gift to the world," Jesus. Jews are seen as unjustifiably fretful about religion in public schools. They are represented by the American Civil Liberties Union, which interrupts Christmas plays and works to ban the singing of carols and Bible reading in a rural elementary school because one Jewish student studies there. For some, Jews stand firmly against biblical principles; for others, Jews know their "Old Testament well" but continue to be "under the law" and believe in "works" to gain their salvation.

Thus Jews and evangelicals live in two different worlds, characterized by differing world views and agendas. However honest and natural their differences, they are also separated by prejudice, stereotypes, and caricatures of one another. Within each community today, one notes an ambivalence toward the other, a simultaneous repulsion and attraction to knowing the other group. Some Jewish leaders question any interaction with evangelical leadership. In spite of the much publicized evangelical resurgence in politics, some Jews believe that the Jewish community is strong enough to stand on its own with the help of its traditional, non-evangelical friends. Others urge more interaction with "conservative Christians," arguing that such an important block of the American public must not be neglected and implying that Jews and evangelicals can join together in a host of mutual concerns.

Most evangelicals are excited by the prospect of getting to know "the chosen people of God," but have little idea of how to go about such a process. When some evangelicals do pursue a course of dialogue and interreligious activity, other evangelicals may accuse them of succumbing to a Jewish plot to control evangelism. The latter group claims that evangelical-Jewish dialogue necessitates compromising the Christian message. For most evangelicals, however, a great hindrance is the church's demand on their time. Much more active in attendance at worship services than their Jewish counterparts, evangelicals are involved in a seemingly endless array of Sunday school classes, morning and evening (and midweek) worship services, small group sessions, etc. Prohibited by time, geography, and knowledge from quality interaction *with* Jews, the evangelical is nonetheless dramatically affected in perception and attitude *toward* Jews by his or her church "world."

SUNDAY SCHOOL MATERIALS

The Jewish afternoon and Sunday school curriculum does not appear to be the intregal influence from childhood to adulthood that it is within the evangelical community. On the elementary level, the Jewish Sunday school curriculum rarely deals with Christianity. As one Jewish educator stated: "We have the children only three or four hours a week; we have to teach them Hebrew, the holiday cycle, some Bible, some prayers, and a smattering of history in quick outline. You want me to teach them about Christianity? I'm lucky if they learn anything about Judaism!"

Even on the secondary level, Jewish students rarely learn about Christianity except in history and comparative religion segments of the studies. Where these materials are used, however, a caution often accompanies the Jewish curriculum that is notably absent in retrospect from the evangelical curriculum. The United Synagogue's *A Curriculum for the Afternoon Jewish School* (1978) stated within the goals of a lesson series on Judaism and Christianity:

> The purpose is not to denigrate Christianity but to differentiate between Judaism and Christianity. The goal is not resentment, disdain or hatred for either Christianity or Christians but differentiation, disassociation and *internalization* of the conviction that Jewishness cannot be blended with Christianity.... The students without rancor, should emerge...with the conviction that conversion is actually disassociation from Jewishness.[2]

As Judith H. Banki concluded in her study of the Jewish curriculum:

> In sum: formal Jewish education teaches relatively little about contemporary evangelicals as a distinct group. About the claims of evangelical Christianity, Jewish education says a bit more. These claims are firmly rejected, but they are rejected without malice or invective, and in the context of a powerful affirmation of religious pluralism and the kinship of all humankind.[3]

Evangelicalism is quite a contrast. For the evangelical, the Sunday school is an important influence from the earliest years of life through adulthood and into the golden years. Many evangelical churches continually pressure their members to observe regular Sunday school attendance as faithfully as the Sunday morning service—in other words, *every* week. Therefore the perceptions formed by the four major distributors of Sunday school literature (David C. Cook Publishing Company, Gospel Light Publications, Scripture Press Publications, and Standard Publishing Company) toward Jews and Judaism have an important effect on evangelical attitudes.

Ever since 1963, when Dr. Bernhard Olson's influential study, *Faith and Prejudice*, was published, it has become commonplace to link Christian curricular materials to the formation of negative attitudes about Jews and Judaism. Olson demonstrated that this linkage is extremely complex: prejudice is not directly correlated with theological orientation or style of scriptural interpretation. Nonetheless, prejudice—anti-Semitism, in particular—was found across the board in the thousands of denominational educational materials Olson studied. Since his study, many Christian publishers and denominations have become aware of the nuances of negativism regarding Jews and Judaism in their materials and have undertaken systematic efforts to rid them of prejudice. Subsequent investigations of Christian curricula are always in order.

In 1984, a study was conducted on themes relating to Jews and Judaism in the materials by the first three major publishers listed above.[4] This research concentrated on materials produced for the spring quarter (March-May 1984) and evaluated teacher's manuals, student guides, workbooks, looseleaf handouts, and other curriculum aids for ages two years old to adult. An important finding was that the "Christ-killer" theme—the most potent religious force in forming anti-Jewish attitudes—was absent from most of these materials, except in selected adult electives. Especially in the materials for young children, there was not even a hint of Jewish responsibility for the death of Jesus. Instead, a high regard for the heroes and heroines of the Hebrew Bible was instilled through a wide selection of study aids.

Through these evangelical materials, Israelite men and women of faith became the child's examples of faithfulness to God. The errors that the Israelites made were correlated to the errors that the child makes. God's love and mercy toward those, who failed from time to time in the Hebrew Scriptures, resemble God's love and mercy toward children today. The enemies of the Israelites are portrayed as enemies of God. They, in turn, become the child's enemies. Thus biblical stories have valuable morals for children. For example, Primaries (Grades 1-2) discovered that the Israelites worked together to rebuild the Temple and Jerusalem. The teacher's guide emphasized the importance of working together and worshiping together to celebrate God's goodness (Gospel Light). Students explored the life of King Solomon, ascertaining how he used his time and resources wisely and unwisely. The teacher's guide suggested a discussion on the ways children may use their time, abilities, and possessions.

In the David C. Cook materials, Primary-Juniors (Grades 3-4) learned of the life and exploits of Moses, Caleb, and Joshua. Through these great heroes, the young people were taught that God always guides his people if they trust and obey him. Through lessons on the Israelites' wanderings in the wilderness, students learn how God meets different kinds of needs in their own journey through life. Pre-primaries (four and five year olds) prefaced a study on the life of Jesus with several weeks on the life of Daniel, David, and Abraham as heroes of the faith (Scripture Press). Subsequently, Jews were portrayed as the friends of Jesus.

These benign portrayals of "Jews" are in contrast to another theme found in the same publishers' materials. In an adult elective on the Book of Acts, the Christ-killer theme is clearly evident. Gospel Light Publications chose to feature Paul E. Pierson's *Themes From Acts* as their weekly resource tool. Each member of the class received this paperback, studying a chapter a week. Pierson is a Presbyterian minister who served as a missionary in Brazil and Portugal for seventeen years. He received his master and doctoral degrees from Princeton Theological Seminary and pastored the First Presbyterian Church of Fresno, California before becoming dean of the School of World Mission at the evangelical Fuller Theological Seminary. Dealing with Peter's message in Acts 2, Dr. Pierson wrote: "Yet the Jews, led by their priests, had engineered His condemnation and handed Jesus over to pagan rulers to be crucified. But even though they were guilty of his death, they had unconsciously fulfilled the purpose of God. He had revealed through His prophets that the Messiah should suffer and die for the sins of many."[5] Conjuring vivid images of Jews and Judaism in his discussion, Pierson continued:

> Martin Luther often said we must hear the bad news before we can hear the Good News. Peter's message, if true, must have appeared to be the worst possible news to the crowd. They and their leaders

had not only rejected the long-awaited Messiah; they had put themselves clearly in opposition to God by crucifying Him! Was it any wonder they were cut to the heart and cried for help!

Peter's message is a marvelous example of the preaching of the cross. His hearers realized as never before the depth of sin and its effects. It was both collective and individual, national and personal. Not only had their leaders rejected the Messiah and been responsible for His murder; they too had been personally involved and were responsible. Some who were there had no doubt been part of the mob which had shouted, "Crucify Him!" Now they felt desperate.

Peter answered their cry with amazing Good News. They were not lost; they were not irrevocably rejected by God. Through repentance and faith in this crucified Messiah they would receive two gifts greater than any they had ever hoped for.[6]

For Dr. Pierson, the first gift was "the forgiveness of their sins" (the greatest sin being their complicity in the death of Jesus"). "It was an indication of the greatness of God's power and love," he informed both Sunday school teacher and student, "that He could take that seemingly tragic event and make it the means of redemption even for murderers of His Son." The second gift was the Holy Spirit. For Pierson, "the Jews," both ancient and modern, are emphatically in need of salvation, without which they cannot atone for the crime.

Although the evangelical publishers of Sunday school literature had provided teaching guides of nearly every conceivable kind to help prepare teachers, not one statement warned the teacher against fostering negative images of Jews and Judaism. In fact, a Scripture Press high school elective, *Dr. Luke Examines Jesus*, stated bluntly: "Since only Jewish money can be used in the temple, the money-changers are making outrageous profits by changing foreign currency into Jewish money at sky-high exchange rates."[7] It seems reasonable to presume that intensively negative images of scriptural Jews and Judaism can lead to negative attitudes toward modern Jews. At the very least, the negative orientation of religious education cannot help in the formation of a positive or even a neutral civic attitude.

A content analysis of the curricular materials of four major publishers of evangelical Sunday school materials was conducted for spring 1988. These materials were, disturbingly, more negative than their counterparts four years before. That is because many of these March-May 1988 resources dealt with the death of Jesus. Consequently, the Christ-killer theme and related anti-Jewish stereotypes and caricatures increased. It is important to spend some time on each evangelical publisher's materials in this study to ascertain the complexity of the evangelical experience, as well as to determine the problem areas in the evangelical curriculum.

Gospel Light Publications

Gospel Light Publications did provide "Adventure through the Bible" take-home papers which shared the story of the Passover and talked about the importance of family traditions, thus implicitly portraying Jews in a good light. But Paul Pierson's *Theme From Acts* continued to be offered as an adult elective and, unfortunately, its rhetoric was replicated in the standard lesson plans for most ages. For example, teachers of Juniors (Grades 5-6) were given backgrounders on the predicament of three leaders, namely, Caiaphas, Pilate, and Herod. "Caiaphas, as the high priest, represented the Jewish people before God," the teacher's manual explains, describing the composition of the Sanhedrin. "But despite his power, he could not carry out the Sanhedrin's verdict of death. That was his predicament—how to coerce the Roman authorities to execute Jesus."

The teacher is advised that Pilate was a mere pawn of the Jewish community's animosity toward Jesus. "The predicament faced by Pilate was entirely different," the background meditation explained. "Pilate as an experienced Roman leader, saw through the trumped-up political charges against Jesus. Not wanting to give in to the Jews, Pilate put off the problem of what to do with Jesus by sending Him to Herod."[8]

Entitled "Betrayed and Tried," the teacher's manual conveys the view that "the Jews" engineered Jesus' death. The child is taught that the "chief priests were trying to get people to testify against Jesus so they could put Him to death," "the Jewish leaders were having a difficult time building a case against Jesus," "the Jews had taken Jesus to see the governor," "the Jewish leaders were trying to frame Jesus," etc. It is recommended that the class sing: "Were you there when *they* crucified my Lord?"

The lesson plan for four- and five-year-olds does not mention "the Jews," but rather states that "other people and their leaders were angry and jealous...they didn't want Jesus teaching the people about God." "So the leaders started making plans to kill Jesus," the teacher is to say. "The angry people hurt Jesus...and Jesus let them kill Him."[9] Citations from the Gospels which relate Jesus' death and resurrection are listed for the teacher. Middlers (Grades 3-4) are encouraged to read the account with their instructor. These Gospel Light materials stress that "Jesus allowed Himself to be arrested, tried and sentenced to die because He loved us and was willing to take the punishment for our sins." Children's "memory verses" emphasize Jesus' willing sacrifice of his life and the wonders of his resurrection.

The predilections of the individual Sunday school teacher and the way he or she tells the story has much to do with the student's perceptions. Yet in the materials there is little, if any, counter-balance to the anti-Jewish images conveyed. One East Coast evangelical college student upon studying the Holocaust recalled sorrowfully that her Sunday school teacher had called it the "Holy Cost" to the Jewish people for rejecting Jesus. There is no way of knowing whether this kind of pedagogy is the exception or the rule.

Scripture Press

Scripture Press's "The Bible-in-Life" Sunday school curriculum takes a similar approach to Jesus' death and resurrection as the Gospel Light curriculum. Nursery (Ages 2-3) and Kindergarten (Ages 4-5) learn of Jesus' enemies and friends:

> We've seen how Jesus did only good things for everyone. You would think that everyone would love the Lord Jesus and want to be His friend.

> But, some men didn't love Jesus. When He did kind things these men became angry, because they couldn't do the things Jesus could do. They couldn't make sick people well or forgive people's sins. They

didn't like to see people praising Jesus, waving palm branches and singing to Him. They wanted the people to praise *them*, not Jesus.

That's why they got together and said, "Let's kill Jesus. Then the people will forget about him and do what *we* say."[10]

Key consideration, however, is to be given to the young child's acceptance that Jesus is alive, loves children, and helps people. The stories about Jesus are to show God's love and His desire for the love of the child.

As in most evangelical literature and sermons, the Pharisees do not fare well in this curriculum. The Juniors (Grades 5-6) begin their section on the Good Shepherd with this explanation: "The Pharisees of Jesus' day turned their backs on people who did not know and keep all their religious rules. They didn't care about those people at all. But Jesus did. He talked about those lost people as sheep who needed a shepherd."[11] In one of the following March 1988 lessons, the fifth and sixth graders were taught to link the Pharisees with Satan in "Satan's plot against Jesus":

> There is nothing Satan ever wanted to do more than get rid of Jesus. On the night of the Passover, Satan's plot to destroy Jesus seemed to be working. Satan stirred up the chief priests and Pharisees. They were filled with envy and fear of Jesus. Then Satan brought together Judas, a false disciple of Jesus, and the chief priests and Pharisees. The plan to kill Jesus was set in motion.[12]

This lesson emphasized the need to be an "overcomer," and the memory verse was 1 John 4:4; "Greater is He that is in you, than he that is in the world."

Scripture Press's high school teaching guide used a five-week study of the life of Jesus to introduce a four-week study in Habakkuk and Malachi. The goal was to relate the rejection of Jesus to the rejection every teenager faces, the problems Jesus faced to the problems teens face. The unit theme was "Recognizing Jesus as King." While "the Jews" do not appear in the lesson plan, the Pharisees and others are held highly accountable for the rejection of Jesus, and the crowds are "hard," "dull," and "closed" in their attitudes. Using Matthew 12 as a text, the opposition of Jewish officialdom is portrayed as follows:

> While most of the people hesitated, the religious officials (priests and scribes, Pharisees and Sadducees) decisively rejected and opposed Jesus all the way.
>
> First, they tried to strike at Him through His disciples, but Jesus exposed and rebuked them for their commitment to ritual rather than to compassion for people (Matt. 12:1-8).
>
> Then they tried to condemn Him for healing on the Sabbath (12:9-10). Such healing was illegal according to their warped traditions, but not according to Scripture. When Jesus again revealed their lack of love, they went away even more determined to destroy Him (12:11-14).
>
> As Jesus continued to perform healing miracles (12:15-22), many people seriously wondered, "Is not this the son of David?" (12:23), meaning they thought He was the Messiah. This threatened the Pharisees and they began to insist that demonic powers were behind Jesus' miracles—a theory Jesus proved foolish (12:24-28).[13]

If the teenagers link "Pharisees" to "Jews" (and certainly the Bible passages they are to look up do so), Jewish tradition emerges as "warped," characterized more by "ritual" than by "compassion." Jews were determined "to destroy" Jesus. Of the people, the lesson concludes: "Though the crowds didn't actively oppose Jesus as the religious rulers did, He knew that the same hardness was creeping into their hearts."

The *Youth Illustrated* student Bible study magazine that these high schoolers carried home with them after Sunday school was more direct. It stated that the "Jewish people didn't expect or want the kind of kingdom Jesus described, so they turned Him off," that "the Jews thought the Messiah would turn all people to himself," and that "the Jews expected to rule with the Messiah when He came."[14] Jesus' response to each situation is suggested for the student's response in the midst of rejection.

David C. Cook Publishers

For the younger children, the David C. Cook materials emphasize Jesus' friends, his triumphal entry into Jerusalem, and his resurrection (to the near exclusion of his trial and death). In fact, the teacher's guide for the Nursery (Ages 2-3) explains:

Do not expect your 2s and 3s to understand the full meaning of Jesus' death and resurrection. Most of your preschoolers will think that Jesus was sleeping or that He was very sick or that He just wasn't able to be with His friends for a while. That's all right. Your goal in teaching this lesson to young children is not to be sure they understand death, but to emphasize the joy of Jesus' resurrection.[15]

Four- and five-year-olds are taught to forgive others and to love others because God loves them.

Yet even at this tender age, Jewish "law" is contrasted to the teaching of Jesus. Jesus appears to be separated from his Jewish community in the following May 1, 1988 teacher's "Bible Background" material for four- and five-year-olds. It states:

To our twentieth-century standards, the laws of the Jews and Romans of Jesus' time seem harsh.

Jewish law allowed a person to be stoned to death for adultery. The Romans crucified rebels. And an entire family could be sold into slavery or thrown in prison for inability to pay a debt.

Because of the harshness of the times and the hardness of human hearts, Jesus stressed the need of forgiveness. He taught forgiveness in the Lord's Prayer, by His own example, and through parables.

Jesus taught us to pray: "Forgive us our debts, as we forgive our debtors" (Mt. 6:12). The Jewish people thought of sins as debts. In Luke, the word "sins" is used instead of "debts" (Lk. 11:4). Jesus went on to teach that if we do not forgive others, God will not forgive us (Mt. 6:15).

There is no more beautiful example of forgiveness than Jesus' example on the cross. There He forgave not only the thief next to Him, but those who crucified Him (Lk. 23:34,43).

Jesus' parables on forgiveness include the prodigal son and the unforgiving servant, today's lesson.[16]

In contrast, the Primary (Grades 1-2), Primary-Junior (Grades 3-4), and Junior (Grades 5-6) Sunday school materials study the lives of such biblical figures as Elijah, Daniel, and Ezra with deep respect for Jewish history and accomplishments.

David C. Cook Publishing Company takes Junior High and Senior High school students through a study of the prophets in the March through May 1988 units. Junior High students cope with issues such as the call to serve, renewal, greed, injustice, war, and hypocrisy. In dealing with hypocrisy, the prophet Micah's call for justice is used for Senior High school students, but the Pharisees are not mentioned. Instead, hypocrisy is brought home as "a game some Christians play most of the time." The next section asks, "Aren't we all phonies in one way or another?" Micah, however, is Christianized. "For Micah," the lesson notes, "true worship of God was an everyday matter, not for Sundays only. He rebelled against 'religious people' who went through the forms of religion and then went out and forgot all about others." The Book of James in the Christian Testament is referred to as well.[17]

The Easter segments, however, link the prophets' references to the Messiah to Jesus. Junior High and Senior High students are not drawn to "the Jews" crucifying Jesus or the Pharisees as scoundrels, although the rejection of the religious leaders of Jesus' day is mentioned. Nevertheless, the question is asked: "Why is it so important that Jesus be the One that the Old Testament prophets were referring to?" The answer concludes: "If Jesus was not *the* Messiah, then the correct belief would be in line with today's Judaism, which celebrates waiting at Hanukkah, waiting for Someone who hasn't yet come. The Bible itself is useless, too, as Jesus is the Cornerstone of both Testaments."[18]

It is the adult manuals in the David C. Cook materials which most clearly castigate the Jewish leadership for Jesus' death. "The Jews continued to bring trumped-up accusations against Jesus," the Palm Sunday manual states, pointing out that "the Jews" had charged Jesus with the religious offense of blasphemy. Since this held no weight with Pilate, the Jewish officials came up with "secular" offenses, "political crimes carefully calculated to attract the attention of the Roman governor." The account continues:

> It had become customary for the Roman governor to release one prisoner at the annual Feast of Passover. Possibly this was intended as a token gesture to mollify the more zealous Jews.
>
> By his own investigation, Pilate had found Jesus to be innocent of the charges brought against Him by the Jewish leaders. He discerned it was pure jealousy over Jesus' popularity with the multitudes that caused the chief priest and elders to want Him dead. Therefore,

Pilate decided to offer Jesus as the one to be released. He assumed that the jealousy was confined to the rulers, and that Jesus was loved by the population at large... No doubt Pilate thought that when he gave the people a choice—innocence vs. guilt, and truth vs. lawlessness—they would surely choose Jesus over Barabbas.

But exactly the opposite happened. The chief priests and elders succeeded in stirring up those present to such an extent that reason lost out and mob rule claimed the day. As a result, the multitudes clamored for Barabbas (Mt. 27:21). Their choice was made.[19]

"So to the Jewish leaders' bad choice to reject Jesus and the mob's bad choice to call for His crucifixion was added Pilate's bad choice to back off and eventually give in to popular pressure," this section of the lesson concludes. "Most likely not all the people went along with the crowd," the next section explains, "but enough did that the cry for Jesus' crucifixion sounded like one voice (Lk. 23:21)."

While the lesson calls for the teacher to lead a discussion on the dangers of "going with the crowd," a later discussion concludes that Jesus was in perfect control of the situation, laying down his life for the Sunday school class members and their neighbors as well as the people of all generations. "Jesus was in perfect control of the situation," the lesson notes. "He had told the Pharisees during His ministry, 'No man taketh [my life] from me, but I lay it down of myself. I have power to lay it down, and I have power to take it again.' (Jn. 10:18). And that is exactly what happened."

Despite Jesus' voluntary sacrifice of his own life, the Jewish leaders are ridiculed for their "tragic choices." According to the lesson, they were wrong about Jesus' identity, ministry, authority, and salvation. The significance of their error is described in this fashion:

Wrong choices. These two words characterize the chief priests and elders of Israel. At every opportunity they decided against Jesus and for themselves.

Their problem was one of attitude. The leaders were comfortable with a religion based on self-righteousness. When Jesus came along, He messed things up—as they were concerned. He challenged them to dump their hypocrisy and called them to account for their legalistic attitude toward spiritual matters.

Things are no different today. Many are content to merely go through the motions of religion. There couldn't be a worse choice to make.

Who is Jesus Christ to you? What are you doing with Jesus in your own life? Whose voice persuades you? These are hard questions. But each person must confront them squarely and answer them seriously in order to avoid making wrong choices.

The "right choice" about Jesus avoids "the mistakes made by the chief priest and elders." The lesson concludes: "To choose Christ is to choose life; to reject Christ is to choose death... It's your choice. What will you do with Jesus?" As we shall see in the next chapter, evangelical Sunday school materials, as well as sermons, books, etc., continually exhort the student to witness to his or her faith.

The adult teaching aids that the teacher used for these lessons included handouts on "The Hebrew Sacrificial System" and "The Last Supper" (explaining the Passover meal). The teacher also was to use a large drawing of the dress of the Hebrew high priest. One of the last teaching aids was a summary chart of the Book of Hebrews in the Christian Testament entitled "The Sacrificing Priest is also The Priestly Sacrifice." It declared in bold print that "the Book of Hebrews shows the relationship of the Christian faith to Judaism." The center section, "Tracing Key Themes," expounds:

BETTER

Everything about the New Covenant is better than the Old Covenant, because "Jesus [is] the mediator of the new covenant" (12:24).

* The Son a better revelation (1:1-3).
* Jesus better than angels (1:4).
* A better hope (7:19).
* A better testament (7:22).
* Jesus a better Priest (8:1-6).
* A better covenant based on better promises (8:6).
* A better sacrifice (9:23).
* A better and enduring inheritance (10:34).
* A better resurrection (11:35).
* A better future (12:24).

WARNING

If there was accountability under the Old, how much more under the New! (2:1-4; 3:7-19; 6:4-8; 10:26-39; 12:25-29).

The May 8, 1988 lesson, "God's New Covenant," declares: "The Hebrew sacrificial system looked forward to Christ's sacrifice of Himself, and so it became obsolete when Christ died. While the Old Covenant was based on following the rules and regulations of ceremonial worship, the New Covenant is based entirely on what Christ did for us on the cross." While there was "nothing wrong" with the Old Covenant (for it was "the right thing at the right time"), the "limited effectiveness" of the Old Covenant necessitated the New Covenant—"God had a 'better' plan in mind."[20]

Standard Publishing Co.

In recent years, Standard Publishing Company has gained an expanded following in the evangelical Sunday school market. Its "Classroom Stories for One-Year-Olds" provides a glimpse at how ideas are ingrained at a very young age. "This is my church. Church is a happy place," the very first entry teaches. "At my church, I sing about Jesus," the little toddler is later taught, "At my church, I pray to God." Soon the Bible is brought to the consciousness of the child. The large print, decorated "story book" reads:

Here is a Bible at church. The Bible is a special happy book. My teacher reads to me from the Bible. I "read" the Bible too! The Bible tells about Jesus. I like the Bible. I like to read the Bible at church.

The key words the child is to learn for the 1988 spring quarter are: "Church, Happy, Sing" (March), "Church, Sing, Pray" (April), and "Church, Bible, Jesus" (May).

Very early in the Standard curriculum, however, attitudes toward the Pharisees are established. While the Nursery students (two- and three-year-olds) are taught that "even more wonderful is the fact that Jesus was a friend to all, regardless of race, sex, social standing, or vocation," the text relates:

As the Bible story points out, Jesus was not without enemies during

His earthly ministry. Two groups of religious leaders were especially set against Him. The Pharisees were one group who were constantly trying to trick Jesus. They were overly concerned with the minutest interpretation of the law. They continuously addressed devious questions to Jesus, in hopes of proving Him guilty of breaking the law (See Matthew 22:15-22.)[21]

"If you feel that your children are too immature to handle the facts of Jesus' death," the teachers manual continues, "then omit this part of the story and dwell on the happy breakfast Jesus and His friends shared."

The spring 1988 curriculum for four- and five-year-olds, however, begins honing in on the Jewish community more directly. "The Jews could not believe Him (Jesus), and they were so angry with Him that they were ready to stone Him," the teacher's "Lesson Background" explains.[22] When the lessons move into the life of Paul, the manual relates: "Since the Jews could not refute his arguments, they reacted the same way they did with Stephen— they determined to kill him... But with the help of his Christian friends, Saul (Paul) escaped in a basket lowered over the city wall at night."[23] The teacher's manual has a number of references to "the Jews," but often the student's storybook uses words such as "bad men," "shouting crowds," "angry men," "mob," and "mad" men. The series is entitled, "Tell About Jesus," and the teacher is instructed to inform the child that "you don't have to be a preacher to tell somebody about Jesus. You don't even have to be a grown-up. You can tell somebody about Jesus even though you are only a four- or five-year-old. Who can name someone he has told about Jesus? Whom will you tell this week?"[24]

Middlers (Grades 3-4) and Juniors (Grades 5-6) pursue the theme, "Seek God's Friendship" in Standard Publishing's spring 1988 curriculum. Most of their attention is focused on the Hebrew heroes of the faith. For Palm Sunday, however, Isaiah 53 (the Suffering Servant) is used and for Easter a "Victory!" section is incorporated. "Who judged Jesus?" the middlers are asked. The proper response: "Pilate and the Jews." A child is then requested to read Matthew 27:31 ("After they had mocked him, they took off the robe and put his own clothes on him. Then they led him away to crucify him"), and the teacher asks, "Where does this verse tell us Jesus was taken?" The proper response: "To be crucified."[25] Juniors actually build a cross and are encouraged to put on a play where the announcer states in part: "The Jews said He was stirring up trouble and accused Him of blasphemy—claiming to be the Son of God."[26]

All of these lessons stress the resurrection of Jesus, insisting on the importance of his abiding love. In asking the rhetorical question, "Why teach this lesson?" the teacher's manual answers:

> The fact of the resurrection is the foundation of the Christian faith. Although third-and fourth-grade children may understand only in part the significance of the event, they need to be introduced to the basic facts that form the essence of the faith: Jesus was born of a virgin, thus being God in the flesh; Jesus died for our sins; Jesus was raised from the dead to assure our eternal life. Help the children rejoice in the truth of the resurrection. Emphasize the victory that He gave over spiritual death. Don't be concerned if they don't grasp all of the importance of the facts. Yet share the essence of the faith with these youngsters who will themselves within the coming months and years make their own decisions to follow Jesus. Give them good reasons to make that choice.[27]

The story of Jesus' passion and resurrection is a necessary part of Christian education. Nevertheless, evangelical Sunday school curricula show definite lack of sensitivity to the anti-Jewish, even anti-Semitic implications of their approach. Most evangelical theologians would agree that it is ludicrous to blame Jews of all generations for the death of Jesus. Christian theology teaches that the sins of every man and woman necessitated the death of Jesus and that Jesus laid down his life voluntarily. Popular evangelical songs stress the theme, "Because of me He died." Even the Sunday school materials seldom neglect to emphasize this theme.

But this theological judgment rarely offsets the vivid images of a specifically Jewish guilt that arise from presentations of the Christian Testament. Irresponsible statements which foster negative images about Jews and Judaism need to be monitored; a sensitivity needs to be acquired. For anti-Semitism is certainly antithetical to the teaching of Jesus, as both Jewish and Christian scholars have affirmed.

In ascertaining the attitudes of the four major publishers of evangelical Sunday school materials, one notes a stress on the same scriptures and prooftexts that have suffered misinterpretation for centuries. Although these publishers have provided teaching guides and suggestions of every kind to facilitate an accurate portrayal of the Bible and improve class attendance and teaching techniques, the danger of fostering negative images of Jews and Judaism is never countered. The great number of writers from varied backgrounds, the breadth of the topics, the demand for the subject matter, the ignorance of the problem, and the lack of sensitivity to anti-Semitism in Christian thought create a barrier to evangelical-Jewish relations. The problem, in fact, transcends conservative theology. Rev. David Simpson, when director of the National Council of Churches Office for Christian-Jewish Relations, openly expressed his concern over their constituent denominations' Sunday school literature in 1983.

Ironically, this overview of evangelical Sunday school curricula, while it might bring a shudder to Jewish readers, would also surprise evangelicals. These thoughts and expressions come so naturally to evangelicals that they would be shocked to think that their Sunday school materials were engendering anti-Jewish attitudes—that indeed the Sunday schools and their teachers could be contributing to anti-Semitism. Most evangelicals are very responsive to a more accurate portrayal of Pharisees, the first-century milieu, classical Judaism, and the modern Jewish community. They only need to be educated and sensitized to both history and proper biblical interpretation. The task of undoing caricature, insensitivity, and misinterpretation is a constant uphill battle, for prejudice is being fostered at all levels of evangelical education.

Regrettably, evangelical Bible institutes, colleges, and seminaries provide a constant ridicule of the Pharisees in lectures and in sermons. To emphasize the value of Christianity, Judaism is often portrayed as a dead, legalistic religion.

JEWISH PERCEPTIONS OF EVANGELICALS

For the Jewish community, the kind of Christian teaching encountered in evangelical Sunday schools and sermons is viewed as a deep and enduring source of anti-Semitism. In his recent book *The Christian Problem: A Jewish View* (1986), Stuart E. Rosenberg stated at the outset: "Anti-semitism and anti-Judaism, history teaches, feed upon each other; they are twin phenomena."[28] Theologically evangelicals are lumped together with all traditional Christians of the past and present. For the average Jewish person, anti-Semitism and evangelicalism go hand in hand. Evangelicals are seen as "Elmer Gantrys," "redneck racists," "narrow-minded bigots," and "religious fanatics."

While Jews would not normally be aware of what occurs in evangelical Sunday schools and seminaries, or of the content of evangelical preachers' sermons, they certainly would not be surprised. Evangelicals are expected to believe in the sort of anti-Jewish diatribe found in dramas such as the Oberammergau Passion Play and its many American imitations. Although the text of the play has been amended somewhat, Jews are still portrayed as corrupt, vengeful antagonists of Jesus. The actors depicting Jewish leaders in the play are dressed in strange costumes with horned hats, while Jesus and his followers are dressed in simple flowing robes. Jewish law and the Pharisees are depicted as cruel, rigid, vindictive, and merciless. There is no positive link in the play between Jesus and his Jewish contemporaries. For three and one-half centuries this passion play has been held at least once a decade, and today more than a half a million people attend this emotion-producing spectacle. Jewish people would *expect* evangelical sermons to follow the same horrifying trend as the Oberammergau presentation.

The perception of the evangelical as unenlightened and religiously intolerant is coupled with apprehension about their public presence. As Rabbi Joshua Haberman has put it, Jewish critics of the "Bible Belt mentality" see it "not as a mere aberration but as a formidable threat to our entire democratic system. Comfortable in what they believe to be the secular pluralism of twentieth-century America, these critics are alarmed and horrified by the nationwide following of fundamentalist preachers such as Jerry Falwell, Jimmy Swaggart, and Pat Robertson. There are widespread fears that a resurgence of popular Bible study and preaching, and the growing political strength of its promoters, would lead us, step by step, to fanaticism, censorship, the suppression of dissent, the subversion of First Amendment rights, and finally, the establishment of a quasi-totalitiarian Christian theocracy."[29] Rabbi Haberman has succintly captured the anxieties the evangelical resurgence evokes in many American Jews.

What are the reasons for this anxiety? One reason might be termed "cognitive otherness." Evangelicals appear to Jews as persons whose beliefs about the world in the most general sense are radically different from their own. The universe of the evangelical is pervaded by divine influence. Events in the individual's life, no matter how ordinary or trivial, are ascribed to divine intervention. And such intervention is actually sought. On the other hand, Jews are aware that evangelicals often take "Satan" seriously, that is, as something (actually as someone) more than a metaphor. Evangelicals also hold to doctrines of Scripture most modern Jews find incredible. The belief that Scripture is inerrant, that is, that Scripture is an unimpeachable witness to not only faith and correct morals but also to facts of history and cosmogony, trades on a set of assumptions about human life and the universe that are unimaginable for most modern Jews. Finally, the application to contemporary events of biblical scenarios of the course of history, derived from the prophets and the apocalyptic writings, is utterly foreign to Jews. This "cognitive otherness" makes the evangelical appear at times incomprehensible, at times menacing to the Jew. To hold the beliefs that evangelicals apparently do requires, many Jews tend to think, a sacrifice of intellect; indeed a sacrifice of cognitive citizenship in the modern world.

In addition to their division over the cognitive requirements of modernity, Jews and evangelicals are divided, as has been suggested, by the ancient Christian-Jewish hostility. Although evangelicals, as Christians, are candidates for a generalized Jewish suspicion, their emphasis on evangelization evinces special concerns. One gets the impression that Jews consider evangelicals to be more serious Christians than nonevangelicals. Put negatively, the ancient poisons of anti-Judaism are feared to be more alive in those whose Christianity is more raw, unrefined, unreconstructed. To the extent that evangelicals represent that "old time religion," they represent a Christianity relatively undiluted by the "civilizing" elements of modern culture. This thesis (which is quite false, as it turns out) allows Jews to relate today's evangelicalism to yesterday's persecutorial Christianity. Other Christians are seen as more predictable fellow citizens of the modern world, while evangelicals are menacing survivals from premodernity. They might be thought of as a curiosity, like the Amish, were they not perceived as threat.

This section will explore in more detail the different perceptions that Jews have had of the evangelical movement. It will also consider some of the initiatives undertaken by Jewish organizations to enhance communication and understanding between the two groups.

Fischel's Fears

Writing in *Midstream* (December 1982), Jack R. Fischel decries the tendency in the Jewish community to accept the hand of friendship from conservative Christians. He complains: "There are those within the Jewish community, however, who see little to fear from the likes of a Jerry Falwell or a James Robinson. This confidence in the friendship of fundamentalists towards Jews is bolstered by the strong support which many evangelical fundamentalists give to Israel."[30] He goes on to depict the ostensibly disturbing components of this support. First, these Christians are "dispensationalists," which means that Israel is important to them only because of their (from the Jewish point of view, bizarre) scenarios of history. The Jewish return to the homeland signals the penultimate chapter of history. We are now poised on the brink of an apocalyptic consummation of history in which Jesus will return, the Jews will accept him (at least some of them), and the world will be plunged into a final cataclysm followed by an eternal reign of peace. While this scenario invests recent Jewish history with profound meaning for fundamentalists, it also allows for a certain callousness toward that history as well. The Holocaust is but a necessary step on the march to divinely intended triumph. The proliferation of nuclear weapons and trends that destabilize the world order are also positive signs of the implementation of God's final plan. Alas, according to Fischel, the failure of American Jews to "return" to Israel marks them out for "negative stereotyping." While Jews who live in Israel are "treasured" by fundamentalists, American Jews are seen as "a symbol of all that is grossly material in our society."

Fischel credits the fundamentalists with a deep ambivalence toward Jews, arguing that they see Jews in a positive light according to their dispensationalist historiography, but are prone to traditional Christian anti-Semitism as well. He asserts that there is "ample evidence to suggest that the older association which Jews have made between anti-Semitism and fundamentalism continues to linger on." In fact the principle difference between hard-core, old-time fundamentalist anti-Semitism is that the modern variety is masked or transformed by the emphasis on conversion.

"The differences between old-time fundamentalist anti-Semitism and the present stance of the movement rests, perhaps, on the greater emphasis on saving the souls of Jews than in engaging Jews in an adversary relationship." Fischel is so deeply troubled by the missionary intentions of some evangelicals and fundamentalists that he counts them to be as serious a threat as the anti-Semitism of some of America's most notorious bigots. "The anti-Semitism may have mellowed but the stereotyping is alive and well as is the missionary activity." "As long as Jews are concerned with survival as Jews in America," he concludes, "fundamentalist-Jewish relations must be monitored very carefully."[31]

For Jack Fischel, fundamentalist-Jewish relations are as the prophet Jeremiah's image of the broken reed: the relationship will break and stab those who hold to it in the hand. Or to change metaphors, the fundamentalists are a Trojan horse, full of hostile effects for those who admit them into the gate.

Fischel was criticized by a number of proevangelical Jewish writers in the November 1983 *Midstream*. Reform Rabbi Joshua Haberman questioned the author's knowledge of fundamentalist belief, practice, and opinion. Finding it inadequate, he countered: "My own opinion, based upon a study of the available literature and long years of acquaintance with fundamentalists, is that we have sufficient grounds for much closer theological under-standing. We can cooperate not only on Israel, but on a whole range of social and moral problems in terms of our shared biblical tradi-tion."[32] Another respondent, Rael Jean Isaac, argued that biblically based support of Israel is the strongest kind of support and de-serves Jewish reinforcement. She credited Fischel with the correct perception that there are "very real cultural differences" separating the two communities. "But why does it follow that efforts to bridge the gap are wrong? Fischel sees danger where there is oppor-tunity."[33] Isaac strongly favored dialogue and cooperation between the two communities.

Another strong plea for increased understanding between the two groups came from the late National Director of the Anti-Defamation League, Nathan Perlmutter. Writing in a liberal monthly, the *Reconstructionist* (December 1985), Perlmutter urged the Jewish community to free itself from the view of evangelicals promoted by the press and media.[34] He called for questioning the assumptions that lead the Jewish community to fear "a mindlessly militant fundamentalist Golem filled with passionate intensity about all the wrong things." Perlmutter tried to dispel the view that fundamentalism is an intrusive newcomer on the American scene by offering a brief lesson in the history of the movement. Tackling the serious concern that fundamentalism is "inextricably inter-woven into the fabric of the American Right and thinks, feels and votes the same ultra-conservative way about all social and political issues." Perlmutter called attention to a national survey of evan-gelical voting behavior, *The Evangelical Voter* (1984). The survey showed that the evangelical is usually a Democrat, and—in Perlmutter's words—supports two to one "the proposed Equal Rights Amendment, the dissemination of birth control information in public schools, the right to abortion, and the massive use of government funds to find a cure for AIDS." The voting habits of evangelicals parallel Gallup Poll findings about all Americans.

Perlmutter then contrasted the solid support evangelicals have given to Israel with the history of criticism and hectoring generated by the mainline National Council Churches. Having laid out the evidence, he concluded:

> Are we to reject Fundamentalist friendship for Israel because its scriptural foundation unnerves us? Is our bias showing? Do we await the day when these fire-and-brimstone preachers will issue a blast of old-fashioned anti-Semitism and we can issue in turn an exultant, "See, we told you so?"
>
> I would suggest that it is high time for American Jews to start, as the human relations pastors put it, "a meaningful dialogue" with Fundamentalists.[35]

Perlmutter ended with a call to be self-critical. Our "smug assumptions" are clouding our vision, he said.

Jack Fischel and Nathan Perlmutter represent thousands of American Jews in their attitudes toward evangelicals and evangelical-Jewish relations. Fischel's viewpoint, undoubtedly, garners a much larger following. Between these two poles, the Jewish community vacillates on the evangelical resurgence, often deciding on an ad hoc basis, community by community how much or how little to do with conservative Christians. While individual rabbis or Jewish communal professionals in the communities face these decisions continuously, some agencies within the organized Jewish community long ago decided to routinize and build "normal" evangelical-Jewish relations.

Early Jewish Outreach

As national director for interreligious affairs of the American Jewish Committee (AJC), Rabbi Marc H. Tanenbaum was heavily involved in Jewish-Christian dialogue, especially among mainline Protestants and Catholics. Already in the 1960s, however, Rabbi Tanenbaum had his eye on the evangelical community. He invited evangelical leader Russell T. Hitt, Editor of *Eternity* magazine, to dinner in an effort to set up conversations between Jewish and Protestant leaders. In a correspondence dated November 25, 1963, Hitt was hopeful that the dialogue could begin and gave Tanenbaum a year's subscription to *Eternity* magazine.[36]

Contact contined, and the consultation between Jewish and Protestant leaders (mainly evangelical) occurred in New York. On March 9, 1966, Russell Hitt thanked Rabbi Tanenbaum, stating: "I am sure reaction to our consultation was good on both sides. I personally was greatly helped although I am awed by Jewish scholarship."[37] At that time, actions were being taken to make connections with the Southern Baptist Convention, to have Rabbi Tanenbaum address the Evangelical Press Association at its annual convention, to organize another consultation, and to publish a special issue of *Eternity* devoted to Jews and evangelicals.

This seminal issue of *Eternity* appeared in August 1967 during the crucial aftermath of the Six Day War. In the editorial section of the magazine, under the heading of "Dialogue, Love and Witness," the editors of Eternity *publicized* for the first time their consultation of more than a year before with the American Jewish Committee. Emphasizing that a dozen evangelical leaders and a dozen Jewish leaders had been invited, the editorial commented:

> This unpublicized meeting was arranged to enable leaders of the two groups to share points of view and to understand one another better. Too often, we have long felt, does the Jewish community get the wrong idea of conservative Protestants. The only conservative Protestants that many Jews are aware of are anti-Semitic bigots.

> One of the thorniest of problems in Jewish-evangelical relations is the problem of witnessing, or as Jews see it, the attempt to proselytize.

> G. Douglas Young, author of "Lessons We Can Learn from Judaism," (page 22), shared with us the following quotation from a newsletter of the World Council of Churches' Committee on Judaism and the Jewish people. It is especially appropriate in discussion of the problem of witnessing.[38]

The six-paragraph statement from the World Council of Churches was printed in its entirety. The statement began by insisting that the "Christian brings to the dialogue with the Jew the hope that all men would acknowledge Jesus Christ as God, Savior, and Lord," but that the "Christian can do no more than witness. Conversion is a function of the Holy Spirit" (see chapter 4 for more detail on this statement).

Dr. G. Douglas Young was a conservative evangelical who had little contact with Jews until he became dean of the seminary and professor of Old Testament at Northwestern Schools in Minneapolis, Minnesota in 1953. In 1954 he met Sam Scheiner, the executive director of the Jewish Human Relations Council in Minneapolis. Although this evangelical and this Jewish person seemed to have nothing in common (in fact the founder of Northwestern Schools, fundamentalist William Bell Riley, was widely perceived within the Jewish community to be an anti-Semite), Young and Scheiner developed a strong friendship as they worked to improve Christian-Jewish relations and educational programs in the Twin Cities area. They worked with the black community as well.

It was Samuel Scheiner who, together with Senator Hubert Humphrey, arranged for Young to take his first trip to Israel in 1956. This led to an invitation from Yigael Yadin to join in an archaeological excavation the next summer. Such positive experiences led to Young's founding of the Institute of Holy Land Studies in Israel (1958). Late in 1963, Young and his wife, Georgina, moved to Israel. Little wonder that both the evangelical and Jewish community found in G. Douglas Young a reference point for future relationships. In a published article, Young declared early on to evangelicals:

> The very existence of modern Israel loudly proclaims that Judaism has survived two millennia in diaspora and thus it can neither be decadent nor of no interest to God. The existence of the new State of Israel should force every Christian back to St. Paul's mystery, back behind the sins of the early Church so long and so sadly perpetuated, back to the Bible itself where it is clear that God has a continuing interest in Jews. There should come an awakening all over the world, a desire to see the values that God enabled Jews to perpetuate, the values He intends to keep on using.[39]

Insisting that "God still has someting to teach us through the Jewish people," Dr. Young listed the qualities he had learned over the past decade from his interaction with Jews. These included caring for their own; religious values; living, working and growing together in spite of differences in background and belief ("a message surely which God would have Christendom heed today," Young noted); a proper church-state relationship and attitude; survival even under intense persecution; faithfulness; "loving our neighbors as ourselves"; helping others without a conversion motive; the value of and need for education. Young maintained that "these values are biblical values" and that "God is speaking to us today through them (the Jewish people)."

The editors of *Eternity* magazine in the 1960s had come to believe wholeheartedly in this message, and the positive values of Jewish tradition were being presented in this popular, national, evangelical periodical. In huge letters on the cover, this issue was entitled: AND YOUR NEIGHBOR AS YOURSELF. Certainly dialogue and consultation had achieved significant results. Both Rabbi Tanenbaum and Sam Scheiner had a right to be proud.

The article following Dr. Young's was "Our Subtle Anti-Semitism" by Belden Menkus. Mr. Menkus pulled no punches when he told evangelicals: "We must honestly admit that far too many of us do not know the Jews in our community as real persons." Strongly objecting to the "high pressure salesmanship" that had dominated much of evangelical-Jewish relations to date, Menkus emphasized that "we are 'saved to tell others'—not called to *convert* them." Declaring that the Holocaust is the evangelical's problem ("Jews died like animals because we did not care"), he sternly criticized the "bigots among us," both those who are in the open and those who are polite and silent. "What is needed is a correction of perspective," Menkus stated. "Our Jewish friend or neighbor is not an impersonal *prospect*. He or she is a vitally important person of worth as an individual and of value in the context of his understanding of his relation to God."[40]

The response to *Eternity's* issue on evangelical-Jewish relations was positive. One of the letters expressing appreciation was from a famed evangelical educator, Frank E. Gaebelein (the son of fundamentalist prophecy teacher, Arno C. Gaebelein). Living in Arlington, Virginia, Frank Gaebelein would forge a solid friendship with Reform Rabbi Joshua O. Haberman of the prestigious Washington Hebrew Congregation in Washington, D.C. Gaebelein would even lead a weekly Bible study at the congregation in the early 1980s, and Rabbi Haberman learned much about the diversity of the evangelical movement (and the possibilities for dialogue). In turn, Gaebelein would learn the sensitivity of the Jewish community to "Jewish" missions, "Hebrew" Christians and "Messianic" Jews, and while not compromising his witness, cherished his friendship with the Jewish community.[41]

The National Conferences

The American Jewish Committee continued its activity with evangelicals throughout the decade. The culmination of its ongoing contacts came in December 1975, when evangelical and Jewish leaders came together in New York City for the First National Conference of Evangelical Christians and Jews. It was a congenial beginning on the national level to erase the stereotypes and caricatures that confronted each community, while attempting to get to know one another more personally. Cosponsored by the American Jewish Committee (Marc H. Tanenbaum's department) and the Institute of Holy Land Studies (G. Douglas Young's educational institution based in Jerusalem), the twenty hours of formal dialogue had been set in the lives and experience of both Young and Tanenbaum more than a decade before. Younger leaders, however, such as Marvin R. Wilson, Professor and Chairman of the Department of Biblical and Theological Studies at Gordon College in Wenham, Massachusetts, and A. James Rudin, assistant national director for interreligious affairs of the AJC, put in considerable effort and time to make the dialogue a success. Wilson and Rudin would go on to spearhead evangelical-Jewish relations in the following years. Their personal friendship would make possible the education and friendship of numbers of others in their respective communities.

This conference centered not on evangelism and witness, but rather on Scripture, theology, and history. The papers of the participants were published by Baker Book House (an evangelical publisher) in 1978 as *Evangelicals and Jews in Conversation on Scripture, Theology, and History.* Jewish leaders and scholars were able to dispel some of the myths that had been projected about

Judaism and to give their own perspectives. For example, Michael Wyschogrod, Professor of Philosophy at Baruch College, in his paper, "Judaism and Evangelical Christianity," pointed to David Flusser's book *Jesus* (1969) which portrayed the founder of Christianity as a Torah-observant Jewish man "whose disagreements with the Pharisees are very much in the spirit of the perennial intra-Jewish debates so characteristic of rabbinic literature." Professor Wyschogrod reminded evangelical Christians that they should not overlook passages such as Matthew 5: 17-20 and Matthew 23:2-3, where Jesus states that he did not come "to abolish the law and the prophets" and that the "doctors of the law and the Pharisees sit in the chair of Moses...pay attention to their words." Paul also, it was suggested, remained a Torah-observant Jew.[42]

In fact, Michael Wyschogrod told the conference participants that although the "anti-Jewish tone of some aspects of Christianity can be traced to the Pauline polemic against the law," Paul's thought could be interpreted "in accordance with rabbinic thinking." "This is how any rabbi, past or present, proceeds in discouraging gentile conversion," he explained of Paul's seemingly harsh words in Galatians. "As an apostle to the gentiles, Paul's purpose is to preach Christ crucified and risen to the gentiles and, in view of contrary opinions emanating from Jewish Christian circles in Jerusalem, to dissuade gentile circumcision and acceptance of the yoke of the Torah." About faith and works, Professor Wyschogrod elaborated:

> When Paul says that man is justified by faith and not by works of the law, he is saying nothing that is strange to Judaism. A Jew who believes that man is justified by works of the law would hold the belief that man can demand only strict justice from God, nothing more. Such a man would say to God: "Give me what I deserve, neither more nor less; I do not need your mercy, only your strict justice." If there are Jews who approach God in this spirit, I have never met nor heard of them. In the morning liturgy that Jews recite daily, we find the following: "Master of all worlds: It is not on account of our own righteousness that we offer our supplications before thee, but on account of thy great compassion. What are we? What is our life? What is our goodness? What is our virtue? What is

our help? What is our strength? What our might?" The believing Jew is fully aware that if he were to be judged strictly according to his deeds by the standards of justice and without mercy, he would be doomed. He realized that without the mercy of God there is no hope for him and that he is therefore justified—if by "justified" we mean that he avoids the direct of divine punishments—not by the merit of his works as commanded in the Torah, but by the gratuitous mercy of God who saves man in spite of the fact that man does not deserve it. From this it does not follow that obedience to the commandments of the Torah has ceased to be obligatory for the Jew, just as it does not follow from the Pauline teaching of justification by faith and not by works of the law that the Christian may become a libertine and do as he wishes as long as he retains his faith. It is imperative for the Jew to do everything in his power to live in accordance with the commandments. At the same time, he is aware that he will not succeed fully and that he is therefore in need of divine mercy.[43]

"It is, then, quite incorrect to distinguish between Judaism and Christianity as if the former puts its emphasis on works while the latter, its emphasis on faith," Michael Wyschogrod summarized. "Both, it seems to me, emphasize works while realizing that the mercy of God is nevertheless essential."

Under such teaching, stereotypes and caricatures propounded by ministers and Sunday school curriculums alike began to fall. By the Second National Conference held at Trinity Evangelical Divinity School in December 1980, evangelical theologian Donald G. Bloesch of the University of Dubuque Theological Seminary presented "Sin, Atonement, and Redemption" and was followed by Seymour Siegel of the Jewish Theological Seminary and his paper "Sin and Atonement." In the Third National Conference, held early in 1984 at Gordon College, Jewish scholar David R. Blumenthal, Professor of Religion at Emory University, presented "The Place of Faith and Grace in Judaism," while evangelical scholar Walter C. Kaiser, Jr., of Trinity Evangelical Divinity School, elaborated upon "The Place of Law and Good Works in Evangelical Christianity." As shall be seen in the next chapter, the area of mission and proselytism was tackled by the second conference, and these proceedings were published as *Evangelicals and Jews in an Age of Pluralism* (1984). The papers from the third conference were published in *A Time to Speak: The Evangelical-Jewish Encounter* (1987).[44]

During the first conference, both Jewish and evangelical scholars took on the Christ-killer theme. Asher Finkel, Professor of Graduate Jewish-Christian Studies at Seton Hall University, concluded after approaching the controversial passages in the Christian Testament: "Alas, the reader of the passion narrative has lost sight of the original ritualistic background and as a result misunderstandings have occurred."[45] Evangelical historian Edwin M. Yamauchi of Miami University in Oxford, Ohio gave a fuller presentation of the trial and crucifixion of Jesus, elaborating on the many divergent Jewish and Christian viewpoints (including "extreme positions"). "One very important area where evangelicals can work against anti-Semitic prejudices," Professor Yamauchi insisted, "is in the field of the Sunday school curriculum. At the very least, the Jewish background of Jesus and his disciples has often been eliminated; at the very worst, the Jews have simply become the villains."

> We conclude then that in spite of an inevitable conflict over basic doctrines, evangelicals with their high regard for the Old Testament as well as the New Testament must recognize the Jewish background of their roots, and join their Jewish friends in a spirit of humility and compassion in a community of effort against the prejudices which are endemic to fallen men. They must be particularly vigilant against the specter of anti-Semitism which may be unconsciously fostered by a false or careless interpretation of New Testament passages.Only then will they deserve a hearing for the gospel which they profess.[46]

Considering the questions "Who Killed Jesus?" and "Is the New Testament Anti-Semitic?" Kenneth S. Kantzer, past editor-in-chief of the evangelical *Christianity Today* magazine and Dean of Trinity Evangelical Divinity School, asked in the second conference for a balanced interpretation of the accounts, insisting that evangelicals "must guard against the unconscious anti-Semitism in themselves and others that lies concealed in the structures of society" and asserting that evangelicals must "demonstrate in tangible ways their abhorrence of anti-Semitic actions...(declaring) a crucial truth to the Gentile world at large: *to attack Jews is to attack evangelicals, and such attacks will be registered by evangelicals as attacks against themselves.*[47]

Conveners of conferences between evangelicals and Jews soon recognize that each group initially has differing agendas. Evangelicals are interested in a more theologically oriented agenda, in deepening their knowledge of the Jewish roots of the Christian faith. "What do they believe about Messiah, sin, atonement redemption, and interpreting Scripture?" is the question that is often asked. Jews, on the other hand, immediately think of a social, "this-worldly" agenda. "Let's talk about human rights, social action, religion, and politics." In the national conferences *both* agendas were incorporated with a pleasantly surprising, broadening effect. Jews learned that evangelicalism has a social conscience. Evangelicals learned that modern Judaism has a dimension of theological expertise. Discussions and interaction became a profitable and enjoyable enterprise for both. The three major national conferences between evangelicals and Jews tackled topics such as "The Meaning of Israel," "Response to Moral Crises and Social Ferment," "Religious Pluralism," "Moral and Spiritual Challenges of the Eighties," "Mission and Proselytism," "Self-Definition," "Shared Nightmares," "Church and Synagogues at the End of the Twentieth Century" as well as the basic theological topics (Messiah, law, grace, faith, good works, the Bible, etc.). The groups encountered and shared their history and their impact, for good and for ill on American culture.

Just prior to the third national meeting, the conference cochairpersons, A. James Rudin and Marvin R. Wilson, issued a "Conference Call" that would serve as the basis for a constructive evangelical Christian-Jewish dialogue of the future. The ten points proved that progress had occurred for some evangelical and Jewish leaders:

1. We are united in a common struggle against anti-Semitism. We are outraged by the continued presence of this evil and pledge to work together for the elimination of anti-Semitism and all other forms of racism. We are committed jointly to educate this present generation and future generations about the unspeakable horror of the Holocaust.

2. We categorically reject the notion that Zionism is racism. Zionism, the Jewish people's national liberation movement, has deep roots in the Hebrew Scriptures, no less than in the painful history of the Jewish people.

3. We are committed to support Israel as a Jewish state, within secure and recognized borders. We also recognize the Palestinian Arabs have legitimate rights. We pledge our joint effort in behalf of a just and lasting peace not only between Jews and Arabs but among all peoples of the Middle East.

4. No government is sacred, and no government's policies are beyond criticism. But we strongly object to the practice of holding Israel to a different standard of conduct and morality from that applied to all other nation-states, especially to those committed to Israel's destruction.

5. We affirm the eternal validity and contemporary relevance of the Hebrew Scriptures as a primary source of moral, ethical, and spiritual values. And we pledge to work together to uphold and advance these biblical values in our own society and throughout the world.

6. We pledge to uphold the precious value of religious pluralism in our society. We strongly condemn those who would use unethical, coercive, devious, or manipulative means to proselytize others. Witness to one's faith must always be accompanied with great sensitivity and respect for the integrity of the other person lest religious freedom and pluralism be threatened.

7. We will seek to overcome any popular stereotypes, caricatures, and images that may contribute to one faith community falsely perceiving the other. To further this end, we pledge to continue to examine the rich spiritual legacy that Judaism and evangelicalism hold sacred together as well as their profound differences of belief.

8. We share a common calling to help eliminate inhumanity and injustice among all humankind. We also jointly resolve to work together to prevent nuclear annihilation and to pursue the path of world peace.

9. We share a joint commitment to uphold the principle of separation of church and state in the United States.

10. We pledge to deepen our joint involvement in the struggle to achieve human rights and religious liberty for our coreligionists in the Soviet Union and elsewhere in the world.[48]

William Sanford LaSor, a retired seminary professor who was active in Christian-Jewish relations in the 1960s and 1970s, noted in his foreword for *A Time To Speak* that from the additional names involved "the circle is growing larger." LaSor paid tribute to the foresight of the first national gathering sparked "by Rabbi Marc Tanenbaum and Dr. G. Douglas Young." "Whereas the first conference began with an undercurrent of suspicion about each other's motives," LaSor recalled, "the second conference was distinguished from the beginning by its trust and candor."[49]

William Sanford LaSor is an example of a Professor of Old Testament at Fuller Theological Seminary who came face to face with Christian-Jewish dialogue on the local level (West Coast), and who progressively became sensitized to Jewish concerns and anti-Semitism while holding firmly to his evangelical belief system. In *Judaism*'s special issue, "Interfaith at Fifty: An Evaluation of the Movement by Catholics, Protestants and Jews" (Summer 1978), LaSor was asked to contribute the article, "An Evangelical and the Interfaith Movement." Writing on triumphalism, LaSor confided: "I once held some such view, but I have come to see that it is not consistent with Biblical teachings, particularly those set forth in chapters 9-11 of Romans. I believe that the redemptive purpose of God is organic. It has been working through the ages and is still working. I reject any idea that God was suddenly forced, by Jewish unbelief, to put into action 'Plan B.' I, the Gentile, am the outsider, and by God's grace we Gentiles have been brought into God's plan of salvation. If there is any triumphalism, it is the victory of God that we pray for and work for."[50]

Yechiel Eckstein

Most leaders in evangelical-Jewish dialogue realize that there are pressing needs for their local communities to get to know one another in an effort to dispel some of the caricature and stereotyping that is so prevalent. Indeed, in some cities local dialogues increased. Women's groups in some areas (both evangelical and

Jewish) got together to break down some of the barriers. G. Douglas Young's handpicked successor, Clarence Wagner, Jr., continues the Bridges for Peace organization for which Dr. Young had such great hopes of dispelling prejudices on the local level. Wagner continues Young's publication, *Dispatch From Jerusalem*, as well. Impatience and fatigue in the face of constructive dialogue appears to be the current nemesis in evangelical-Jewish relationships. Both groups are involved in dialogue on several fronts, and leaders willing and able to participate are busy with many other tasks. Many more lay persons need to become involved in their local areas to help out frustrated leaders. Publication efforts may help arouse evangelicals and Jews to the task at hand, but those willing to learn and to make themselves vulnerable to a new relationship (bridging the "two worlds" of evangelicals and Jews) are desperately needed.

One successful instigator at the local as well as the national level is, ironically, an Orthodox rabbi, Yechiel Eckstein. A former national codirector of the Interfaith Affairs Division of the Anti-Defamation League of B'nai B'rith (ADL), this graduate of Yeshiva University became involved in dialogue with the evangelical community in the mid 1970s. Seeing stereotypes broken down systematically in nearly miraculous fashion, he helped organize an unpublicized conference in 1978 between evangelicals and Jews in Chicago, where he was based, and began forming study groups and sessions. Clearly noting the vacuum in relationships between Jews and conservative Protestants, Yechiel Eckstein left the ADL to focus on evangelical-Jewish relations, branching out in approach to pentecostal and charismatic evangelicals. His Holyland Fellowship of Christians and Jews was founded in 1982. His radio program, "Ask the Rabbi," answers many of the questions that Christians have about Jews and Judaism. He is a frequent guest on radio and television programs across the nation and has been featured in a number of evangelical periodicals as well as secular newspapers. He lectures on college and seminary campuses as well. His book, *What Christians Should Know About Jews and Judaism* (1984), was published by an evangelical publisher, Word Books, and is now in its third printing.

The passion of this fourth-generation rabbi, however, is to bring evangelicals and Jews closer in social as well as political endeavors. At a large meeting in Palm Beach, Florida, in December 1986, for example, he explained to the religion writer of the *Fort Lauderdale News* that doctrinally conservative Christians were being overlooked in interfaith relations. "Evangelicals often don't think of Jews as real people," Rabbi Yechiel Eckstein related. "They think of Jews as potential Christians, as objects to be missionized. Or Jews are objects of curiosity—people of the Bible, very religious and moral. If they meet real Jews who don't measure up, the Christians may deny they're real Jews." "Both problems," Rabbi Eckstein insisted, "are from lack of a relationship with, or exposure to, real Jews. That's one of the things I'm trying to change."[51]

Yechiel Eckstein also pointed out that Jews stereotype evangelicals. "They think all born-again Christians are like Jerry Falwell. They think the movement is a monolith that is trying to Christianize America, diminish civil liberties and destroy the separation of church and state." Rabbi Eckstein believes the answer is arranging for both groups to meet one another and to share common concerns on the local level. Setting up local chapters throughout the nation of the Holyland Fellowship is one of his primary goals. In 1987, he set up two local chapters in southern Florida—the very area where his *Fort Lauderdale News* interview and meetings took place. While other leaders may be getting discouraged or impatient at the enormity of the task, Rabbi Yechiel Eckstein has made it clear that he is in "for the long, long haul"—the duration, with realistic evaluation of the problems to be encountered. Whether or not the insensitivity of some evangelical leaders and some evangelical publications concerning the Willowbank Declaration (see end of chapter 1) will dampen his ardor remains to be seen.

4

THEOLOGIES IN CONFLICT: MISSION AND WITNESS

At a recent national dialogue between Christians and Jews, a well-respected Roman Catholic speaker was asked by a concerned participant, "Where are the evangelicals in this conference?" The speaker chuckled and quipped, "That's all we need....them, here, passing out their tracts!"

Many Jews would agree. Evangelicals are often portrayed as cultists, lurking around corners with gospel tracts and luring literature, feeding upon the unsuspecting. Most Jews consider conversion to Christianity as "spiritual genocide"; for if it succeeded on a large enough scale, the Jewish people, as Jewish people, would cease to exist. Jews who have become committed Christians are considered by the Jewish community to have abandoned the Jewish peoplehood, and to some Jews, any evangelistic effort is definitely anti-Semitic. Others would suggest that Christians should witness to the unconverted gentiles and leave the Jews alone.

While the debate over evangelism is not foreign to mainline Protestants and Catholics (even in the ecumenical community, there is no consensus on whether or not Christians should attempt to evangelize Jews),[1] the broad sea of evangelicalism by its very name and historic practice looms as a target for special criticism. Evangelicals practice traditional Christianity, and traditional

Christianity has been tirelessly evangelistic, spreading the "gospel message" to the ends of the earth. Modern evangelicalism is indebted to the revivalism of earlier centuries, a revivalism that attempted to permeate the nation and the world "for Christ." Statements by Jesus to "go and make disciples of all nations, baptizing them in the name of the Father and of the Son and of the Holy Spirit" (Matthew 28:19) and "Open your eyes and look at the fields! They (souls) are ripe for harvest....I send you to reap" (John 4:35-38) have been quoted for centuries in the Eastern and Western churches. Mark 16:20 records that the early disciples of Jesus "went out and preached everywhere," because Jesus had told them personally that "repentance and forgiveness of sins will be preached in his name" (Luke 24:47) and "you will receive power when the Holy Spirit comes on you; and you will be my witnesses in Jerusalem, and in all Judea and Samaria, and to the ends of the earth" (Acts 1:8). Witness is as integral to traditional Christianity as the observance of Passover is to Judaism.

ROLE OF WITNESS IN EVANGELICALISM

This does not mean that every evangelical today preaches enthusiastically to everyone he or she meets. Witness encompasses example as well as words. From the youngest age, however, evangelicals are taught that they should share their faith out of a responsibility to God, out of a thankfulness "for what Jesus has done" for them, and out of indebtedness to humankind. Sermons encouraging evangelicals to witness often stress that evangelicals have the "life preserver" to save a "drowning" human being. To not "give out" that preserver is a criminal act. They are God's emissaries, they are told, to tell the world the "good news." Jesus said, "You did not choose me, but I chose you and appointed you to go and bear fruit—fruit that will last" (John 15:16). Clergy explain that Jesus spoke a few verses earlier in this passage about "love," exhorting his hearers to "Love each other as I have loved you. Greater love has no one than this, that he lay down his life for his friends" (John 15:12-13). Sermons teach that as Jesus loved the world and gave his life for it, each Christian is to love the world and to tell the world what Jesus did, even if Christians must undergo death, imprisonment, or embarrassment. Missionary and evangelist, the apostle Paul, is pointed to as he declared of his mission: "For Christ's love compels us" (2 Corinthians 5:14).

Contrary to popular opinion, it is not easy for most evangelicals to witness to their faith. Young and old are bombarded Sunday after Sunday with their responsibility to evangelize. Often when they speak to someone about their faith, it is with fear and trepidation and out of a keen sense of responsibility, religious commitment, and love. In all fairness, evangelical theology teaches that one must not coerce or trick a human being to "accept Jesus as their personal Savior," for only the Holy Spirit of God can "convict and convince" the unbeliever. Evangelicals are taught to obey the spirit of God, to use common sense, to be ethical in witness, and to avoid rude behavior and angry arguments. In dialogue, Jewish leaders soon found that evangelical leaders deplored any duplicity in presenting the gospel message to Jewish people. Deceitful techniques and lack of respect in Jewish evangelism was mourned by evangelical and Jew alike. Evangelicals insisted that undue pressure on a prospective convert was out of order and that a Christian's task was to be a faithful "witness" to the truth of God's love. Often when evangelicals speak of missions, they are speaking of their responsibility to the world-at-large. A recent trend is to support missionary enterprises to unevangelized foreign cultures and to permeate countries closed to traditional missionary approaches.[2]

It is important for the Jewish community to realize that when one simply asks evangelicals to give up "witness," one is asking them to give up their faith and belief. While an evangelical may not attempt to evangelize the Jewish person next to them, most guard vociferously their right to do so. One popular evangelical magazine in the spring of 1988 sought to have a debate by evangelical theologians over whether or not one should witness to Jewish people, only to find that those who would disparage evangelism completely, were not considered evangelicals. Nevertheless, evangelist Billy Graham stated some years ago that he did not agree with missionary enterprises aimed solely at Jewish people, and the American Jewish Committee awarded this *evangelist* with their first National Interreligious Award. The citation noted that Graham had strengthened "mutual respect and understanding between evangelical and Jewish communities." Years before, Billy Graham had received the Anti-Defamation League's Torch of Freedom Award.

Practically, Jews and evangelicals who are friends have little problem over witness on the personal level. Ironically, Jews often want to know what a Christian believes once mutual respect and an honest relationship have been established. But the fact that evangelism exists, vexes Jewish-evangelical relations. Sometimes a Jewish leader will confess of an evangelical colleague in dialogue, "I, at times, get the feeling that he would like to convert me." A few Jewish leaders have totally accepted evangelical (and Christian) mission and witness as part of the Christian faith-principle, but they have clearly drawn the line at "Hebrew Christians" and "Messianic Jews"—groups they view as deceptive and untenable.

The role of evangelism in evangelicalism is clearly seen in William W. Wells, *Welcome to the Family: An Introduction to Evangelical Christianity* (1979). Published by Inter-Varsity Christian Fellowship, a student evangelistic movement active on college and university campuses, the book was designed to explain to a new convert the "genealogy" of their evangelical faith. "Becoming a Christian is a lot like getting married," the book begins. "You get family in the bargain." It continues:

> The wedding may leave you with blurred memories of new faces. But gradually the faces become familiar, and you begin to develop a bond with some of the relatives. The evangelical family is like that. When you first commit your life to Christ, you feel pretty much alone. But then you discover that you have become a member of a whole family of people who are also committed to Christ...Evangelicalism is a significant part—but only a part—of what is commonly called Christianity. It is not a denomination (like the Baptists, Lutherans, or Presbyterians); it is, rather, a perspective on the Christian faith that is held by many people from many different denominations. I personally consider it, with all its weaknesses, to be closest to the normative Christianity of the New Testament.[3]

After covering sections on the Bible, church history, the rise of revivalism, and the basics of spiritual life, *Welcome to the Family* concludes with chapter 12, "Reaching Out In Christ: Ministry to Others."

This chapter is significant, because it details for the new convert the mission of the church and the role of evangelism. "When we accept the gift of salvation offered by Jesus Christ, we not only receive a new relationship with God, we also become members of the body of Christ," *Welcome to the Family* explains. "Just as life in relationship with God is both a gift and a task, so living in relationship with God's people is both a joy and a duty. We were commanded by Jesus Christ to 'love one another.' That love is to extend not only to other Christians, but also to non-Christians the world over. Because of their commitment to live in obedience to their Lord, evangelicals accept a share in the mission of the church."[4]

In the same manner as evangelical sermons and evangelism texts, *Welcome to the Family* links church growth to outreach. It asserts:

> God has ordained that the universal church will not die. But a local congregation, like all other organisms, may either grow or die out. When Christians in a local church take the attitude that outreach is unnecessary and turn their sights inward, that congregation begins to die. Fortunately the converse is also true. When a local congregation intentionally devotes its energy to reaching beyond its boundaries, that body of believers grows. The church has been called upon to reach beyond itself for two reasons: to take the gospel to those who have not yet heard the message, and to stand for justice, unity and healing in a world full of injustice, pain and suffering.[5]

"Why should the church propagate the gospel? Evangelism seems to imply that Christianity is the only true religion. Is this the case?" Wells's *Welcome to the Family* rhetorically questions. The answer: "Evangelicals respond with a unanimous yes. This is one of the places where the evangelical perspective on the Christian faith differs most clearly from more liberal perspectives."

William Wells's commentary on the evangelical faith in this

book is also consistent with most evangelical sermons and books on the subject. He continues:

> There have been many great religious thinkers throughout history who have taught people how to live with regard to spiritual things. If Jesus were merely a great teacher, on a par with other great teachers, then evangelism would be unnecessary. But evangelicals hold that Jesus is more than the greatest of religious teachers. He is rather the culmination of God's revelation. Jesus is the incarnation of almighty God. He is Emmanuel, which means "God with us." When Jesus said, "I am the way, and the truth, and the life; no one comes to the Father, but by me," he claimed absolute uniqueness for himself (Jn. 14:6). He claimed that salvation was available only through himself.
>
> If the Bible were merely the product of religious reflection, then the church's concern to propagate the gospel would indeed be out of place. But evangelicals have always insisted that God has revealed himself through the Old Testament, the New Testament and pre-eminently through Jesus Christ. Is the Christian message true? Yes. But that is not the primary point. The primary point is that the message is *God-given*. Herein lies the exclusive claim of Christianity.
>
> This exclusive claim does not imply that there is no truth or value in other religions. But it implies that the greatest truths are found in a biblical faith. We read the Bible because God has promised to speak through his Word.
>
> We read other religious literature with the awareness that it may be profoundly moving and helpful, but that it is not the inspired Word of God. That is why Christians feel that it is a service to tell others about Christ. But in the end this is not the central issue. The central issue is that God commanded to proclaim to all people the message of his love and forgiveness available through Christ's unique sacrifice. Evangelical Christians are committed to obeying that command.[6]

For Wells, along with tens of millions of other evangelicals, *evangelism* is simply "the process of sharing your faith with others." Whether publicly before large groups or privately with a neighbor, witness must occur because God commanded it.

While admitting that missionaries historically have been guilty of cultural chauvinism, William Wells and other evangelicals believe that the solution is better training for missionaries, not withdrawal from the evangelistic enterprise. And evangelicals seem to believe that in many cases the gospel itself is inherently disruptive; therefore, contention does not necessarily mean that his mission work has gone wrong. They explain that Jesus himself warned his followers that his message would at times cause division. The evangelical Christian, it is said, does not have the luxury of religious relativism that his or her more liberal compatriots have.

There are actually several different levels of religious expression by any group of faith, including evangelicals. The first level is what the religion says of itself, that is, its theory and theology. The second level is the actual practice of the adherents—the day-to-day life, which may differ considerably from the theoretical first level. The third level may incorporate the historical changes and cultural contributions that have occurred over a period of time, as well as the diverse organizational subgroups that relate to the larger religious system.

In reality, these levels of actual practice and cultural changes contribute to the fact that most evangelicals are *not* evangelizing or attempting to proselytize every day or week or month. Yet evangelical Sunday school curriculums do their best to encourage evangelical witness. Children as young as four and five years are taught that "all children need the Savior" and "we can tell others about Jesus." Elementary Sunday school teachers, as well as Junior High and Senior High teachers, are given instructions on how to lead a child to "the Lord Jesus." These materials boldly present the gospel message in a variety of forms. Teenagers who have "accepted Christ" are required in some lessons to witness to at least one person about Jesus during the week and to report back to their classmates. Teachers' manuals explain that "witnessing for Jesus Christ is the natural overflow of a life that He has touched, filled, and is in the process of transforming." Teachers are encouraged to help their students' "understanding of the gospel and the role they can play in reaching other people for Christ."

Building moral values and social concern is an integral part of the evangelical Sunday school curriculum, but evangelism is never forgotten. A representative example is Scripture Press's "goals for kingdom living." After discussing the high schooler's leadership, membership, personal relationships, social responsibility, and rewards, the materials state:

> Every organization needs goals—its reasons for being. The kingdom's goals are: (1) to strive for the salvation of every person, as is the Father's will (Matthew 18:14); (2) to serve, especially the spiritual needs of others (20:28); (3) to preach the gospel to the entire world in preparation for Christ's second coming (24:1-14); and (4) to make disciples and teach them Jesus' commands (28:19-20).[7]

A corresponding adult lesson on Isaiah 53 (the Suffering Servant) concludes: "Let several volunteers tell the class about Christians who faithfully witnessed to them when they were unbelievers. Then have each class member think of someone he knows who is an unbeliever and decide how he could share Christ's love with that person this week."[8]

Evangelical believers "witness" in a variety of settings. The massive electronic church (television and radio) is largely evangelical-owned, evangelical-operated, and evangelical-oriented (see next chapter). Today most of the independent missions in the inner cities are run by conservative evangelicals. They reach out not only to derelicts, but also provide Sunday schools for children in poverty-stricken housing projects. Evangelical motorcycle enthusiasts established The Christian Motorcyclists Association in 1975, after Herb Shreve became convinced that "God wanted a Christian organization dedicated to reaching motorcyclists with the gospel of Jesus Christ." In a few short years, this organization grew to a membership of over 27,000 with 270 chapters across the United States and Canada. Membership letters are still coming in, including applications from South America.

Shreve, who claims that he is "Riding For the 'SON,'" and who takes 2 Corinthians 5:20 as his inspirational verse of Scripture ("We are therefore Christ's ambassadors, as though God were making his appeal through us. We implore you on Christ's behalf: Be reconciled to God"), explained:

> The main purpose of this ministry is to share the gospel of Jesus

Christ with motorcyclists. This purpose is achieved by attending motorcycle rallies and/or tours and conducting worship services. God has charged me with this responsibility and I literally travel tens of thousands of miles each year, holding many, many worship services, fulfilling His mission through me. Hundreds of motorcyclists have turned to Christ during these services. Other methods of sharing Christ with motorcyclists are being developed to make The Christian Motorcyclists Association even more effective.

Members of this group include former members of the Hell's Angels and other disorderly motorcycle gangs, converted to evangelical Christianity and witnessing to their former compatriots.

Even evangelical holiness groups, such as the Church of the Nazarene, whose members are generally very conservative in lifestyle, have similar groups of weekend motorcycle enthusiasts. The Nazarene's Agape Riders do not have many former motorcycle gang members, but are working-class riders out for fun and witnessing, often as married couples. In addition, evangelical truckers have initiated similar groups, and some "preaching truckers" have gone into full-time ministry by driving semis, pulling trailers with chapels and study centers inside. They conduct worship services at truckstops across the nation.

Tens of thousands of evangelicals have dedicated themselves to foreign mission fields, supported either by their own denominations or by raising their own support from individuals and churches to serve with independent evangelical missionary organizations. They are in a great part responsible for the phenomenal growth of Christianity in the Third World. It is estimated that by the year 2000, the churches of the Third World will comprise about 60 percent of the world's Christians![9]

KEY '73 AND THE JEWISH RESPONSE

The relationship of evangelism and outreach to church growth has not been lost on the mainline Protestant denominations, who are struggling to keep the membership that they have. In recent years, these denominations have been implementing programs of church development, while Methodists and Presbyterians have been asserting their evangelical heritage more in conferences. Even

Reform Judaism has initiated a fledgling program to reach mixed families in its midst.

The World Council of Churches (WCC) has not been oblivious to such developments. In fact, the WCC has used the terms "mission" and "evangelism" in a variety of ways. American Methodist, John R. Mott (1865-1955), was a fervent evangelical who was influenced by evangelist Dwight L. Moody to dedicate himself to the cause of world missions. Mott believed that Christian ecumenism was essential to support effectively the Christian missionary enterprise and to make an impact upon the world. He spearheaded the drive for a thoroughly ecumenical world organization, and in 1938 became the vice chair of the provisional committee of the World Council of Churches. In 1961, the International Missionary Council, with which he had been associated for forty years, became the Division of World Mission and Evangelism of the WCC. This gave the ecumenical body more direct contact with the Third World. A WCC declaration, adopted 1961, stated that "the World Council of Churches is a fellowship of Churches which confess the Lord Jesus Christ as God and Savior according to the Scriptures, and therefore seek to fulfill together their common calling to the glory of God, Father, Son and Holy Spirit." The Russian Orthodox church joined the WCC the same year.

The August 1967 issue of *Eternity* magazine reprinted the Statement of the WCC's Committee on Judaism and the Jewish people regarding witness to Jews. The evangelical periodical, which did not condone the WCC and ecumenism, believed the six-paragraph WCC directive to be "appropriate" in the discussion of the problematic area of evangelism among the Jewish community. The WCC statement began:

> The Christian brings to the dialogue with the Jew the hope that all men would acknowledge Jesus Christ as God, Savior, and Lord. This is the most "sensitive" element in dialogue, but to refuse to acknowledge this hope would be dishonest. Should the Christian try to "convert" the Jew? The question is meaningless because the Christian can do no more than witness. Conversion is a function of the Holy Spirit.
>
> What do we mean by "witness"? Its highest form is love. Some

would remind us at this point that the Christian has shown precious little love to the Jew over the centuries. We have already confessed that this is true. We can only hope for new beginnings, for it is still true that the highest form of witness is love. It is only when the love of Christ is manifest in the deeds of the Christian that the Jew—or any man—will find himself compelled to ask questions about the Source which inspires that love.

But does "witness" also include words—even persuasive words? Yes, of course it does. Some would say that because the Christian has been loveless he has lost the right to speak the words. It is true that the words of witness are repugnant without the presence of love. But it is also true that no Christian is ever "worthy" enough to speak about Christ to another man. If the Christian were to wait until his love fully matched his words, silence would prevail forever. After all, it is precisely because all men are "unworthy" that we speak of Christ at all.[10]

The World Council of Churches' statement then repeats words that were familiar to the evangelical, "Implicit in what we have been saying is the fact that the Christian is bound to obey the missionary command of his Lord. Witness is not optional. To fail either to love in the name of Christ or to speak in the name of Christ is to betray Christ."

The WCC's committee put the Jewish community on alert that "those who enter into dialogue with Christians must realize that they are in dialogue with men who are 'under orders' from God. It is thus impossible for the Christian to abandon his hope that all men would acknowledge Jesus Christ as God, Savior, and Lord." Nevertheless, the statement concluded:

But there are other ways to betray Christ. One such way is to advocate Christ in such a way that the advocacy involves coercion, either subtle or direct. Surely this is as abhorrent to Christ as it is to the one who is subject to it. To love a man is to respect his freedom— including his freedom to say "No" to Christ.

Thus Christian witness is the servant of both hope and restraint: a hope which may often have to go unspoken, but which ought always to be accompanied by words of persuasion where there is welcome for them; and a restraint which repudiates all forms of coercion and at every moment disdains to violate the freedom of the other man.

The evangelical could live with such a statement, and that it was sent to *Eternity* by G. Douglas Young for use in its issue on Christian-Jewish relations signifies that an evangelical friend, such as Young, could hold firmly to his theology and yet be sensitive to the Jewish colleagues that he loved.

During this period, a growing interest in a united national evangelistic thrust began. American church leaders had become alarmed that half of the U.S. population remained outside the churches and synagogues, and on any given Sunday only one-half of those church members attended a service. Carl F.H. Henry, editor of *Christianity Today*, had his colleague, Gene Kucharsky, draft an editorial in 1967 that would prod evangelicals to cooperate in a national network to evangelize their home communities.[11] When the editorial appeared, it stimulated more response than any editorial in the magazine's entire history. A conference was held at the Key Bridge Motel in Washington, D.C., and the evangelistic campaign came to be known as "Key '73."

Subsequently, 140 denominations committed themselves to the effort, including the Southern Baptist Convention, the United Methodist Church, the Assemblies of God, the Presbyterian Church, U.S., the Lutheran Church—Missouri Synod, the Church of the Brethren, the Salvation Army, and the Moravian Church in America. Organizations such as the Billy Graham Evangelistic Association, the Navigators, Inter-Varsity Christian Fellowship, and Campus Crusade for Christ also took an active part. Roman Catholic bishops gave Key '73 their official approval. The *New York Times* labeled it "the biggest evangelistic campaign ever undertaken ecumenically in the United States," and an organizing committee was named in 1972 under an executive director, Dr. Theodore A. Raedeke of the Lutheran Church—Missouri Synod.

Key '73 supported the divine inspiration of the Bible, while skirting the divisive issue of biblical inerrancy. It declared that a new society could only be created by spiritually reborn men and women, and for this purpose the universal church had to experience inner renewal. It affirmed that salvation was deliverance from the bondage of sin and that the primary mission of the church was to confront men and women with Christ's "good news" of reconciliation and redemption. The death of Christ was viewed as an atonement for sin—Jesus, as the Son of God, dying in the place of the believer. In spite of some reservations, Dr. Donald G. Bloesch, professor of theology at the University of Dubuque Theological Seminary, told the readers of *The Christian Century*: "With its emphasis on Bible study and on bearing witness to the gospel by both word and deed, Key '73 fits in well with this new mood in ecumenical circles. Rightly, it calls the church to its primary mission: the proclamation of the gospel and the conversion of souls."[12] The Key '73 *Congregational Resource Book* explained: "Key '73 carries the vision of every unchurched family in North America by being visited by someone who comes with loving concern to share his faith in Christ." The concept touched the evangelistic heartstrings of even the mainline churches.

The excitement is clearly seen in the American Baptist journal, *Foundations*. In an editorial in the January-March, 1973 issue, John E. Skoglund announced the journal's involvement in the November 1972 working session with the American Baptist Theological Advisory Board and the staff of the Home Mission Agencies in conjunction with active members in Key '73. Of the cooperative evangelistic effort, Skoglund wrote: "Key '73 has discovered that no easy answers can come to man's questions; therefore, it is seeking to shape its keys to understanding and adjustment theologically, sociologically, psychologically, and historically...the conference sought to understand modern man in relation to the Good News of the Christian faith. It is hoped that the papers in the next issue of Foundations will become widely useful as local congregations and area groupings move into active participation in Key '73."[13]

The subsequent Key '73 issue was sent to all American Baptist ministers. Jitsuo Morikawa began the first article by exulting: "There is no question that Key '73 is an incongruous surprise. We expected so little, and so much is happening, inside of us as well as outside of us."[14]

But what could the Jewish community expect from such a program? To Jews, ominous signs were beginning to appear. *Christianity Today* devoted its January 19, 1973 issue to Key '73. Harold

Lindsell, the new editor-publisher, proudly noted: "The seed of Key '73 was planted in the offices of *Christianity Today*. Following a challenging editorial in this magazine the Key Bridge meetings were held, and out of them developed Key '73." Lindsell asked the faculty of Fuller Seminary's School of World Mission and Institute of Church Growth to write articles and strategies useful to all Key '73 participants. In "What Key '73 Is All About," Arthur F. Glasser, Dean and Associate professor of Missions, related:

> Recently a Jewish Christian approached a prominent "prophetic teacher" known for dramatizing the significance he sees in the epochal establishment and survival of the State of Israel. "Do you love the Jews?" He was taken back, and protested. "My ministry is largely devoted to analyzing the place of Jews in God's program for the ages." "Yes, but are you in contact with any Jewish people, seeking to lead them to Jesus Christ?" Under this persistent probing, the pathetic moment came when he confessed he did not have even one Jewish friend. How different from the Apostle Paul's abiding burden for Israel and his ceaseless efforts to win them. What good is eschatology if it does not issue in evangelism?[15]

To Glasser, a graduate of Union Theological Seminary, New York and a former missionary to China, the Key '73 statement to "confront every person in North America with the gospel" certainly included the Jews.

Rabbi Solomon S. Bernards, Director of the Department of Interreligious Cooperation of the Anti-Defamation League of B'nai B'rith, responded to such assertions, representing the common view of the Jewish community toward Key '73, when he wrote:

> As an American and as a Jew, I react with considerable ambivalence to the Key '73 evangelistic campaign, which will be "calling our continent to Christ." I affirm the right of all Christian (and other) individuals and groups to proclaim their witness as vigorously and forthrightly as they are able. But the apparent monolithic, triumphalist tone and approach of the Key '73 outreach disturb me. I fear that the campaign may result in a backlash of resentment against the religious enterprise as a whole.
>
> As a believing person, I welcome concerted efforts to give public visibility to religious commitment and principle; but at the same time I am troubled by Key '73's seemingly narrow focus on

individual salvation, and even more by what appears to be a simplistic pietism, which is likely to weaken, if not seriously to undermine, the commitment to active religious concern for a just and compassionate society.

As a student of Christianity, I understand Key '73 to be an expression of its preoccupation with evangelism as a core article of faith. Simultaneously, I am worried about the effect of this proselytizing effort on the Jewish community and especially on the current Jewish-Christian dialogue.[16]

"The Key '73 campaign would introduce a new form of public piety: church bells ringing at noon every day; offices, department stores and supermarkets called upon to halt their activities for a daily period of meditation and/or supervised prayer; every house on every block of every city, town and village systematically canvassed for the distribution of New Testament tracts and other evangelical materials," Rabbi Bernards explained. "No doubt some people will welcome this new climate, but many others will resent these intrusions on their privacy."

The triumphalism of such an endeavor deeply worried him, as he related one leader's statements that in a year or two the whole United States (and eventually the world) may be converted to Christianity. "Imagine how leaders of non-Christian faiths will react," Rabbi Bernards noted, "when they learn of plans for their quick liquidation and extinction from the world scene." He continued:

> in the effort to win great masses of people, (Key '73) will tend to pitch the evangelical message at the common-denominator level of biblicism and simplistic theology, with the heaviest emphasis on emotional appeals...in the desire to "convince," it will tend to disparage and downgrade other faiths and value systems... A new intensified campaign for converts to Christianity is bound to affect the Jewish community. Like other Americans, Jews will be approached at work and at home and urged to accept a tract or to attend a rally—in short, to respond to the Key '73 appeal. And there's the rub!

The Jewish experience with Christian evangelism is obviously longer than that of any non-Christian group in history. After all, Jesus was a Jew and the first Christians were Jews. This experience has been and continues to be extremely painful and sorrow-laden. The Gospels record both the initial overtures to Jews and the Christians' frustration at Jewish resistance to these overtures. The New Testament also records the charges laid against the Jews by those frustrated Christians: blindness, stubbornness, demonic perverseness, unredeemed decadence, corruption and degeneracy, etc., etc. Will Key '73 evangelizers be similarly malicious in consequence of their inevitable disappointment with Jewish prospects?

Clearly, mass-based evangelical enterprises such as Key '73 are bound to induce jitters in the Jewish community. It takes seriously the possibility of losing some of its members to Christianity (and every loss, whether of one or of many, is a matter of deep concern). But above all it foresees the resurgence of tension, anxiety and bitterness on both sides that this evangelical effort will bring about.[17]

For Rabbi Bernards, the Jesus People with their "devoutly memorized phrases and passages" and their "peculiar type of enthusiasm and Jesus worship" were actually proponents of a "crypto-anti-Semitism." Worse were the evangelists recruited from the ranks of converted Jews, who "unfairly and inauthentically" called themselves "Hebrew Christians," "completed Jews," or "Jews for Jesus." They were "riding on the coattails" of Key '73.

Solomon Bernards was very disturbed that Billy Graham had declared in a television interview that "a lot of Jewish people are coming to believe in Jesus. Now they may not believe in him the way I do. They say that they are not leaving Judaism, they're accepting Jesus as a fulfillment of their Judaism." Rabbi Bernards concluded:

All of this threatens a setback for Jewish-Christian conversation—an enterprise based on mutual respect and trust. Already those sectors of the Jewish community which have been suspicious of Jewish-Christian dialogue from the start are beginning to assert that their suspicions have proved well founded—that the nice things Christians have said to Jews during the past few years were a calculated process intended to "soften up" Jews for the baptismal font. I hope responsible Christian leaders will allay these suspicions by repudiating the effort of Key '73—or for that matter any future evangelical campaign—to proselytize Jews.[18]

He was gratified, however, that the local clergy association of

Richmond, Virginia, only agreed to cooperate with Key '73 as long as local Jews were not proselytized.

Rev. Theodore A. Raedeke, the executive director of Key '73, responded to Jewish critics by suggesting that Jews mount their own evangelistic campaign. "In America," the Lutheran clergyman declared, "we have the privilege of propagating our faith." He expressed shock that "any religious organization enjoying similar privilege would rob us of this freedom." Evangelical statesman, Carl F.H. Henry, took Rabbi Bernards's comments "as indulging in fantasy." Noting to *Christianity Today* readers (April 13, 1973) that Rabbi Marc Tanenbaum also scathed Key '73 as an opening for anti-Semitic feeling, "an assault on the honor, dignity, and truth of Judaism," Henry recoiled, "Yet when Jewish spokesmen today imply that evangelical Christians are bent on coercing Jews into becoming Christians, they are so far wrong as to be comical." Carl Henry found the "growing number" of Messianic Jews to be a "voluntary" phenomenon, "a remarkable spiritual development."[19]

Christian critics of Key '73 began to appear more frequently in print as the year progressed. Reinhold Niebuhr's magazine, *Christianity and Crisis*, entitled its March 19, 1973, issue, "Key '73: The New Evangelicalism." Articles devoted to the subject were highly critical of the endeavor, treating it on one hand as a danger and on the other as a farce. The writers were not unmindful that the endeavor came at a time when fringe sects were singling out the Jewish people as special targets for proselytizing. Other religious leaders agreed. Sixteen members of the tri-faith Philadelphia Task Force on Women in Religion issued the following statement in the Spring 1973 issue of the *Journal of Ecumenical Studies*:

> We cannot support or condone the stated goals of Key '73. Specifically, we stand with our Jewish sisters in opposition to implied attempt to proselytize Jewish citizens of North America (not to mention persons who are members of faiths other than Jewish or Christian). Secondly, we challenge the tremendous expenditure of money for this enterprise. It would be better spent in striving to solve some of the pressing social problems of the day, rather than in attempting to convert all Americans to a monolithic view of Jesus and of God. Thirdly, we deplore the sexism inherent in the composition of the planning groups for Key '73,

demonstrated by the extremely limited number of women involved in the project.[20]

An issue of *Dialog: A Journal of Theology*, which was dedicated to "Key '73: Evangelism" (Winter, 1973) featured an easy-open pop can on the cover emblazoned with the insignia "Key '73." Although the editor, Carl E. Braaten of Chicago's Lutheran School of Theology, had chosen a wide spectrum of scholars to write on the issue (some who had barely heard of Key '73), most of the articles were highly critical of the campaign.

A number of denominations had chosen to stay out of Key '73 from the beginning, although this did not preclude individual members or congregations from becoming involved in the campaign. The United Church of Christ, the United Presbyterian Church, U.S.A., and the Episcopal Church officially reacted negatively to the enterprise. The National Association of Evangelicals chose *not* to be involved in Key '73, as did also most independent fundamentalist churches (plus fundamentalist denominations such as the Association of Regular Baptists). Billy Graham clarified his reported statements by emphasizing that he frowned on "proselytizing that is coercive" and emphasized that he had not been "directly involved in the developing organization of Key '73." While he did not exempt Jews from the "persuasive invitation" of the gospel, Billy Graham noted that he did not agree with missionary organizations aimed only at the Jewish people.

In *Confessions of a Theologian: An Autobiography* (1986), Carl F. H. Henry tried to put the best light on the "achievements" of Key '73. "Key '73 achieved certain commendable goals; it was hindered, however, by the refusal of independent fundamentalist churches to cooperate in a witness to Jesus Christ that involved also ecumenically affiliated churches," he wrote. "A further deterrant came through ecumenically aligned spokesman who under bureaucratic pressures sought to make social justice rather than personal evangelism the forefront thrust." Of the Jewish response, he commented:

> American Jewish spokesmen assailed Key '73 as "anti-Semitic" because of its Christian intention to confront every American with

the claims of the gospel of Christ. Any effort that embraced evangelization of Jewry was interpreted as a covert attempt to erase Jewish culture and identity; some Jews even likened a comprehensive Key '73 thrust to Auschwitz and Buchenwald. Secular religion editors generously publicized such frenzied assessments.[21]

"After condemnatory statements had done their damage," Henry somewhat bitterly remarked, "Rabbi Marc Tanenbaum acknowledged that Key '73 was not anti-Semitic after all."

Evangelicals, like many other Christians, did not assess Key '73 in the positive light that Carl F.H. Henry continued to see the campaign. Most scholars, theologians, and lay people felt that it was a "giant fizzle," a "failure," and "better forgotten." In fact, an entire generation of evangelicals have appeared without an inkling that Key '73 ever existed. That this evangelistic effort nevertheless captured the attention of the nation and garnered the support of such a large number of congregants, clergy, organizations, and denominations (both liberal and conservative), underscores the power that the Christian doctrine of evangelization holds over a general segment of the population.

That it was opposed by fundamentalists and the National Association of Evangelicals breaks down stereotypes nurtured for decades. Liberals, however, were captivated by the evangelistic spirit in Key '73—to build the kingdom! Conservatives were enthralled by the same challenge—even to the point of cooperating with liberals. The Jewish community was reminded once again what a fragile minority they were in a "Christian" culture. But they could also note, with some relief, how quickly Key '73 passed from the scene and was forgotten.

"HEBREW" CHRISTIANS AND "MESSIANIC" JEWS

The fears associated with converted Jews involved in missionary movements toward the Jews, however, continued to escalate. While such movements had been in America for generations and Rabbi Isaac Mayer Wise had given ample indication of their presence (see chapter 2), a resurgence of pietistic faith and evangelical Christianity in the 1960s contributed to the rise of "Jews for

Jesus" young people. "If you'd told me a year ago," a businessman exclaimed to *Life* magazine in May 1971, "that I'd have a son who'd carry a Bible wherever he went, who'd drop out of college to become a Christian missionary, who'd argue on the *wrong* side of the Scopes trial issue, I'd never have believed you. And neither would he!" "Some times I almost wish they *would* go back to something simple like smoking a little grass," Mrs. Lynne Seiffer, a travel agent completing her master's degree in library science told the same journalistic staff. "Drugs I can try to understand, but this? This is creepy." Parents in Rye, New York, had come face to face with the "Jesus Movement."[22]

And so had the news media. *Time* magazine dubbed it "The Jesus Revolution." NBC and CBS ran television news stories on the movement. *The Readers Guide to Periodical Literature* was forced to add the one-line caption, "Jesus freaks," which in turn informed the investigator, "See Hippies—Religion." Even evangelist Billy Graham took cognizance of the movement by writing the book, *The Jesus Generation* (1971), in which he accurately noted that "the secular media was just finding out (what) had already been going on for several years."[23]

Indeed, the "Jesus Movement" had been growing in the 1960s. It brought forth a vibrant charismatic movement that is visible today in the electronic church and Pat Robertson's Christian Broadcasting Network and Regent University (formerly CBN University). It also fostered changes in the Hebrew Christian Alliance of America (HCAA), which was virtually without a youth movement in the 1950s and early 1960s. Since its inception in 1915, the Hebrew Christian Alliance of America had been a key disseminator of information on Jews and Judaism to the evangelical community. Both independent Hebrew Christians and those affiliated with mainline denominational groups (such as the Presbyterians and Methodists) belonged to the association. The driving motive of these members was *evangelism*, and the evangelism of the Jewish people (they believed) fell squarely on their shoulders.[24]

Fundamentalist-evangelical in theology, the members of the HCAA believed that Jesus could return at any time to take them with him (in the "rapture"), and later, set up his kingdom on the earth. They believed that the Jewish people were lost to an eternity in hell if they did not accept the Christian gospel. Insisting on strengthening existing Jewish missionary enterprises, they endeavored to foster more "missions" and more outreach. They found, however, that the evangelical community was constantly questioning them as to whether or not they were "too Jewish," "judaizing," and separating themselves from gentiles. Some evangelicals feared a "Hebrew Christian Church" that would "rebuild the wall of partition between Jews and gentiles in Christ," and Hebrew Christians were often encouraged to marry gentile Christians. Other evangelicals seemed quite disinterested in supporting an effort to evangelize Jewish people.[25]

In an attempt to join the mainstream of the fundamentalist-evangelical movement, the fledgling Hebrew Christian Alliance of America, early in their history, opposed "Messianic Judaism" as heresy. In 1917 the HCAA position was spelled out quite clearly in an editorial which began: "We felt it our duty to make it clear that we have nothing to do with this so-called 'Messianic Judaism,' in any shape or form, nor have we any faith in it." It continued:

> Their grand sounding designation is a misnomer, for it is neither "Messianic" nor "Judaism." It does *not* describe any movement of Jews in the direction of recognizing our Lord Jesus as the Messiah, but an agitation on the part of some Hebrew Christian brethren, who have much to learn as to the true character of their high calling of God in Christ Jesus. To venture into such compromises would not only prove weakness, but our whole Christian testimony would be endangered.[26]

Insisting that the early Jewish Christians gave a "bold testimony," the HCAA concluded that these Messianic Jews felt that "by observing Jewish ceremonies and customs" they would demonstrate their "national continuity" and would win Jews, but such an effort, "history and experience prove," was doomed to failure.

Quoting Naphtali Rudnitsky, they heartily agreed with his conviction: "But if, in truth, we, as Jewish Christians are to claim unity with our people, then there is a much more excellent way open to us (I Cor. XII:31)—unfeigned devotion to Jesus, and untiring wooing of the heart of our brethren through His

Gospel." Regarding the traditional Jewish view toward such "Messianic Judaism," he asserted:

> This law-observing Judaism will not be contented were we to observe its national religious customs and yet believe in Jesus: if we would have its recognition we must deny Christ. This is the price required by the synagogue for our approach to it. Alas! some have paid this price who began by seemingly harmless "observances."[27]

The HCAA underscored its opposition to the "misguided tendency" of Messianic Judaism, pointedly declaring *"we will have none of it!"* The members stated that they wanted "to know nothing save *Jesus only!"* The editorial concluded: "We are filled with deep gratitude to God, for the guidance of His Holy Spirit, in enabling the Conference to so effectively banish (Messianic Judaism) from our midst, and now the Hebrew Christian Alliance has put herself on record to be absolutely free from it, *now and forever."*

For a half century, the Hebrew Christian Alliance of America was successful in this endeavor, and Jewish leaders (while not condoning evangelism) certainly agreed that observing Jewish rituals and ceremonies was deceptive and made mockery of Jewish tradition. The initiator of the despised Messianic Jewish proposal was Rev. Mark John Levy, a minister from a Jewish background who had engineered the passing of the following "memorial" in his Protestant Episcopal Church General Convention of 1916:

> Our Jewish brethren are free to observe the national rites and ceremonies of Israel when they accept Christ (as the Messiah), according to the clear teaching of the New Testament and the practice of Christ and the Apostles.[28]

Levy ironically stayed within the fellowship of the Hebrew Christian Alliance of America. A later casualty, however, was Hugh J. Schonfield, the writer of the *Passover Plot*, a book that caused considerable controversy in the 1960s. Few realize that Schonfield was a vibrant Hebrew Christian in the 1930s and was responsible for a scholarly study in defense of Messianic Judaism entitled, *The History of Jewish Christianity* (1936). In the face of intense "rebuke and misrepresentation," Hugh Schonfield endeavored to hold fast to his Christian ideals, writing in 1940 that he still had "love for and confidence in my Hebrew Christian brethren." Nevertheless, a veritable battleline had been draw between the philosophy of "Hebrew Christianity" and the philosophy of "Messianic Judaism." Bitter with the struggle, Schonfield never returned to Judaism, but proceeded in the 1950s to become a mystic and a pantheist.[29]

It is a great irony that the Hebrew Christian Alliance of America, the organization that stated that it would be "absolutely free of Messianic Judaism, now and forever," would by 1975 have its name changed to "The Messianic Jewish Alliance of America" (MJAA). The Jesus movement of the 1960s had given a surge of youth to the organization—youth that progressively wanted to maintain their Jewish heritage and Jewish lifestyle. The Israeli-Arab Six-Day War in 1967 was also an extremely important influence among young and old. To Hebrew Christians, as to prophetically minded fundamentalist-evangelicals, the "last days" appeared to be upon the church. They believed that God was going to raise up his 144,000 Jewish evangelists to bring the gospel message to the whole world. The gentile was to be soon phased out as the Jew took over his rightful place of esteem in prophetic events. Gentiles were caught up in the excitement as well. Shira Lindsey, the gentile daughter of a Dallas Pentecostal evangelist, converted to Judaism in Boston and moved to Israel in 1970. Although the rabbis in Boston later annulled her conversion, she continued to maintain that a Jew could continue to be Jewish and still accept Jesus as the Messiah. Other gentiles would follow her lead in converting to Judaism in order to evangelize more effectively among the Jewish community. Over the cries of the old guard of the HCAA ("This is revolution!"), the younger members over-whelmingly voted in Messianic Judaism and the quarterly became *The American Messianic Jewish Quarterly*.[30]

One of the prominent members of the former Hebrew Christian Alliance of America was Martin ("Moishe") Rosen, a totally assimi-lated and gentilized Hebrew Christian who worked for many years as a missionary for the American Board of Missions to the Jews. In the summer of 1970, he left his position in New York City and journeyed to San Francisco to evangelize in the midst of the Jesus movement. The San Francisco Bay Area was a center for Jesus people activity, and Rosen began using slogans such as "Jesus made me kosher" and "Jews for Jesus." Like the slogan "Drink Coca-Cola" as an advertising gimmick with worldwide impact, the slogan "Jews for Jesus" began to be used by the media. So novel was the expression, that some synagogues and Jewish community centers were inviting members of this "Jews for Jesus" movement to address their groups. The Northern California Board of Rabbis had to issue a statement in March 1972 against this practice. They declared: "We deplore that Jewish groups see fit to invite the movement's representatives to be part of their program. We do not deny them the right to their aberration, but we can insist that there be no misunderstanding about the nature of this group as having no relationship whatsoever to Jewish religious sentiment." In September 1973, Rosen incorporated his missionary enterprise to the Jewish people as "Hineni Ministries" (literally "Here am I" ministries). As Rosen told Baptist writer James Hefley in the period during the Key '73 campaign: "Our movement is small...A couple of years ago we had to work to make ourselves known. We slapped up posters and passed out handbills on the street. Now the media are coming to us."[31]

Rosen clearly stated that his organization was "an arm of the local church," and that he and his staff were primarily evangelists "to effectively win and disciple Jewish people." The doctrinal statement upon which Hineni Ministries was founded reads clearly as an evangelical statement of faith.[32] Rosen himself is fundamentalist-evangelical in belief, and he sought to funnel Jewish converts into Christian "fundamental" churches. Jews for Jesus also began to thrive on confrontation with Jews, both in publicity and in finances. The media picked up on the novel disagreements "among Jews," and the more Rosen publicized the confrontation, the more money his organization received from their Christian backers (for it "proved" that these missionaries were accomplishing something). Rosen wrote about the "confrontation tactics":

> In order to effectively carry out the Great Commision, we came up with our tactics for evangelism. They are based on Biblical examples

and especially those outlined in the Book of Acts. We call our unique method of outreach "Confrontation Tactics." Though the word "confrontation" might have a negative connotation, its dictionary definition reads, "to cause to meet or face." We want God to use us as instruments to cause people to regard the person of Christ and to face the decision to serve God through His appointed Messiah. By this we do not mean that we force our convictions or beliefs on anyone who expresses a desire not to hear. We feel firmly that only the Holy Spirit can impel people to consider the claims of Christ and persuade them to open their hearts to Him. Our responsibility, as evangelists, is to place ourselves in positions where we can be used of God, directed by the Spirit, to encounter people and speak His Word in a loving, attractive and convincing manner.

Martin ("Moishe") Rosen's Jewish evangelistic enterprise, doctrine, attitudes, and confrontation tactics were spelled out in a six-page communication entitled, *What Evangelical Christians Should Know About Jews For Jesus; A Confidential Report: NOT To Be Distributed To Non-Christians.* Today the organization has a multi-million dollar budget and over one hundred representatives.

Initially, modern Messianic Jews were involved in forming Messianic "synagogues" that would prevent the assimilation of Hebrew Christians and Jews for Jesus. The *congregation* was distinctive of the Messianic Jews, and they deplored Rosen's "confrontation tactics." Some privately tried to talk to him about the "overly" confrontational manner and disrespect of the Jewish community he exhibited. Rosen's evangelistic seminars for Christians on "witnessing" to Jewish people were seen as events that stereotyped and caricatured the Jewish people. To journalists, a number of the Messianic leaders would explain that "Jews for Jesus is just a small group of 40-100 Hebrew Christians in a West Coast missionary enterprise that is very vocal and widely publicized." Rosen's influence in the new Messianic Jewish Alliance of America (MJAA) waned, and his political position was wrestled from him. Philadelphia's Beth Yeshua Messianic congregation and their many followers in congregations around the country have an abiding animosity toward Rosen, and he toward them. The former are in control of the MJAA at present.

Nevertheless, by the mid-1980s, Rosen had not only formed his own congregation in New York City, but had a number of key leaders of the Messianic Jewish leadership lecturing for Jews for Jesus at substantial sums. Congregations of Messianic Jews who wished a more traditional Jewish practice historically have been doomed to opposition and failure, and some Messianic Jews now worship at regular synagogues because they consider the Messianic synagogues to be "a charismatic Christian service with a few Hebrew words thrown in." A few "Messianics" have thrown in the towel on what they consider "Christian aberration" of Jewish ideals—they have simply converted to Judaism and renounced their belief in Jesus Christ.[33]

Leaders in the evangelical community have been hesitant to criticize Moishe Rosen and his Jews for Jesus organization. For years he has had a great influence on evangelical opinions and the evangelical media. In *Christianity Today's* Key '73 issue, for example, Arthur F. Glasser's statement on Jewish evangelism seems to have been influenced by Jews for Jesus, and this Dean and Professor at the School of World Mission at Fuller Theological Seminary may have been quoting Rosen. Donald McGavran, Senior Professor of Missions at the same school, wrote "The Dividends We Seek" for that same issue, an extremely positive view of Key '73. In *Momentous Decisions in Missions Today* (1984), he wrote of Rosen:

> Moishe Rosen, founder of Jews for Jesus, is one of the few missiological geniuses of our day. In the early sixties he recognized that Jews were hearing the gospel as a proposal to leave "us" and join "them." He invited Jewish people to become—not Christians, heaven forbid!—but *Jews* for Jesus, or Messianic *Jews*, or fulfilled *Jews*.

> Operating in the white light which insight casts on the scene, many thousand Jews, perhaps fifty thousand, have become baptized believers in Yeshua Ha Maschiach. Thus they have entered into salvation. They accept the entire Bible as the Word of God. They will rejoice around the throne of God with us and all other believers from every nation, tribe, and tongue.

> Rosen recently commented on a letter he had received from a Jewish friend. I quote first from the letter and then from Rosen's revealing comments. Both illustrate the present hiddenness of the Jewish people.[34]

Rosen's Jewish "friend" stated that he believed the Christian gospel "as soon as I understood it" and that most Jewish people had never really "heard" the gospel message. He explained that his Jewish teachers had no understanding of Christianity and that "too many good Christians fear to speak of Jesus to us, lest we be offended." The twenty-six-year-old friend added: "Believe me, being offended is better than being condemned for eternity!" A lengthy explanation by Rosen then follows. Both he and McGavran try to portray the Jewish people of America as one of the "hidden peoples" and "new" field of "unreached peoples" (as much as some obscure African or Asian tribe). In another section of McGavran's book, Rosen is lauded as "the insightful executive of Jews for Jesus."[35]

Jewish leaders are not amused by such portrayals. In the April 24, 1981 issue of *Christianity Today* magazine, Rabbi Marc H. Tanenbaum declared that so-called Messianic Jews had forsaken the Jewish faith. Rabbi Tanenbaum explained to evangelical readers that "Judaism is incompatible with any belief in the divinity of a human being." He wrote:

> Jewish tradition allows that Gentiles can believe in the Trinitarian concept, termed in Hebrew as shittuf (partnership). Belief in shittuf, Judaism affirms, does not constitute idolatry for non-Jews, but does so for Jews. Jews, born of a Jewish mother, who become so-called Messianic Jews, are bound by the Covenant of Sinai, which explicitly excludes the possibility of any belief that God shares his being in any partnership with any other being (Exod. 20:2-6; Deut. 4:15-21).
>
> While humanly one might emphathize with Messianic Jews who wish nostalgically to retain some cultural linkages with the Jewish people—whether for guilt or other emotional reasons—in point of fact, reenacting Jewish rituals of the Sabbath, the Passover, the bar mitzvah, without commitment to the convictions they symbolize, soon make a mockery of their sacred meanings.
>
> When those rituals are employed as a ruse or a device to trick other Jews into believing that they can remain both authentic Jews as well as authentic, believing Christians, that is nothing less than deception, which is not worthy of any high religion such as Christianity.

Rabbi Tanenbaum also related that "Judaism believes that all

Gentiles are obligated to observe the seven Noachian principles of moral and ethical behavior in order 'to be assured a place in the world to come.'" This Jewish view is prevalent today, but even medieval Jewish teachers seem reluctant to grant Christianity a full Noahide status, and some Jewish scholars have suggested that this is a recent phenomenon to accommodate the current Jewish emphasis on pluralism.[36]

While the Jewish community had to cope with a Jews for Jesus organization that raised funds by publicizing the opposition they were receiving from rabbis and other Jews in the midst of "confrontational tactics," Christians were appalled at the Jewish Defense League (JDL) and antimissionary movements that met Hebrew Christians and Messianic Jews with violence and scare tactics. These opponents of missionary activity among the Jewish community were also able to glean millions of dollars for their illegal operations, to the consternation of many Jewish leaders. In the latter 1970s and early 1980s, radical Jewish movements unleashed strong-arm tactics against the Messianics. In Toronto, from 1978 to 1980, a "Jews for Judaism" organization funded by the JDL and a radical Orthodox congregation threw rocks, hurled insults, threatened, and cajoled a small Messianic congregation. They were finally stopped when the local Jewish community, a Jewish newsman, and the general press exposed their dastardly deeds. In Pittsburgh, a leader of the Anti-Missionary Institute (AMI) promoted violence and deprogramming. He had converted to Christianity through Campus Crusade for Christ, but had had a falling out with the organization. A former National Collegiate Athletic Association (NCAA) wrestling champion, his hatred for Messianic Jews was difficult to contain as he lectured on "Cults and Missionaries" and gained funds to fight the "Messianics." He was replaced by a devoted young man, who told the AMI that there would be no further violence "or *we* will send you to the police."

The opposition began to border on the absurd, disgusting Jew and Christian alike. In Los Angeles, Ahavat Zion Synagogue (one of the most traditional of all Messianic congregations) had their Torah scroll stolen by two JDL members. While running away with it, the JDL thieves dropped the scroll in a sand box at a nearby playground. One JDL member declared that he would not call it theft, but rather "liberation." The *Los Angeles Times* reported: "The police say it was grand theft, the Jewish Defense League calls it 'liberation' and the Jewish establishment doesn't want to talk about it." The newspapers reported that the Torah scrolls were recovered, but the alleged thieves were upset because the police confiscated their skullcaps "for evidence." The next month (Sunday, March 23, 1980), a dozen JDL members picketed the congregation and hurled rocks through the windows. Rabbi Kenneth Cohen of Young Israel Congregation marched with them, declaring to reporters that "many rabbis support the JDL," but they do not become active for "political reasons" and for fear of getting involved. The Board of Rabbis of the Jewish Federation Council disputed Cohen's claims.[37]

While these incidents were sad, and many in the Jewish community acknowledge that violence and persecution toward Messianic Jews would no more diminish them than Christianity's attempts in the past eliminated Judaism, it was not the JDL that forced the closing of one of the only traditional Messianic congregations in the United States. A Hebrew Christian on the Executive Board of the Southern California District Council of the Assemblies of God denomination confiscated Ahavat Zion's building (owned by the Assemblies) because they were *too Jewish*.

There are sensible and educated responses to the Jewish Christianity phenomena within the Jewish community. For example, the Jewish Community Relations Council of New York created a task force on missionary activity whose purpose was to alert and educate the Jewish community and to develop appropriate responses towards proselytizing. One of the results of this publication effort was the booklet, *Jews and "Jewish Christianity"* by David Berger and Michael Wyschogrod. It was published by Ktav Publishing House in 1978 and has been widely distributed since 1980. Berger and Wyschogrod maintain that although their goal is "to retrieve for Judaism every possible Jew," they will address the individual leaning toward Jewish Christianity "with the respect that any sincere person who seeks truth deserves." They emphasize that their approach is attempted with honesty and love. The authors explain:

Nowadays, many Jews who hear about Jews involved with Christianity attribute such involvement to lack of Jewish education and/or psychological problems. It is true that many Jews, both old and young, lack a proper Jewish education. And it is also true that many persons today have psychological problems. But religious choices can rarely be explained just on psychological grounds. In one way or another, a person is responding to God and to spiritual realities. The spiritual realm involves man's soul, and that is deeper than the mind that the the psychologist can understand. There will be no attempt here to "explain away" your interest in Christianity by reducing it to a psychological or educational problem. If your Jewish education is weak, then you ought to improve it, and this booklet will play a small role in so doing. But above all, you can be sure that you are being taken seriously on a religious and spiritual level.[38]

Jews and "Jewish Christianity" methodically analyzes the differences between Christians and Jews in six brief chapters, ending the last and main chapter with this thought: "Furthermore, every form of 'Jewish Christianity' in existence today teaches Jesus as God and not only as Messiah. Any Jew who embraces this belief commits idolatry. While he does not thereby cease to be a Jew, since a Jew always remains a Jew, he commits one of the gravest sins of which a Jew is capable. It is imperative that Jews know this."[39]

TRENDS

For Christians and Jews, who often view one another from a perspective of stereotype and caricature rather than actual interaction, June 1987 was significant. Rev. Bailey Smith, the former president of the Southern Baptist Convention, was again being censured. Infamous for his statement, "God Almighty doesn't hear the prayer of a Jew" and cited as an example of a repentant fundamentalist when he met with Jewish leaders and traveled to Israel as an act of reconciliation, the now itinerant evangelist and member of the Board of Directors of the bankrupt PTL ministry, told a conference of Southern Baptist evangelists in St. Louis that unless they (the Jewish people) repent and get born again, they don't *have* a prayer!"

During the same month, the 199th General Assembly of the 3.1 million member Presbyterian Church (U.S.A.) passed a controversial paper, "A Theological Understanding of the Relationship Between Christians and Jews," after downgrading its status from "policy statement" to "study paper," and changing statements on Israel. Rev. Benjamin Weir, who had just returned after being held hostage in Lebanon for sixteen months, had made an impassioned plea to scuttle stronger statements in support of Israel. He told the assembly that he would find it "very difficult to live with the paper" if it called Israel the promised land for Jews. The study paper was changed to reject the notion that the state of Israel fulfilled God's promise to the Jewish people, declaring: "The state of Israel is a geopolitical entity and is not to be validated theologically." A small but very vocal group of Hebrew Christian Presbyterian ministers had supported the original Israel portion, but criticized "what the paper did *not* say." Rev. Herbert Links, Executive Director of the Committee on the Christian Approach to Jews, Presbytery of Philadelphia, and a self-styled "compeleted Jew," circulated the paper "But What About the Jews?" He complained that "the tone of the document advocates dialogue with Jews rather than a sharing of the gospel." Rev. Links asserted: "In any modern 'interfaith dialogue' there's always a Jewish hidden agenda which disallows any discussion regarding the real issue— the Messiahship of Jesus. How then can there be honest 'dialogue' between Jews and Christians if He is excluded?"[40]

If the Presbyterian statement was embroiled in controversy even as a "study paper," the 1.7 million member United Church of Christ's (UCC) affirmative *resolution*, made at its June 1987 convention in Cleveland, Ohio, was destined for continued bickering and contention. To pass the declaration at the General Synod meeting, the resolution committee had to fight strong opposition to even get it on the floor; and floor leaders had to delete references to Israel's "right to exist." Surprisingly, the final resolution did pass smoothly, expressing that Judaism and Christianity were equally legitimate and asking forgiveness for the historical Christian anti-Semitism that denied Judaism's validity. While Dr. Robert H. Everett, pastor of Emanuel Church, Irvington, New Jersey, insisted that the resolution put "the UCC on record as being in the forefront of Jewish-Christian relations" (Everett was asked by officials to draw up a study paper on the issues of covenant and land), he acknowledged that "the UCC has been, on a national denominational level, rather hostile to Israel and we had expected problems in this area."

The strong feelings which encompass the broader scope of Christian-Jewish relations in the United States do not occur spontaneously or in a vacuum. The Presbyterian paper had been presented originally in 1983; the UCC resolution resulted from various study committees over a three-year period. Bailey Smith made his original infamous remark in 1980 and was criticized by fundamentalists and evangelicals (in addition to liberal clergy-persons). As we have seen, Christian-Jewish dialogues entered a new era of rapprochement during the 1960s, and considerable interaction and conferences among selected national leaders occurred in the two decades that followed.

In Protestantism, mainline denominational groups, such as the United Church of Christ, are huge conglomerates of members of many different theological persuasions—with many different approaches to Christian-Jewish relations. Within a year, the UCC resolution had been assailed from both sides of the theological spectrum. Conservatives have accused the resolution of "giving away the whole theological store." Some have gone as far as to state that "for our revelation to be true, Judaism has to be false" and "the church is definitely the successor institution to Judaism." At the other end of the spectrum, liberal challengers insist that any validation of Judaism empowers Zionism, a philosophy that they view as "imperialistic" and "racist." Jewish leaders have been alarmed at such anti-Zionist rhetoric from the National Council of Churches' administrators and United Church of Christ opponents, since it verges on hatred and anti-Jewishness. They have taken note of deep pockets of anti-Semitism within liberal and mainline Protestantism, a phenomenon that both liberal and conservative Christian participants in Christian-Jewish dialogue sadly admit.

Within the ecumenical community there is no consensus on whether Christians should attempt to evangelize Jews. The area of mission and witness remains blurred and diverse in even the most liberal of Christian circles, Catholic or Protestant. Rev. Allan Brockway, programme secretary for Jewish-Christian relations of the World Council of Churches, Geneva, underscored this fact in a June 1987 article in *One World* (a WCC publication). The United Methodist minister quoted from "Ecumenical Considerations on Jewish-Christian Dialogue" (1982), a position paper commended to the churches of the WCC by the Executive Committtee. Brockway acknowledged that these three different positions are still being taken by member churches and ministers:

> There are Christians who view a mission to the Jews as having a very special salvific significance, and those who believe the conversion of the Jews to be the eschatological event that will climax the history of the world. There are those who would place no special emphasis on a mission to the Jews, but would include them in the one mission to all those who have not accepted Christ as their Saviour. There are those who believe that a mission to the Jews is not part of an authentic Christian witness, since the Jewish people finds its fulfilment in faithfulness to God's covenant of old.

In this larger context of Christian-Jewish relations and Christian attitudes toward mission and witness, evangelical-Jewish relations today are more perceptively viewed.

As evangelical-Jewish relations have matured through three national dialogues (1975, 1980, and 1984) and numerous local conferences in cities throughout the United States, the seeds of conflict (as well as understanding) seen in the denominational struggles and individual agendas surface also among evangelicals. Evangelical theologian Donald G. Bloesch of the University of Dubuque Theological Seminary, a participant in the Second National Conference of Evangelicals and Jews (1980), a conference where mission, witness and proselytism were clearly discussed, has expressed concern that both the Presbyterian study paper and the UCC resolution "tend toward universalism and religious relativism." Ken Myers, an evangelical member of the Presbyterian Church, USA (PCUSA), and editor of *This World* and the newsletter *Public Eye*, noted that he was "struck by how many assertions of the Westminster Confession (the founding confession of Presbyterianism) are compromised if one accepts the

teaching of the new PCUSA statement." A number of evangelical
Reformed leaders are concerned that Jews will not accept as "good,
decent Christians" those who cannot share such universalistic statements.

In contrast, other evangelicals remark confidentially that both
the Presbyterians and the United Church of Christ were honestly
trying to deal with the historic anti-Semitism within the church and
the problems vexing Christian-Jewish relations. These evangelicals
believe that the declarations tend to make Christians on the local
level more aware. One evangelical leader observed that in spite of
the problems, the declarations were "a breath of fresh air" in the
stagnant denominational air of anti-Jewish rhetoric. There is little
doubt among those at either end of the spectrum, however, that the
evangelical-Jewish dialogues made them more perceptive to
Jewish fears about mission, witness, and proselytism, and more
sensitive to the overall picture. Hebrew Christians and missionaries to the Jews have, unfortunately, tried to discourage such
interaction. Moishe Rosen has complained frequently about evangelicals who have, in dialogue with Jews, opposed Jews for Jesus
and their tactics. Harold A. Sevener, president of the American
Board of Missions to the Jews, accused antimissionary efforts by
the Jewish community of seeking "to cause a rift between evangelical churches and missionary agencies such as ours."[41] Perhaps
their complaints are indicative of the fact that evangelicals and
Jews have developed friendships and understanding that many
religious analysts believed were impossible.

The seeds of honest dialogue were evident even before the first
national conference. In a letter to Rabbi Richard Rocklin of the
Conservative Temple Israel (Charlotte, North Carolina), Leighton
Ford, a popular evangelist on the Billy Graham Evangelistic Association team, felt that it was "better to state honestly my calling
as a Christian to be an evangelist" and that there was "no point in
weaseling about this if we're going to have honest encounter." Rev.
Ford explained:

> One of my friends has suggested to me that this dialogue is not the
> occasion for polemics, apologetics, or evangelism. On the whole I'm
> inclined to agree. But I do have a problem with his advice. Since I

believe the Scriptures are the Word of God, I have to take seriously the teaching given (in what Christians call the New Testament) to go into all the world and preach the gospel to every person. My faith compels me to take this teaching seriously. I think one of your own scholars has remarked that the great commission is as Christian as a prayer shawl is Jewish! For me to disclaim a desire to evangelize all peoples would be dishonest. And yet it is not my intent to turn this dialogue into a platform for proselytism. That would be grossly arrogant.[42]

"You may see that, as an evangelist, my taking part in this dialogue is delicate," Leighton Ford noted. "Some of our Jewish friends will no doubt suspect the worst: that I am there to try to evangelize them. And I'm sure some Christians will probably also suspect the worst: that I am not going to try to evangelize!" But Rev. Ford felt that both communities could work together in spite of their differences, asserting in conclusion: "If Jewish leaders who are equally concerned for spiritual and moral renewal could stimulate a companion movement in their own community, who knows what might happen to bring a new beginning to America? And who knows what God might do to bridge the gulf between us which no human can bridge?"[43]

William Sanford LaSor, Professor of Old Testament at Fuller Theological Seminary in Pasadena, California (who along with Jewish scholar, Ellis Rivikin of Hebrew Union College-Jewish Institute of Religion, was given the topic "The Messiah" in this first conference) would explain in 1978 that such honest dialogue and abstinence from arrogance would make it "possible for me to have a dialogue with a Jewish friend on the subject, dialogue that is meaningful and, I hope, helpful to both of us." He noted that he continually reminded himself "that I am the outsider, I am the gentile, and all that I ever learned about the Messiah I learned from Jews—pre-Christian, Christian, and non-Christian." Of his interfaith dialogue he concluded:

> In interfaith activities, my own faith has become richer and more meaningful. From the Jew I have my God, my Bible, my faith, my Savior. I am, to use Paul's words once more, "debtor to the Jew." From my Jewish friend I have learned to examine my beliefs and my actions more carefully, and I have learned something of his faith and

life. He has helped me, and if I have helped him, too, I am glad. Faith
is not a goal; it is a commitment to God by which we move toward
His goal by His leading. Interfaith dialogue should not, and does
not, require the denial or removal of parts of that faith; rather, it
should result in the increase of faith, of commitment to God's
redemptive work. In that spirit I participate in the interfaith movement.[44]

Rabbi Balfour Brickner wrote a letter to *Worldview* the same year,
stating: "It is not the gospel that is a threat to the Jews. The threat
is from those who use the gospel as a club to beat others into a brand
of belief and submission with which they may disagree or find no
need."[45]

In discussing the problem of proselytization, Vernon C.
Grounds, president emeritus of Conservative Baptist Seminary in
Denver, Colorado, summarized to the Second National Conference
between evangelicals and Jews in 1980:

> Thus in the end the problem is not *why* but *how*: as undeserving
> recipients of redemptive love how can we lovingly share the gospel
> with Jewish non-Christians? If we share it prayerfully, graciously,
> tactfully, honestly, sensitively, and non-coercively, we will not be
> guilty of the proselytizing that understandably disturbs Rabbi Bal-
> four Brickner...Our evangelism, if love-motivated and
> love-implemented, will fall within the category of witnessing ap-
> proved by Rabbi Bernard Bamberger: "I see no reason why
> Christians should not try to convince us of their viewpoint, if they
> do so decently and courteously; and I believe that we Jews have the
> same right."[46]

"One might devoutly wish that he were a theological genius and a
sociological wizard capable of undoing the Gordian knot of Jewish-
Christian relations," Dr. Grounds whimsically related. "But that
tangle, I fear, will stay tied until, an evangelist might exclaim, the
millennium has dawned."

A number of Jewish scholars have maintained that a proper
Jewish education and family-oriented participation in the life of the
Jewish community is actually the best determent to conversion.
When Blu Greenberg, author of *On Women and Judaism* (1981) and
How To Run A Traditional Jewish Household (1983), flew to Chicago
from New York especially to deliver her paper, "Mission, Witness,

and Proselytism," to the second conference, she not only related her "great ambivalence" toward Christian mission, but pulled no punches in letting the evangelical representatives know how painful proselytism was to the Jewish community. "In light of the three criteria (used by the general Jewish community) then—election, historical anti-Semitism, and the normative event of the Holocaust—the idea that only through Christ will Jews be save is out of order," she declared. "Let me say it in undialogic fashion. It is obscene!" Near the end of her forthright analysis, however, she confided:

> Having said what I said earlier about mission-proselytism, let me make one final comment. Although I've called it obscene and have described it as spiritual rape, somehow I don't feel personally threatened. I think that is because I feel very strong as a Jew, not in the sense of power but in terms of commitment to my tradition and my people. I so love being Jewish—the Jewish Sabbath, the traditions, the Torah, the liturgy, the history—that nothing could entice me away, even, I believe, on pain of death. What's more, through the miracle of election, through diligence and good fortune, my husband and I have been able to generally pass these feelings on to our five children. So while I am intellectually and theologically critical of mission-proselytism, the issue does not have as much emotional impact on me as, say, the tensions in the Middle East or the Soviet treatment of Jewish refuseniks.[47]

"Thus, as a Jew secure in her tradition, I am in a sense both free enough and distanced enough to learn something else from Christian mission," Blu Greenberg concluded. That is, "that if you love something so deeply, you do not keep it only to yourself or your family or your immediate community. You reach out to share it with others, including those who are on the fringes, who are the misfits, the marginals, those who do not have the support systems of family and friends."

Rabbi Yechiel Eckstein, another Orthodox observer of evangelical-Jewish relations, summed up well these "theologies in conflict" when he said: "Evangelicals and Jews will have to come to grips with the fact that while they share many values and goals, their central commissions, in fact, clash. For the principal conviction shaping the backbone of the evangelical identity is world evangelism, to proclaim the gospel of Jesus Christ to all people, including Jews. The most central force guiding Jewish life today, especially in the aftermath of the Holocaust, on the other hand, is to survive as Jews." Rabbi Eckstein, who is possibly one of the most active Jews involved with evangelical-Jewish relations on the grassroots level today, has hope. "This clash does not necessarily mean, however, that evangelical-Jewish relations are ultimately doomed to failure," he wrote, "Hopefully, it will be possible to build a *modus vivendi*, an Hegelian-type synthesis from the conflict between the two communities' core self-definitions. To sustain any kind of positive relationship, however, both will have to engage in a 'give and take' process, affirming their central commissions, albeit in a way that is least objectionable to the other."[48]

5

POLITICAL AGENDAS

In *The People's Religion: American Faith in the 90's,* George Gallup, Jr., and Jim Castelli explain that "Groups with the largest proportion of members under 30 and the strongest track record on evangelization have the best chance of increasing their share of the population; those with the smallest proportion of members under 30 and the weakest evangelization efforts stand to decrease their share of the population." Using the latest survey techniques, these authors claim that evangelicals "are likely to increase their representation in the general population" while Jews "are likely to decrease their proportion in the general population." Noting that evangelicals currently account for 45 percent of all Protestants, these pollsters suggest that in the 1990s "it is likely that evangelical Protestants will outnumber non-Evangelical Protestants" and that the mainline Protestants would be moving to the sidelines.

These authors also observed that such "religious affiliation" is related directly to "political affiliation." Summarizing their statistics on political agendas, Gallup and Castelli report:

> We have seen that religious affiliation is related to political affiliation. Will America's changing religious makeup shift its political balance? Yes and no. Republicans will gain some advantage if white evangelicals and Mormons make up a larger proportion of the population and Jews make up a smaller proportion; Democrats will gain if Catholics, black evangelicals and the unaffiliated make up a larger proportion of the population and mainline Protestants make

up a smaller proportion. These changes may have a greater impact in certain regions or states, but, all in all, neither party may gain a real advantage.[1]

Such statistics were little comfort to many in the Jewish community who feared the evangelical resurgence into politics in the 1980s, who battled the growing strength of the Republican Party, and who deplored the conservatives who sought "in Jesus' name" to Christianize America. A weak maintenance of the status quo seemed too much to bear.

ATTITUDE AND VOTING PATTERNS

As we have explained in chapter 1, the evangelical and Jewish communities generally differ in their voting patterns. Nevertheless, it is important to note that evangelicals are much closer to the voting norm in the United States than the Jewish community. In the early 1980s, sociologists Stuart Rothenberg and Frank Newport insisted in their book, *The Evangelical Voter*, that "the evangelical voter is in many ways not so different from the American voter," and surveys in the latter 1980s confirmed these findings.

Gallup and Castelli agreed, finding that white evangelicals were "the most conservative group in the country on social issues" (such as abortion, the women's movement, gun control, race relations, homosexuality, tolerance of atheists), while on most measures Jews were "the most liberal whites in America." And yet, importantly, they point out that many of these differences are "of degree, not of kind." Significant majorities and pluralities of Jews and evangelicals support more aid for education; support civil rights; insist they would vote for a qualified black, Jew, or woman for president; support the existence of labor unions and an increase in the minimum wage; support AIDS education and values education in the public schools; support increased government spending for social programs; and even support stronger gun control measures.[2]

While individual Jewish leaders have pointed to such statistics in an attempt to foster more dialogue and cooperation between evangelicals and Jews, the Jewish community is far more reticent to forge friendships with the evangelical community than with most other groups. Many of the factors that have been covered in previous chapters have contributed to this attitude. Like Nathan Perlmutter and a few other Jewish leaders before him, Rabbi Joshua O. Haberman attempted to allay such Jewish fears in 1986, citing statistics concerning evangelical diversity and evangelical-Jewish consensus on many social questions. Rabbi Haberman concluded that in view of the 60 million evangelical Christians in the United States "would any rational Jew question the importance of developing dialogue with them?" The answer to his decade-long effort was provided in 1988, when 34 percent of the Jews surveyed by the AJC stated bluntly that "many" fundamentalist Protestants are anti-Semites. Privately, numerous Jewish leaders conveyed their belief that "building bridges" with the evangelical community would never occur. In their estimation, the two different worldviews transcended general areas of agreement—some Jewish leaders privately indicating that even if the evangelical community renounced evangelism, they believed the general Jewish community would never be friends with the evangelical community. In major Jewish organizations, a strong opposition to Jewish-evangelical dialogue has been in effect during the 1980s and seems to be escalating as the twenty-first century approaches.[3]

Such opposition exists at a time when the evangelical world faces its strongest obstacles in the areas of political power and, ironically, formidable challenges in areas where evangelicals have been supportive of Jewish political agendas. For example, fundamentalist-evangelical support for Israel has greatly influenced attitudes in the larger evangelical movement during the twentieth century. Today such views are challenged as never before. In addition, fundamentalist-evangelical distrust of the Christian state has strongly influenced twentieth-century evangelical political attitudes. These views, too, are challenged today as never before.

Support for Israel

The *Nationwide Attitudes Survey* of evangelicals conducted for the Anti-Defamation League of B'nai B'rith in September 1986 concluded that over 56 percent of the evangelical community had a favorable view of Israel. In spite of the fact that this survey included a large percentage of mainline Protestant evangelicals who were part of organizations that opposed Israel or denominations that had little official regard for Israel, only 10 percent of the evangelicals surveyed reported an unfavorable view of Israel. In response to their own polls, Gallup and Castelli stated bluntly: "After American Jews, the strongest supporters of Israel in the United States are white evangelical Protestants. And while blacks are the least likely group to describe themselves as "pro-Israel," black Protestants who are evangelicals hold a more positive view of Israel than those who are not."[4]

Both studies suggest that it was the importance of Israel in evangelical theology that influenced such views. The theology referred to is none other than the fundamentalist-evangelical "premillennial" prophetic interpretation discussed in chapter 1 and elaborated in chapter 2. As has been shown, this theological perspective in the nineteenth century led many evangelicals to support the fledgling Zionist movement and, after the First World War, committed a large percentage of twentieth-century evangelicals in the 1920s and 1930s to advocate the restoration of the Jewish people to Palestine. This view of the future in the 1930s and 1940s also helped convince many evangelicals of the danger presented by Adolf Hitler and helped them accept the horrid reality of the Holocaust at a time when more liberal Christians were questioning the validity of the event.[5]

Fundamentalist-evangelicals welcomed the formation of the Jewish state in 1948. They reminded the evangelical movement that Israel was important in Bible history and future events. The editors of *Our Hope*, for example, welcomed the new nation with the ten-paragraph excerpt, "Israel Becomes a Nation Again." They declared that "the state of Israel, one of the world's oldest sovereignties, became the world's newest sovereignty at midnight." Alerting its readers to the retreat of High Commissioner, Sir Alan Gordon Cunningham; the selection of the new premier, David Ben-Gurion; the "recognition" by President Harry S. Truman; and the impending attack by five Arab nations, *Our Hope* exclaimed that "Britain has mystified the world by having disarmed the Jews and armed the Trans-Jordan Arabs." Noting the many Bible passages that refer to the restoration of the Jewish people to their ancient land, the prophetically-minded evangelical periodical insisted: "Observe, that in God's sight it is *their own land*."[6]

Mainstream Christian publications sometimes showed the imprint of prophetically minded evangelicals. A case in point is Dr. Daniel Poling, the well-liked editor of the popular Christian monthly, *Christian Herald*. This evangelical publication claimed to be *inter*denominational and *un*denominational, and it had a circulation approaching 400,000 in 1948. A self-proclaimed "gentle fundamentalist," Poling was senior minister of the Baptist Temple in Philadelphia and national cochair of the American Christian Palestine Committee. He was also treasurer for the Children's Memorial Forest in Palestine. Answering unequivocably a reader's question in October 1947, Daniel Poling declared: "I am a Christian Zionist who believes that Palestine should become, as promised, the Jewish state." Welcoming the new state of Israel, he never wavered from that position.[7]

The news analyst for the *Christian Herald* in the 1940s and 1950s was Gabriel Courier. In his "Gabriel Courier Interprets the News" section, he often defended the state of Israel while underscoring the complexity of the situation in the Middle East. When Count Bernadotte, the United Nations representative, was shot by Jewish extremists in 1948, Gabriel Courier cautioned:

> Let's remember that "the Jews" did not do this thing; an irresponsible, lawless, barbarously ignorant Stern gang did it. And when they did it, they may have cut off from their cause the sympathy and resources of millions of friends around the world. Completely innocent, the leaders of Israel and their cause have suffered a tragic blow.[8]

In contrast, many liberal theologians and ivy league academicians took such opportunities to rail against the new Jewish state. Columnist Dorothy Thompson changed her two-decade pro-Israel stance to an anti-Israel diatribe that supported the efforts of the anti-Zionist American Council for Judaism. Credible Christian supporters of Israel in liberal academic circles, such as famed archaeologist William Foxwell Albright and famed theologian

Reinhold Niebuhr, found themselves pressured from all sides to sever their relationship with pro-Israel forces. William Ernest Hocking, Alford Professor of Philosophy at Harvard University, a missionary statesman who had supported Balfour in 1917, became so anti-Israel that he finally joined right-wing extremist efforts to discredit the Jewish state in American Christian opinion.[9]

The biblically and prophetically minded evangelicals were quite a contrast. While acknowledging imperfection in the state of Israel and the plight of the Middle East milieu, the bottom line for these premillennialists was the Jewish right to the land. They concurred with such early members of their movement as William Blackstone, whose petition of 1891 explained, "According to God's distribution of nations (Palestine) is their (the Jewish people's) home, an inalienable possession, from which they were expelled by force... Let us now restore them to the land of which they were so cruelly despoiled by our Roman ancestors." Furthermore, these evangelicals were positive that Jerusalem would be restored to Jewish control. Dr. Wilbur M. Smith, who taught at Moody Bible Institute from 1937 to 1947, at Fuller Theological Seminary from 1947 to 1963, and at Trinity Evangelical Divinity School from 1963 to 1968, declared in his evangelical correspondence course in 1950 that "almost any day or night this prophecy of our Lord (concerning Jerusalem) could be fulfilled." He lived to see the day.[10]

This is the theological mold in which both Billy Graham and Jerry Falwell were nurtured, and in spite of their different positions on the evangelical spectrum, this view of the future permeates their thinking to this day. A 1958 survey conducted by Opinion Research Corporation showed that 74 percent of Protestant clergy in the United States considered themselves to be "conservative" or "fundamentalist." The prophetically minded fundamentalist-evangelical movement had great influence in nurturing a Christian Zionism within this evangelical milieu.

Anti-Israel Rhetoric

Opposition to Israel has always been present in evangelicalism, even in the twentieth century. In Calvinist, Lutheran, and pacifist circles, pro-Zionist evangelicals were assailed and maligned. As more evangelicals took their academic degrees from anti-Israel academics, a cadre of anti-Zionist evangelical professors began to inundate Christian liberal arts colleges and seminaries. As in liberal Christian circles, many conservative missionaries and archaeologists in Arab countries led the way in reevaluating the strong Israel bias within evangelicalism. Editors of evangelical periodicals, such as *Christianity Today* and *Eternity*, began to bend over backwards to include more "balance" on the Middle East.

For example, when most evangelicals (and most Americans) gloried in Israel's phenomenal success during the 1967 Six-Day War, *Christianity Today*'s appointed correspondents were missionaries and archaeologists in Arab lands—correspondents who feared that the Arabs might spurn their Christian enterprise because of Israel's success. Concerned with their own Arab missionary prospects, these correspondents had little use for Jews or Judaism. James L. Kelso, a former evangelical moderator of the United Presbyterian Church, issued such a diatribe against Israel in the July 21, 1967 issue of *Christianity Today* that the editors had to label his remarks an "interpretive appraisal of the Arab-Jewish conflict." Kelso had worked with Arabs for forty-one years and had participated in a number of archaeological expeditions in Palestine. His rhetoric is indicative of the small but growing anti-Israel evangelical contingent that has consistently pecked away at evangelical support for Israel in recent decades. He began:

> How did Israel respect church property in the fighting a few weeks ago? They shot up the Episcopal cathedral just as they had done in 1948. They smashed down the Episcopal school for boys so their tanks could get through to Arab Jerusalem. The Israelis wrecked and looted the YMCA upon which the Arab refugees had bestowed so much loving handcraft. They wrecked the big Lutheran hospital, even though this hospital was used by the United Nations. The hospital had just added a new children's center and a new research department. The Lutheran center for cripples also suffered. At Ramallah, a Christian city near Jerusalem, the Episcopal girl's school was shot up, and some of the girls were killed.

> So significant was this third Jewish war against the Arabs that one

of the finest missionaries of the Near East called it "perhaps the most
serious setback that Christendom has had since the fall of Constan-
tinople in 1453."

Dr. Kelso went on to blame the Balfour Declaration as "the major
cause of the three wars whereby the Jews have stolen so much of
Palestine from the Arabs who have owned it for centuries." He
expounded upon the Arab refugee problem, the mothers and
babies he saw suffering in the camps "in the bitterly cold winter of
1949-50," interjecting that "Mary and Christ received better treatment at Bethlehem than the Arab refugees did that winter."

Missionary and archaeologist came together in a duet of anti-
Israel rhetoric in his following statements. The United Presbyterian
pastor exclaimed:

> A missionary who has worked constantly with Arab refugees through
> the long years since Israel became a state in 1948 speaks of them as
> "human sacrifices to political ruthlessness." It is the most accurate
> statement I know. Sometimes it was actual human sacrifice, as when
> 250 Arab men, women, and children were massacred at Deir Yassin.
> I know that massacre well, for one boy who was fortunate enough to
> escape that massacre later worked for me on my excavations. There is
> deep horror about all this history in the fact that great numbers of
> Christians in the United States applaud Israel's crimes against Arab
> Christians and Arab Muslims. How can a Christian applaud the
> murder of a brother Christian by Zionist Jews? The Arab church is as
> truly the body of Christ as the American church.[11]

This last question, unfortunately, came to dominate both liberal
and conservative Christian propaganda against Israel. Either in
blatant denouncement or a secretive whisper, the anti-Israel argument took the form of anti-Jewish thought, that is, how can you
support the non-Christian Jew against you Arab brother? Only the
prophetic biblical theology of the grassroots evangelical movement continues to stem the tide and hold the dike against the
constant ravages of such rhetoric today—a rhetoric increasingly
being heard in the halls of education of the evangelical movement.

Some *Christianity Today* readers were appalled at Dr. Kelso's
interpretation, and their edited letters in following issues showed
shock and dismay. Elias Newman of Minneapolis wrote of his

"chagrin and disillusionment," while Rev. Harold P. Warren of First Baptist Church in Oak Park, Michigan, emphasized that many of Kelso's statements "are contrary to the facts as I know them." Warren's church was attempting to build a good rapport with the Jewish community, and he believed that "it is time for Christians to speak out on behalf of Israel and be identified as friends of Israel." In the September 29, 1967 issue, Benad Avital, first secretary of the embassy of Israel in Washington, D.C., responded to Kelso's "emotional charges."

The following year, Dr. William Culbertson, president of the Moody Bible Institute of Chicago, supported the Jewish restoration to the land of Israel in an article citing relevant biblical passages. Before becoming president of Moody Bible Institute, Dr. Culbertson had been bishop of the New York and Philadelphia synod of the Reformed Episcopal Church. A graduate of Temple University and of the Reformed Episcopal Seminary, Culbertson mentioned the Arab refugee problem at the end of his article, his "heart" going out to them. But in the face of the fact that "Israel has incorporated hundreds of thousands of refugees" into its economic and social life, Dr. Culbertson asked, "Why have not Arab countries (especially those rich in oil) done more to help their own?" Dr. James Kelso countered with fifteen anti-Israel points. Again, Kelso began by reminding *Christianity Today's* readers that "10 percent of the Arab population is Christian."[12]

One of the pro-Israel, fundamentalist-evangelicals who Kelso and other anti-Zionist evangelicals have taken to task is the popular evangelist, Billy Graham. When Graham's World Wide Pictures released the film, *His Land*, in the fall of 1970, anti-Israel evangelicals lashed out. They were horrified that the film presented a strong and positive premillennial view of Israel, and they were appalled at the film's pro-Israel advertisements, one of which stated:

> Israel today is a living testimony to the words of the Old Testament prophets, and a portent of the triumphant return of Christ...The rebirth of the State of Israel by the United Nations decree on November 29, 1947, is by far the greatest biblical event that has taken place during the twentieth century.

Dr. Bert De Vries, an evangelical professor of history at Calvin College, strongly disagreed with *His Land's* pro-Jewish stance, writing in the *Reformed Journal* about such glorification: "So this argument, drawing a wrong conclusion from faulty premises, is false. Nevertheless, it has served to convince many Americans that the founding of Israel on Arab land was justified. And the failure of *His Land* to see through this argument turns what is supposed to be a celebration of God's faithfulness into a piece of pro-Israel political propaganda."[13]

In a subsequent article, *"His Land* and Prophecy," Professor De Vries declared that "spiritual conversion" was the requirement for the Jewish people to have a title to the Promised Land, and that the Jews long ago forfeited the right to Israel because of their unfaithfulness. De Vries insisted: "Through the prophets God announced to Israel: 'You no longer have a right to the promises I made to you, because you have been unfaithful, you have not kept your promises to Me.'" When fundamentalist-evangelical Cliff Barrows of the Billy Graham Association exclaimed during his narration of *His Land*, "There are just no words for that first glimpse of the Sea of Galilee!" De Vries dryly noted: "These sentimental and emotional speeches bolster the mistaken claim, based on out-of-context quotations of Old Testament references to the land, that modern Palestine is God's own special piece of real estate."[14]

By 1975, Professor Bert De Vries had gone further than any of his evangelical Calvinist colleagues had expected. He announced in his article, "The Palestinian Issue":

> Why then the vehement Israeli reaction to Arafat and the PLO? The PLO call for an end to the state of Israel does not mean the destruction of its Jews, but the destruction of its Jewishness. Arafat proposed to replace Israel with a state in which Muslim, Jew, and Christian will live together in a "democratic, humanistic, and progressive society."[15]

Even De Vries's anti-Zionist colleagues were dismayed at his naiveté, and rejoinders by his friends appeared in the same periodical. Nevertheless, the anti-Israel crusade slowly gained converts within the academic bastions of evangelicalism during the 1970s and in the 1980s, made significant gains.

Most evangelicals, however, continued to support the state of Israel in spite of such constant bombardment. They looked to clergymen, such as Billy Graham and G. Douglas Young. Young wrote to the *Jerusalem Post* (October 31, 1975) that he had "been accused of being a Zionist—a Christian Zionist" by some of his coreligionists. "I would like to take this means of thanking them for this compliment," he added. For Dr. G. Douglas Young, Israel held the key to the welfare of the Jewish community as well as to that of the world. He felt that Bible-believing Christians had a stake in the continued existence of Israel and in Israel's meaning for all humankind. Young summed up his evangelical beliefs in the conclusion of a speech at Cornell University in 1975:

> And so this Christian's view of Israel is that in antiquity Israel has blessed this Christian by giving through the seed of Abraham one who loved me and redeemed me. But in addition to that, this Christian's view of Israel includes...the very deep-seated conviction that there are yet many cultural, educational and other ways in which these people can continue to bless the world as they did through the ancient Judeo-Christian tradition...The Judeo part was not superseded by the Church. The Judeo part is alive and vital today, and we have a great deal in common.

When Young's article, "Israel: The Unbroken Line" appeared in *Christianity Today* (October 1978), an article which sought to provide a positive view of the importance of Israel, the evangelical periodical made certain that an anti-Israel article followed it (without telling Young that they had attempted to nullify his words by rejoinder).

On October 30, 1977, Billy Graham emotionally addressed The National Executive Council meeting of the American Jewish Committee in Atlanta, Georgia. Rev. Graham attacked the Palestinian terrorists and called for United States' rededication to the existence and safety of Israel. His words were reminiscent of the early period of premillennial fundamentalism. In an unusual act, Rabbi Marc H. Tanenbaum, the Director of the National Interreligious Affairs division of the AJC, notified all AJC area directors about Graham's speech and cited it as another example of evangelical support for Israel and opposition to the Palestine Liberation Organization.

EVANGELICAL POLITICS

In the 1960s, evangelicals were clearly evident on the political scene. Avowed evangelicals were elected to Congress, including Republican Senator Mark O. Hatfield of Oregon and Republican Congressman John B. Anderson of Illinois. Hatfield was a member of a Conservative Baptist denomination and had been governor of Oregon before he was elected to the Senate in 1966. He gave the keynote address at the Republican National Convention in 1964. In 1968, Billy Graham had urged Richard Nixon to name Hatfield as his vice-presidential running mate instead of Spiro Agnew. Anderson was an Evangelical Free Church layman and a moderately conservative representative who was elected to the House in 1960. The National Association of Evangelicals named him Layman of the Year in 1974. Both Hatfield and Anderson would forsake their traditional conservative views to vote positively on more liberal moral issues in the 1960s. Hatfield came out firmly against the war in Viet Nam in the mid-1960s. Anderson cast the swing vote in the House Rules Committee for what would become Johnson's Civil Rights Act of 1968. In fact, President Johnson won over many evangelical conservatives for his war on poverty and civil rights program in the mid-1960s, until Richard Nixon began to win them back.[16]

George Gallup's polls in 1966 revealed that 55 percent of the American Protestants voted Republican, while only 35 percent of Catholics and 25 percent of the Jewish community backed Republican candidates. While the Jewish community maintained such a liberal stance during the 1970s, evangelical Christianity was increasingly being seduced by the far right. Although a few evangelical politicians (including Mark Hatfield)[17] warned their community to beware of being deceived by the political process and to avoid the seduction of the bastions of power in the political sphere, evangelicals were delighting in their new-found respect. In spite of the Watergate fiasco and the resignation of Richard Nixon, "born-again politics" was on the rise. When an unabashedly devoted evangelical, Jimmy Carter, became the Democratic Party favorite, conservative Republicans began to portray incumbent

Gerald Ford as a "born-again Christian" as well. President Ford delighted conservative evangelicals when he addressed the joint convention of the National Association of Evangelicals and the National Religious Broadcasters in Washington, D.C., February 22, 1976 (the election year), and mouthed platitudes such as "belief in God" and "belief in the faith of our fathers" will solve "our nation's problems." By the 1980 election year, all three men who vied for the presidency (Jimmy Carter, Ronald Reagan, and John B. Anderson) professed to be "born again."

The New Religious Right

By the time Ronald Reagan was elected to the presidency in 1980, Jerry Falwell had become a household word and "political fundamentalism" was constantly in the news. The appearance of this movement had taken most political analysts by surprise, and its continued growth within the evangelical community was a concern for both Christians and Jews. Christian fundamentalists had been accused in the 1960s of being "apolitical"—castigated for not using the political process in the moral cause of civil rights, poverty, and peace. Outside of their support for Israel, most fundamentalists shunned the political process altogether. Jerry Falwell had stated in the 1960s (as some fundamentalists still do) that a minister was not to be involved in politics and political lobbying. In a 1965 sermon entitled "Ministers and Marches," Rev. Falwell declared: "Preachers are not called to be politicians but to be soulwinners." The next year in *Readers Digest* (May 1966), Sun Oil magnate and benefactor of *Christianity Today* magazine, J. Howard Pew, advised against political activity. Yet compared with 1969-1970, Dr. Robert Wuthnow of Princeton University found "a dramatic rise in attention to political issues during the 1970s" when he conducted a content analysis of *Christianity Today* articles.[18]

What had transpired is that Falwell and others had experienced a change of mind during the new decade. These fundamentalists and evangelicals felt that a crucial part of American life was slipping away from the American people. The Supreme Court decisions, especially the decision on abortion, were a turning point for Falwell personally. A coalition was formed, but not a theological one—rather, a *political* one. A conservative lobby was conceived that included some Catholics and a few traditional Jews. Believing that they were the conscience of the nation and attacking secular humanists as an amoral plague on the American people, the New Religious Right conducted activities on a national scale and represented a geographical distribution that far exceeded the southern Bible belt.

The Christian Voice organization was founded in January 1979 by two California ministers, Robert Grant and Richard Zone. By the middle of 1980, Christian Voice had absorbed several pro-family, anti-abortion, anti-pornography, and anti-gay groups. The organization had a mailing list of over 150,000 laypersons and 37,000 ministers (including 3,000 Catholic priests). In July, 1979, Rev. Jerry Falwell founded the Moral Majority, conducting "I Love America" rallies in the capitals of many states. By the end of the year, over $1,000,000 had been raised through the mailing lists of Falwell's "Old Time Gospel Hour" broadcasts. Both Christian Voice and Moral Majority had the help of the electronic church (Pat Robertson featured Christian Voice on his "700 Club"), and both organizations drew in thousands of independent Baptist ministers who had never considered political action before.

In an effort to reach mainline conservative clergymen, Ed McAteer organized Religious Roundtable in 1980. A former field organizer for the Conservative Caucus and a prominent Southern Baptist, McAteer sponsored workshops that instructed mainly conservative evangelical Methodist, Presbyterian, and Baptist ministers in the art of mobilizing their congregations for conservative causes and candidates. In August 1980, candidate Ronald Reagan expressed his endorsement of the Religious Roundtable at a large Dallas, Texas gathering. The meeting included leading figures of the religious right, numerous national television evangelists, Southern Baptist president Rev. Bailey Smith, and thousands of cheering ministers and laypersons.

Within a few years, many more organizations had sprung up throughout the United States, lobbying through the mail, periodicals, radio, and television. They challenged "liberals" and "secular humanists" for control of education, government, and the

"American way of life." Nevertheless, it is important to note that the large majority of evangelicals stayed aloof from the New Religious Right.

Where most evangelicals and the New Religious Right could agree in 1980 was with regard to Ronald Reagan. Although some leaders in the secular New Right looked to John Connally of Texas to put the United States on the conservative track, Reagan had been cultivated as a palatable presidential candidate for over a decade. As governor of California, Reagan at first supported the Equal Rights Amendment, but later changed his position when conservative opposition mounted. He had fired two staff members who were accused of homosexuality in 1967 and yet signed into law a therapeutic abortion bill the same year (in spite of the anti-abortion lobby in California). As governor, he occasionally attended the Bel Air Presbyterian Church. The pastor of the church, Rev. Donn Moomaw, was an avowed evangelical. Rev. Moomaw insisted that he and Reagan had spent "many hours together on our knees."

For his part, Ronald Reagan increasingly condemned the "wave of humanism" and lauded the Bible as the 1976 presidential race approached. He insisted on the reclamation of "the Judeo-Christian tradition" by turning the nation back to God and declared that there must be "a return to a belief in moral absolutes." Although his 1976 bid fell short, when asked if he had been "born again," Ronald Reagan answered: "I can't remember a time in my life when I didn't call upon God and hopefully thank him as often as I called upon him. And yes, in my own experience there came a time when there developed a new relationship with God, and it grew out of need. So, yes, I have had an experience that could be described as 'born again.'"

As intense disappointment mounted with the presidency of evangelical Democrat Jimmy Carter, the newly organized New Religious Right gloried in Ronald Reagan's perception that God had chosen America and had called the nation to traditional values in order to save the world. In a debate with John Anderson during the 1980 presidential campaign, Reagan asserted that America "was placed here between two great oceans by some divine plan. It was placed here to be found by a special kind of people." As for the present, Ronald Reagan noted, "I have found a great hunger in America for a spiritual revival, for a belief that law must be based on a higher law, for a return to tradition and values that we once had... We are a nation under God." Ronald Reagan also insisted that Americans could "begin the world over again," meet their "destiny," and "build a land here that will be for all mankind a shining city on a hill." Jerry Falwell was satisfied, stating publicly that he personally was going to vote for Ronald Reagan. He clarified for television's "Meet the Press," however, that he was "not endorsing a candidate," because he did not "think any minister has a right to expect his parishoners or those who follow him to follow his cue on voting."[19]

It is ironic that in Ronald Reagan's landslide win in 1980, the New Religious Right claimed that they were responsible for his victory—only to learn that not only were their votes not needed, but also that the entire evangelical vote was not decisive in the Reagan win. Many other factors had played a role, not the least of which was economics and lack of faith in born-again Carter's leadership. Within days of winning, Ronald Reagan began to distance himself from the New Religious Right (until the 1984 election was on the horizon). Evangelicals, however, were not ignored, and Reagan proclaimed 1983 "The Year of the Bible." The same year he addressed the convention of the National Religious Broadcasters in Washington, D.C. and presented the Presidential Medal of Freedom to evangelist Billy Graham. Evangelicals, as well as a large majority of Protestants and Catholics, voted for Ronald Reagan in 1984. In contrast, 66 percent of the Jewish community voted for liberal Democrat Walter Mondale, in what amounted to a colossal defeat.

Evangelicalism had become a highly mobilized political force, and empirical data had documented a change. Between 1953 and 1974, the relationship between theological conservatives and political activity had been investigated in more than a dozen statistical studies. On a national level evangelicals were found to be less involved in politics during this period. In 1971, Charles Glock and Rodney Stark (who had earlier written the book, *Christian Beliefs and Anti-Semitism*) joined other researchers to conclude in *Wayward Shepherds* that "evangelicals concentrate on conversion, and except for occasional efforts to outlaw what they deem to be personal vices, evangelical Protestant groups largely ignore social and political efforts for reform." Ten studies between 1976 and 1981 (seven national and three local) were quite a contrast. These studies insisted that evangelicals had become one of the most politically active religious entities in the United States. They were known in Washington, and politicians began asking themselves, "What will the evangelical community think of this?" Sociologist Robert Wuthnow, in citing such data, questioned:

> How is it, then, that the same religious convictions can so thoroughly discourage political activity at one moment and only a short while later promote it so enthusiastically? How is it that the biblical piety of evangelicals could have blinded them to political concerns at the beginning of the 1970s but only a few years later have allowed them to become politically mobilized?[20]

Professor Wuthnow found his answer in the complexity of evangelicalism, suggesting that the movement should not be viewed as a composition of "neat intellectual dictums governed by canons of rational consistency and elective affinity" or as "static clusters of beliefs organized around simple tenets, such as the quest for individual salvation."

Although the New Religious Right was quite complex as well, to writers, editors, scholars, and lecturers it could be summed up in one Christian fundamentalist minister: Jerry Falwell. Falwell and his Moral Majority became the whipping post for critics and comedians alike. The negative portrayals and the depth of the animosity even surprised the crusty Virginia fundamentalist battler, who had spent most of his life aloof from secular politics. Brown University historian, William G. McLoughlin, accused Falwell of hoping to establish a "Christian America." North American Baptist Seminary professor of theology, Stanley J. Grenz, wrote that he was appalled and surprised "that a Baptist like Falwell would choose the old Puritan concept of a Christian commonwealth governed by Christians as his ideal." Michael Johnson noted in *The Political Quarterly* that "The Reverend Jerry Falwell has at times

been regarded as 'America's Ayatollah.'" And William Willoughby, editor and publisher of the Religion Today News Service, called
the Moral Majority "the most feared religio-political force ever to
emerge on the American political scene."[21]

Later Willoughby also explained in his book, *Does America Need
the Moral Majority?* (1981), that there "was no attack on the Moral
Majority quite so virulent as that of certain Jewish spokesmen." His
reference was to the highly publicized November 22, 1980 speech
Rabbi Alexander Schindler made before the Union of American
Hebrew Congregations (UAHC) semiannual board of trustees
meeting in San Francisco. As president of UAHC, Rabbi Schindler
charged that there was a link between the rise of "right-wing
Christian fundamentalism" and the growth of anti-Semitism in the
United States. "When the head of the Moral Majority demands a
'Christian Bill of Rights,' when the president of the Southern
Baptist Convention tells the Religious Roundtable that 'God Almighty does not hear the prayer of a Jew,'" Rabbi Schindler
intoned, "there should be no surprise at reports of synagogues
destroyed by arson and Jewish families terrorized in their homes."
Schindler was incensed that "Jerry Falwell tells us that only one
brand of politics is acceptable to God," and concluded "that the rise
of right-wing Christian fundamentalism has been accompanied by
the most serious outbreak of anti-Semitism in America since the
end of World War II."

Falwell denied the charges in endless interviews. He insisted
that he did not believe America would ever become "Christian,"
and he affirmed that God hears the prayers "of all people." He
defended the right of Christians to be involved in the political
process and tried to explain how the name Moral Majority came
about. Nevertheless, after eight years of such explanations (and the
failure of such), Rev. Jerry Falwell finally changed the name of
Moral Majority, and in 1988 he decided that the political arena had
taken too much time from his gospel ministry.

Ironically, during the 1970s and 1980s, there was a movement
on the rise that did advocate a "Christian America" and the institution of "biblical law." Because Jerry Falwell and the Moral Majority
were highly visible, they took the brunt for other less palatable

right-wingers, obscuring a movement that was far more dangerous to evangelicals and to Jews. In a campaign report aired September 26, 1980, Bill Moyers reported on the "Bill Moyers' Journal" program: "It is not that the evangelicals are taking politics seriously that bothers me. It's the lies they're being told by the demagogues who flatter them into believing they can achieve politically the certitude they have embraced theologically. The world doesn't work that way. There is no heaven on earth." Seven years later he would narrate a three-part Public Broadcasting series, "God and Politics." "On Earth As It Is In Heaven" was aired December 23, 1987, and in it Bill Moyers detailed a group of "new Puritans," the Christian reconstructionists, who were actively pursuing a "Christian America" before the Moral Majority was founded. That Jerry Falwell and most fundamentalist-evangelicals would have wholeheartedly agreed with Moyer's statement that "there is no heaven on earth" was little consolation in the face of the growing Christian reconstructionist movement.

Christian Reconstructionism

The Christian reconstructionist movement (sometimes referred to as "theonomists" or "Kingdom Now") believes that a society must be created in America that is under the direct authority of "God's law." God's detailed commands revealed in the Torah are mandatory (unless "modified" by dictates of the Christian Testament). Taking their cue from Calvin's Geneva experiment or the Puritan experiment in the Massachusetts Bay Colony, Christian reconstructionists speak in terms of "Protestant nations" and "Christian nations" versus "pagan nations," and instruct Christians to "occupy" in Christ's name, to enforce God's law in every area of personal and national life (including the political sphere), and to gain "dominion" over the earth. The core of their leadership is *postmillennial* in their view of the future, a view that dominated nineteenth-century evangelicalism (see chapter 2). They believe that Jesus Christ will return to earth only after Christians dominate and gain dominion over it. Christian reconstructionists insist that the Christian church will bring in a millennium through evangelism and the gradual imposition of God's law. They maintain that all law is a religious mandate, and that God intends for his detailed commands as revealed to Moses to be the binding "case law" for the person *and* the nation.

The patriarch of this movement is Rousas John Rushdoony. In contrast to Jerry Falwell, who like most evangelicals believes in premillennialism (that only the return of Jesus can bring in the millennium and that the church cannot "create" a Christian nation), Rushdoony in the early 1960s was calling for a second "reconstruction," a reconstruction that would bring the nation's institutions under the dominion of God, back to the biblical roots, reordering society under "God's law." Gaining a small cadre of Calvinistic evangelical followers in the early 1960s (a time when Falwell and many of his followers disdained politics), Rousas Rushdoony established the "non-profit" Chalcedon Foundation in 1966 (it was granted tax exemption in 1968). Two of his disciples, Gary North and Greg Bahnsen, joined him in California for a time and remained in close contact when they moved to other areas to promote the movement.

In 1973, Rushdooney's *The Institutes of Biblical Law* and North's *Introduction to Christian Economics* were published, underwritten by their Chalcedon Foundation. Criticizing the "dispensational god" of many evangelical premillennialists, Rushdoony declared that "this is not the God of Scripture, whose grace and law remain the same in every age." He explained that his *Institutes* were fundamental principles "intended as a beginning, as an instituting consideration of that law which must govern society, and which shall govern society under God." Detailing what he believed to be the Old Testament "civil law," Rushdoony attempted in 800 pages to explain how this biblical "civil law code" could be applied to government.

As might be expected, this attempt was highly controversial as Rushdoony maintained that biblical law must enforce the death penalty not only for murder, but also for adultery, incest, beastiality, sodomy, rape of a betrothed virgin, false witness in a case involving a capital offense, kidnapping, witchcraft, for striking or cursing father or mother, for "prophesying falsely or propagating false doctrines," etc. Later, Rushdooney suggested in his Institutes:

"To the humanistic mind these penalties seem severe and unnecessary. In actuality, the penalties together with the biblical faith which motivated them, worked to reduce crime." He illustrated this by explaining that "when New England passed laws requiring the death penalty for incorrigible delinquents and for children who struck their parents, no executions were necessary: the law kept the children in line."[22]

Such thought continued through Rushdoony's disciple and the "ethicist" of the movement, Greg L. Bahnsen. In his *Theonomy in Christian Ethics* (1977), Bahnsen listed "incorrigibility in children" as a "capital offense against God," along with murder, adultery and unchastity, homosexuality, rape, incest, sabbath breaking, kidnapping, apostacy, witchcraft, sorcery, and false pretension to prophecy. According to Bahnsen, the state is commanded by God to *execute* those who commit the above. "Christians do well at this point to adjust their attitudes so as to coincide with those of their Heavenly Father," Bahnsen wrote.[23]

When the "economist" of the movement, Gary North, decided to publish some of John Calvin's sermons in 1980 because they were "especially valuable in showing how God's law was relevant for the civilization that the Reformers were trying to build," the first two issues of North's *Calvin Speaks* were entitled, "The Execution of Rebellious Children." "If it is possible for children to become so rebellious and incorrigible that they must be put to death," the editor's summary began, "let us learn from this how serious a matter it is to be a parent." The series was launched with the words: "Let us learn from this master in Israel (John Calvin) how to preach and apply this portion of God's holy word."[24] To the Christian reconstructionist leadership, the Christian church had become Israel, the new Jerusalem, and had been given all of the promises once reserved for Jewish people.

The Christian reconstructionists may have remained an obscure movement with odd interpretations had it not been for the rapid rise of the New Religious Right in the latter 1970s. Political fundamentalists were grasping for materials that could argue the case for a "moral America" and were seeking alliances that would be effective in the political arena. The Christian reconstructionists moved into the vacuum with a plethora of materials and well-honed debate techniques. They rapidly became respected members of the Religious Roundtable, the Moral Majority, and other conservative political lobbies. Christian reconstructionists were pro-family, anti-abortion, anti-gay, and anti-pornography—vehemently so! Christian reconstructionists insisted that America was founded as a "Christian America," and they railed against the "secular humanists." Education was the responsibility of the parents and the church. Christian reconstructionists proclaimed that to be brought up according to "God's law," children must be taken out of the control of a tax-supported, state-regulated, "humanistic" school system.

The postmillennial triumphalism of the Christian reconstructionists and some of their "peculiar ideas" were overlooked by the new political fundamentalists. They desperately needed the help of Rushdoony and his cohorts. Since Rushdoony, Bahnsen, and North had spent years trying to convince a wary evangelical community that what the "decadent" United States needed was more *Christian* lawyers to practice more *Christian* law in an effort to bring in a *Christian* society with *Christian* economics to reach the world and make it *Christian*, they had a group of reconstructionist lawyers to help the New Religious Right in their causes. Criticism of the Christian reconstructionists was deemed "false witness" and was a very serious offense in the mind of its devotees. At times they threatened to use their Christian lawyers against critical Christian scholars.

The intimidation worked. Evangelical magazines and journals, such as *Christianity Today*, were strangely silent on this movement in the early 1980s, and only in private would leaders of organizations, such as the Religious Roundtable, shake their heads at some of the "strange ideas" proposed by their Christian reconstructionist members. The editor of the *Evangelical Theological Journal* leaked material to them and asked for their help in editing any critical articles against their movement. Rebuttals were stiffled, and Christian reconstructionists flooded evangelical periodicals with letters criticizing authors who even mentioned in passing the dangers of such movements. Gary North's Geneva Divinity School and his

Institute of Christian Economics were centered in Tyler, Texas, and the Tyler group would brag: "Without admitting it, virtually all the prominent leaders of the so-called 'Christian Right' are getting much of their material, their insights, even their slogans, from the Christian Reconstructionists." A *Newsweek* magazine article (February 2, 1983) would finally label Rousas John Rushdoony's Chalcedon Foundation, located in Vallecito, California, the "think tank of the religious right."

The Christian Reconstructionists were certainly basking in their accomplishments. Their concepts of "God's law" had made inroads into the law school at Oral Roberts University, and this law school was transferred to Pat Robertson's CBN University. CBN University hired Christian reconstructionist professors to indoctrinate their student body, and the Christian reconstructionist leadership appeared several times on Robertson's 700 Club. Great inroads were made into the charismatic and pentecostal movements (a first for ultra-Calvinists), and Pat Robertson was viewed as their Christian reconstructionist candidate in 1988. They worked feverishly for his election.

Criticism of the Christian reconstructionist movement began to mount among the larger evangelical community as evangelicals learned more of the policy and theology of the movement. A number of evangelical leaders had refrained from attacking the movement publicly because of the reconstructionists' fervent support of biblical inerrancy and moral propriety. A debate over the inerrancy of the Bible had been occurring among evangelicals, and Christian reconstructionists had forged alliances with inerrantists in the Evangelical Theological Society.

Former members of the movement, however, began to recount their ordeals, and in 1983 *The Presbyterian Journal* ran a scathing editorial against reconstructionist theology and the divisiveness it was causing in Reformed circles. Editor Jon Zens of the *Baptist Reformation Review* also expressed firm criticism, and a high school social studies teacher, David K. Watson, circulated his critical Calvin College master's thesis on the movement in 1985. In December 1986, an Assemblies of God minister, David Lewis, convened a diverse leadership group of fundamentalists, evangelicals, pentecostals, and

charismatics for a Christian Leadership Summit Conference to confront the heresy of Christian reconstructionism in their midst. One
hundred fifty leaders attended the three-day convocation in
Springfield, Missouri. It also became known that renowned Reformed
theologian, Meredith G. Kline, had issued warnings about the movement in the latter 1970s. Highly respected by the Christian
reconstructionists, Dr. Kline devastated their hopes for a sweep of the
conservative Calvinistic milieu when he wrote in *The Westminister
Theological Journal* in 1978 about Rushdoony's Chalcedon school of
thought: "The tragedy of Chalcedon is that of high potential wasted—
worse than wasted, for its most distinctive and emphatically
maintained thesis is a delusive and grotesque perversion of the
teaching of Scripture." Kline pointed out that the Christian
reconstructionists had "quickly earned a reputation for a cult-like
fanaticism, censoriously disruptive of the Reformed community, ecclesiastical and academic."[25]

It was not until February 20, 1987, that a major evangelical
periodical came out with a cover story on the Christian reconstructionists. In a carefully researched article, cautiously contacting
many reconstructionists, *Christianity Today* magazine ran on its
cover "God's Law for a New Order: What Christian Reconstructionists Really Want," complete with a picture of Mt. Sinai and
tablets of law. The related article inside was entitled "Democracy
as Heresy," and the subtitle declared: "Reconstructionists an-
ticipate a day when Christians will govern, using the Old
Testament as the law book." Editor Rodney Clapp was the author,
and caricatured line drawings of Rousas Rushdoony, Greg
Bahnsen, and Gary North appeared with the text. Although many
of the criticisms and quotes had appeared years before, for the first
time the general evangelical public was confronted by shocking
quotations and thoughts of the movement.

Furthermore, some respected evangelicals criticized the movement in print. Although a quote from his Christian
reconstructionist professor, Joseph Kickasola, appeared in the
article, presidential hopeful Pat Robertson was forced to say that
he had not embraced reconstructionism. "The Lord intends his
people to exercise dominion in his name," the televangelist

noted. "I admire many of these teachings because they are in line with Scripture. But others I cannot accept because they do not correspond with the biblical view of the sinful nature of mankind or the necessity of the second coming of Christ." Pat Robertson underscored that he was premillennial, not postmillennial, and that he did not "expect some kind of reconstructed utopia here on earth." *Christianity Today* also pointed out that Robertson's Dean of the Schools of Law and Public Policy, Herbert Titus, was nurtured in the Christian faith by Christian reconstructionists, and Titus admitted in print that they used "six or seven Rushdoony and North titles for textbooks." When Bill Moyers's series "God and Politics" aired on Public Broadcasting in December 1987, with a segment on Christian reconstructionists, evangelicals were able to view the movement and its leadership (as well as its critics) in living color.

As Christian reconstructionists regroup their political contigent in the 1990s, evangelicals need the support of and dialogue with the Jewish community as never before in their quest for political responsibility, freedom of religion, and the separation of church and state. Ironically, as numbers of Jewish leaders disdain relationships with evangelicals, evangelicals face their gravest dangers from the political right. As a massive voting contingent in the twenty-first century, evangelicalism must not be abandoned or neglected by Jewish leaders.

JEWISH POLITICS

Murray Friedman, in *The Utopian Dilemma: American Judaism and Public Policy* (1985), called for a reevaluation of American Jewry's political priorities, insisting that historically the Jewish community in the United States has been caught between the passion of liberal political ideals and the harsh reality of what is actually beneficial for Jews in America and in Israel. "It was becoming apparent by the early seventies that opposition to the liberal policies supported by many Jewish organizations was rising within the Jewish community," Dr. Friedman wrote. "Poorer and less educated Jews in the lower and middle ranks of the civil service—those, in short, directly affected by the urban crisis—were the most restless. They felt that their more affluent brethren were more distant from urban problems and therefore had less to lose." Friedman explained that "these middle-rank Jews were joined by intellectuals like Earl Raab, Milton Himmelfarb, and Maurice Goldbloom, who argued that liberal Protestant and other upper-class elites were willing to purchase social peace by, in effect, selling out the Jews."[26]

While underscoring the "major reexamination" of views toward American liberalism and Jewish support of liberal public policy, Friedman asked, "How, then, did the Jewish community respond to the new critique of liberalism?" He found that although reactions varied, "on the whole Jewish attitudes changed very little in the late seventies and early eighties." The Jewish community not only held to positions on the welfare state and national defense that were out of step with the "Reagan revolution," but also opposed the New Religious Right agenda against abortion and for prayer and Bible-reading in public schools. "Most Jewish groups now (seem) to feel that the greatest danger to civil rights and civil liberties came from the growth of the Christian Right," Murray Friedman asserted. "This growth touched a particularly sensitive nerve, since Jews have tended to measure their sense of security by the relative openness of the society in which they live."[27]

Sensing that more members of the Jewish community were challenging the utopian strain that had characterized Jewish thought and behavior, Murray Friedman noted that since 1972 it appeared "that one out of three and two out of five Jewish voters have brought themselves to pull the Republican lever" in national elections, and "a high proportion of Jewish voters today clearly identify with moderate Democrats rather than with the party's left wing." The Middle Atlantic states director of the American Jewish Committee argued that this is not a "trivial shift." "Jews, it is true, continue to feel liberal, but a significant number of them have concluded that different voting behavior is not only permitted but needed."[28]

By the 1988 presidential primary campaign, some Jewish political analysts suggested that there was a substantial political change taking place. Herbert L. Solomon, former Assistant Director of the

Jewish Community Relations Council of New York and now on the faculty of Touro College and the Theodor Herzl Institute, suggested in *Judaism* that "the Republicans, at long last, are on the threshold of capturing the Jewish vote." "Beginning about 20 years ago and continuing to this day," he later explained, "gradual changes in Jewish life—social, economic, cultural—are resulting in a loosening of liberalism's hold on Jewish attitudes. Questions are arising whether liberalism is really 'good for the Jews.' Interestingly, and ironically, the very forces that had originally spurred Jews into the liberal fold are now inducing them to consider conservatism as an alternative."[29]

"Jews may, indeed, turn to conservatism (many think they should)," Solomon stressed, "but, so far, they have not shown it in their voting patterns." He attributed this to the fact that "Jews still do not trust conservatives." And the rise of the New Religious Right, in Solomon's estimation, stymied a stronger Jewish vote for the Republican Party in the 1984 campaign. He noted that "the new political thrusts by Christian fundamentalists and evangelical Protestants to 'Christianize' America" was "felt to be a direct menace" by the Jewish community.

Although a number of Jewish scholars, including Solomon, believed that Jews were prepared to switch allegiances in the 1988 presidential election, predicting that nearly one-half of Jewish voters would vote for George Bush, the 1988 election produced few surprises. The Jewish support for the more liberal candidate (Michael Dukakis) over the more conservative one (George Bush) was indicated by every poll. This was perhaps due in some measure to the fact that the religious right wing of the Republican Party was very visible throughout the campaign and also to the fact that Kitty Dukakis was the Democratic Party's nominee for first lady. As early as September 1987, the Jewish magazine *Moment* ran a feature on Michael Dukakis's wife, Kitty, captioned: "Will the First Jew in the White House Be a Woman?"[30] Once again, the Jewish community's vote for president in 1988 was out of step with the rest of the nation. ABC polls recorded a 71 percent Jewish vote for Dukakis and only 28 percent for Bush. The NBC/*Wall Street Journal* poll was nearly the same. The CNN/*Los Angeles Times* poll was more in line with the earlier 1984 results—35 percent for Bush and 64 percent for Dukakis.

Nevertheless, prominent Jewish leaders were active in the Republican victory. Gordon Zacks and Jacob Stein, chair and cochair respectively of the National Jewish Committee to Elect George Bush, were convinced that Bush would run significantly better among Jews in 1988 than did Reagan in 1984. They focused their energies on that effort and had been assured by Bush that they would continue to have direct, immediate access to him. In an interview with *The Jerusalem Post* (August 27, 1988), Jacob Stein, the seventy-one-year-old former chair of the Conference of Presidents of Major American Jewish Organizations, declared:

> I believe that 1988 is the year when there will be a sea of change in the Jewish vote. For years, American Jews have been committed to the politics of nostalgia, voting for the ghost of FDR. But now they see significant changes in the Democratic Party that are inimical to their own interests. For the first time, we are looking to win a majority of Jewish votes.[31]

Gordon Zacks stated in the same article that Jews who had been "lifetime" Democrats had been calling him, offering to contribute money and to go to work for George Bush. "They feel the Democratic Party left them," he asserted. "They said that that party made a quilt in which there was a patch for everyone—but there wasn't a patch for the Jews."

Zacks insisted that many Jews were willing to vote for Ronald Reagan in 1984, but had been offended by Reagan's "ardent endorsement of the evangelical right and its agenda of prayer in the schools and opposition to abortion." Gordon Zacks intimated that George Bush had less fervor for such groups. At the age of 55, Zacks was the chief executive officer of the R.G. Barry Corporation headquartered in Columbus, Ohio, the largest supplier of home footwear in the United States. He was thrilled as George Bush took Ohio's electoral votes in what had been viewed as a crucial state race for the Republicans.

In the precampaign publicity, evangelicals were surprised to learn that there were Jews who were actually "neoconservatives." *Eternity* magazine's October 1988 political issue profiled an interview with Midge Decter, executive director of the Committee for the Free World. "A neoconservative," she told them, "is a liberal with a thirteen-year-old daughter." Paraphrasing prominent neoconservative professor of philosophy Irving Kristol's definition, she added that neoconservatives are "liberals mugged by reality." "The first time you discover, not in your head, but in your nervous system, that there is something beyond you, comes, without question, when you have children," Decter asserted. "You discover that there are lives worth more to you than your own." Espousing family values as well as Western values and virtues, Midge Decter explained to evangelicals how she felt about them:

> I happen to love American pluralism. I think it's the most benign system devised for people to live with one another. I don't believe in the ideal of a medieval Christian society. I don't look with any nostalgia at the Middle Ages. I'm a Jew. The ideas of a pluralist society where we find a common ground in the middle, what Richard Neuhaus calls the "public square," this is a benign human solution to the fact that you and I have everything in common except a belief in the divinity of Jesus Christ.

> I respect your belief. You may or may not respect my lack of belief and from your point of view you shouldn't. But at least we can work out an area in which that is at bay. I am not for ecumenism. Only an attenuated religion can be ecumenical, but that doesn't mean we can't find a saloon where we can park our guns at the door.[32]

"We may accuse each other of error, but both of us are in alliance against atheism," she concluded. "I think atheism and everything implied by it, is our common enemy."

For most Jews, however, the large advertisement in the *New York Times* (November 3, 1988) taken by the National Jewish Leadership Council five days before the election expressed their views and underscored the debate concerning the diverse political agendas of both evangelicals and Jews. "To understand which presidential candidate shares our values READ THE RECORDS...NOT THE RHETORIC. Michael Dukakis shares the values of the Jewish community. George Bush talks about values, but they're not our values," the heading declared. The first of the seven points insisted: "Michael

Dukakis will uphold the principle of separation of church and state. George Bush supports Jerry Falwell, Pat Robertson, and the Radical Right's call for Constitutional amendments supporting school prayer and banning abortion."

Conclusion

TOWARD THE TWENTY-FIRST CENTURY

At present, stereotype and caricature dictate the way evangelicals and Jews generally view one another. Yet it is accurate to say that the composition and orientation of each group contrasts considerably on the American scene. The Jewish community generally cherishes "liberal" ideals, while the evangelical movement insists on "conservative" values. Theological orientation undergirds the evangelical milieu, while social agendas dominate Jewish perceptions.

Further complications arise from the fact that the historic interaction of evangelicals and Jews has determined (almost hauntingly) present attitudes and relationships between both communities. We have seen that impressions from the nineteenth century feed the cauldron of myth and fabrication in the modern folklore of both groups. Inaccuracy often dominates the perceptions of both communities toward one another at the very time that their encounters are destined to increase. The fact remains that the 6 million member American Jewish community and the 60 million member American evangelical community are powerful players on the current political, social, and economic scene.

Nevertheless, this study has shown that individual Jews and individual evangelicals have attempted to overcome such obstacles. In the process, a relatively few have shown that friendships and alliances are possible among these two disparate peoplehoods. Leaders within both communities, however, have faced ridicule and scorn for attempting to foster better relationships on the national scene. Setbacks appear to be a frequent occurrence that may well increase in the twenty-first century.

To the outsider looking in, Jews and evangelicals must be viewed as individuals with similar problems in life. As human beings, they are consumed with vocations, goals and aspirations, raising families, marital difficulties, stress, etc. It is perhaps more difficult for evangelicals to admit such frustrations of daily life because their theological orientation dictates that they have the "peace of mind" that other groups lack. Yet the abundance of Christian psychologists on evangelical radio and television stations, and the accompanying calls by evangelical pastor's wives and the pastors themselves, indicates a belated acknowledgment of such problems. Jews, on the other hand, have to cope as the "outsiders" in a nation that likes to call itself "Christian" and is permeated with Christian motifs. Intermarriage is decimating the Jewish community in America to a far greater extent than conversion could ever threaten to accomplish. Anti-Semitism is far from being eradicated.

Jews and evangelicals hold dear their *identity* and *peoplehood.* This leads to unavoidable complications. Technically, evangelicals cannot deny their witness or they are estranged from their peoplehood. Jews lose their peoplehood if they succumb to evangelical witness. Both groups are fearful of being manipulated by the other. Future conflicts over church/state issues, evangelism, and public demonstration of religious affiliation are inevitable. While these issues often are faced squarely by the few evangelicals and Jews who have established friendships, the perceived dangers negate the possibility of relationships in most cases.

For example, in many instances, both the evangelical and the Jewish communities censor those of their members who pursue such a working relationship. Concerning those involved in evangelical-Jewish relations, evangelicals are accused of "watering-down their faith to court the Jewish desire to undermine evangelism," while Jews are viewed as "naive pawns in the evangelical plan to convert and conquer America." Both Jews for Judaism action groups and Jews for Jesus evangelistic groups have built multi-million dollar budgets by courting these fears. The lack of educational materials accurately explaining both communities to the other permits this absurd fiasco to continue. It is a never-ending cycle that appears to thwart Jewish-evangelical encounters in the twenty-first century. Jews are convinced that they can have nothing in common with evangelicals—that they just do not like evangelicals. Evangelicals are convinced that negative pharisaical traits overshadow Jews and Judaism—the same traits Jesus is thought to have encountered.

Yet there is much that each group might learn from the other. This study has shown social agendas on which evangelical and Jewish leaders have felt that they might work together. If they do, it will spell a new era in American political and social history. Outside of this occurrence, and at the very least, Jews may well gauge American public political opinion by having a closer perception of evangelical attitudes. Evangelicals may well avoid pitfalls in the political and social arena by maintaining close connections to Jewish analysts. Those outside each of these groups may experience the mosaic of America by better understanding and monitoring these diverse peoplehoods. In fact, a world of history and human experience is wrapped up in the roots and development of the Jewish and evangelical traditions. Both of these peoplehoods take a rich past into an uncertain, but intriguing, future.

Notes

Chapter 1. Evangelicals and Jews

1. These are the words of Herbert L. Solomon in his article "The Republican Party and the Jews," *Judaism* 37 (Summer 1988): 281.

2. ABC polls recorded a 71 percent Jewish vote for Dukakis and only 28% for Bush. The NBC/*Wall Street Journal* poll was nearly the same. The CNN/*Los Angeles Times* poll recorded a 24 percent Jewish vote for George Bush, while the CBS/*New York Times* poll was more in line with the earlier 1984 results—35 percent for Bush and 64 percent for Dukakis.

3. Note "Summary of Major Findings" in Steven M. Cohen's *The Political Attitudes of American Jews, 1988: A National Survey in Comparative Perspective*, December 1988, unedited manuscript.

4. Refer to *Nationwide Attitudes Survey, September 1986: A Confidential Report Presented to Anti-Defamation League of B'nai B'rith* by Tarrance, Hill, Newport & Ryan, 156.

5. See "News Items," *The American Israelite* 38 (September 10, 1891): 4. Cf. "Notes," *The American Israelite* 38 (November 19, 1891): 6.

6. Note "Conclusion" in Steven M. Cohen, *Ties and Tensions: The 1986 Survey of American Jewish Attitudes Toward Israel and Israelis* (New York: The American Jewish Committee, 1987), 89-90.

7. Yechiel Eckstein, *What Christians Should Know About Jews and Judaism* (Waco, Texas: Word Books, 1984), 248. Rabbi Eckstein explained: "The classical Jewish response is that a Jew is one who is born of a Jewish mother or who converts into the faith and peoplehood. The various denominations, however, have different standards of conversion so that many Orthodox Jews do not regard Reform or Conservative conversions as valid. This problem is particularly nettlesome today in Israel where all official questions pertaining to religion are determined exclusively by Orthodox rabbis.

8. "Thy son by an Israelite woman is called thy son, but thy son by a heathen woman is not called thy son." (*Kiddushin* 68b)

9. Leonard Fein, *Where Are We?: The Inner Life of America's Jews* (New York: Harper & Row, 1988), 25.

10. Eckstein, *What Christians Should Know*, 248. Rabbi Eckstein continues on the following page: "For many Jews, being Jewish represents an ethnic identification alone, a civil religion, wherein they give charity to Jewish (and other) causes. Beyond that, they identify only minimally in a religious sense. The concept of *tzedakah*, or 'charity,' is a very real one for such Jews, deeply ingrained into their Jewish psyche. In most instances, however, even such secular and unaffiliated Jews mark life cycle events such as birth, death, bar mitzvah, and marriage, through religious observance and with

the presence of a rabbi. Insufficient as such commitments to secular and cultural Judaism are, they nevertheless constitute another way in which Jews today affirm their Jewish identity."

11. Arnold M. Eisen, *The Chosen People in America: A Study in Jewish Religious Ideology* (Bloomington: Indiana University Press, 1983), 182. See pages 4-5 for the earlier quotes from Professor Eisen and a more detailed discussion concerning them.

12. See Cohen, *Political Attitudes* 76. The other quotations are found on pages 75-76.

13. Ibid. Refer to statistic tables on pages 96 and 100.

14. Note Dennis Prager, *Ultimate Issues* 2 (Spring-Summer 1986): 2. This special double issue contains Prager's points and the question and answer sessions that took place after each lecture. It may be obtained for $7.00 by writing *Ultimate Issues*, 2265 Westwood Blvd., Los Angeles, California 90064. Dennis Prager coauthored with Joseph Telushkin the popular books, *The Nine Questions People Ask About Judaism* and *Why the Jews? The Reason For Antisemitism.*

15. Ibid., 4. Prager also emphasized that evil religious people in the synagogue and in the world should not negate the mission or serve as an excuse to abort the mission. Asking this Wexner group to be honest, he declared: "Somehow or other you always hear that evil done in God's name invalidates religion but you never hear that evil done in law's name invalidates law or evil done in medicine's name invalidates medicine or evil done in science's name invalidates nuclear physics. Somehow everything can be perverted and you still know you have to retain its essence but not God and religion. One rotten person goes to synagogue and you have a ready-made excuse not to take religion seriously. So be honest enough and say you don't want to be bugged by religion. I respect that. You don't want to be annoyed by it. Say religion is a pain, that you want to be responsible to yourself, not to a God and not to a Torah, not to a community and not to a religion. O.K. I respect honesty. But please don't tell me that because there are evil religious people, religion is not morally essential." (p. 6)

16. Ibid., 6. Prager ended his first point with these words: "Therefore I am ending the God part with this. We have a mission to spread ethical monotheism. Everything else Jewish becomes meaningless without ethical monotheism. You can give all the money you want to Jewish causes, but as important as that is, ultimately you are not building an edifice that can prevent evil from taking place. While another holocaust will take place, we will continue giving charity. Charity is wonderful but it is not a system for ending evil. That is what ethical monotheism has as its possibility. This is the single greatest gift that we Jews have to give to the world." (p. 8)

17. For both letters see "Dialogue with Readers," *Ultimate Issues*, 2 (Fall 1986): 14.

18. Robert E. Webber, *Common Roots: A Call To Evangelical Maturity* (Grand Rapids, Mich.: Zondervan Publishing House, 1978), 32-33.

19. Bernard L. Ramm, *The Evangelical Heritage* (Waco, Texas: Word Books, 1973), 13-14. Ramm emphasized: "This also means that paralleling the divine Word is the divine Act — Creation, the call of Abraham, the Exodus, the Incarnation, the cross, the Resurrection, and the descent of the Spirit. The Word of God and the Act of God compenetrate so that it is artificial to separate them in any manner."

20. Refer to Kenneth S. Kantzer, "Unity and Diversity in Evangelical Faith," *The Evangelicals: What They Believe, Who They Are, Where They Are Changing*, ed. David F. Wells and John D. Woodbridge (Nashville: Abingdon Press, 1975), 52-54. Kantzer's list of twelve "fundamentals of evangelicalism" are:

(1) the eternal preexistence of the Son as the second person of the one God;

(2) the incarnation of God the Son in man as the divine/human person— two natures in one person;

(3) the virgin birth, the means by which God the Son entered into the human race, without ceasing to be fully God, became also fully man;

(4) the sinless life of Christ while sharing the life and experiences of alien men apart from sin;

(5) the supernatural miracles of Christ as acts of his compassion and signs of his divine nature;

(6) Christ's authoritative teaching as Lord of the church;

(7) the substitutionary atonement in which God did all that was needed to redeem man from sin and its consequences;

(8) the bodily resurrection of Christ as the consummation of his redemptive work and the sign and seal of its validity;

(9) the ascension and heavenly mission of the living Lord;

(10) the bodily second coming of Christ at the end of the age;

(11) the final righteous judgment of all mankind and the eternal kingdom of God;

(12) the eternal punishment of the impenitent and disbelieving wicked of this world.

21. See George Marsden, ed., *Evangelicalism and Modern America* (Grand Rapids, Mich.: William B. Eerdmans Publishing Company, 1984), viii-ix. This book is dedicated to Timothy L. Smith. Regarding the kaleidoscope of modern evangelicalism, Dr. Marsden explains

So on one side of evangelicalism are black Pentecostals and on another are strict fundamentalists, such as at Bob Jones University, who condemn Pentecostals and shun blacks. Peace churches, especially those in the Anabaptist-Mennonite tradition, make up another discrete group of evangelicals. And their ethos differs sharply from that of the Southern Baptist Convention, some fourteen million strong and America's largest Protestant body. Southern Baptists, in turn, have had experiences quite different from those of the evangelicals who have kept the traditional faith within the more liberal "mainline" northern churches. Each of these predominantly Anglo groups is, again, very different from basically immigrant church bodies like the Missouri Synod Lutheran or the Christian Reformed, who have carefully preserved Reformation confessional heritages. Other groups have held on to heritages less old but just as distinctive: German Pietists and several evangelical varieties among Methodists preserve traditions of eighteenth-century Pietism. The spiritual descendants of Alexander Campbell, especially in the Churches of Christ, continue to proclaim the nineteenth-century American ideal of restoring the practices of the New Testament church. Holiness and Pentecostal groups of many varieties stress similar emphases that developed slightly later and in somewhat differing contexts. Black Christians, responding to a cultural experience dominated by oppression, have developed their own varieties of most of the major American traditions, especially the Baptist, Methodist, and Pentecostal. Not only do these and other evangelical denominations vary widely, but almost every one has carefully guarded its distinctiveness, usually avoiding deep contact with many other groups. Viewed in this light, evangelicalism indeed appears as disorganized as a kaleidoscope. One might wonder why evangelicalism is ever regarded as a unified entity at all.

22. Ibid., xi-xii.

23. Carl F.H. Henry, *A Plea For Evangelical Demonstration* (Grand Rapids, Mich.: Baker Book House, 1971), preface.

24. Carl F.H. Henry, *Confessions of a Theologian: An Autobiography* (Waco, Tex.: Word Books, 1986), 387.

25. Ibid., 390.

26. Donald G. Bloesch, *Life, Ministry, and Hope*, vol. 2 of *Essentials of Evangelical Theology*, (San Francisco: Harper & Row, 1979), 235.

27. Ibid., 238-39.

28. James Leo Garrett, Jr., E. Glenn Hinson, and James E. Tull, *Are Southern Baptists "Evangelicals"?* (Macon, Ga.: Mercer University Press, 1983), 126.

29. Ibid., 182.

30. Nationwide Attitudes Survey, September 1986, for ADL, 11.

31. Note the interview with Bill Bright entitled "New Life 2000: By the End of This Century!" in *Mission Frontiers* 11 (November-December 1989): 12-14. *Mission Frontiers* is the bulletin of the U.S. Center for World Mission. Another article in this issue, "Fresh Thinking on Muslim Missions," calls for the renewal of Christian evangelism among Muslims.

Chapter 2. Roots and Reactions

1. John 3:16 reads: "For God so loved the world that he gave his one and only Son, that whoever believes in him shall not perish but have eternal life." John 3:3 reads: "In reply Jesus declared, 'I tell you the truth, unless a man is born again, he cannot see the kingdom of God.'" Hebrews 9:28 reads: "So Christ was sacrificed once to take away the sins of many people; and he will appear a second time, not to bear sin, but to bring salvation to those who are waiting for him." These quotes are from the *New International Version* of the Christian Testament, a current favorite version among evangelicals.

2. Although Lutheranism in particular and Protestantism in general would at times be woefully intolerant toward those of other religious persuasions (even within their own religious community!), the principles of individual conscience and freedom of religious belief have been cherished by individual Protestant groups throughout history. In fact, most Protestant groups have at one time or another appealed to these "God-given rights."

3. Note David A. Rausch and Carl Hermann Voss, *Protestantism: Its Modern Meaning* (Philadelphia: Fortress Press, 1987), 41-74, for a discussion of Puritanism, Pietism, and the philosophical and theological crosscurrents that countered the Age of Enlightenment and challenged its premises.

4. The nine "evangelical principles" or articles adopted by the Evangelical Alliance were published as follows:

1. The Divine Inspiration, Authority, and Sufficiency of the Holy Scriptures.

2. The right and duty of private judgment in the interpretation of the Holy Scriptures.

3. The Unity of the Godhead, and the Trinity of Persons therein.

4. The utter depravity of human nature in consequence of the Fall.

5. The Incarnation of the Son of God, His work of Atonement for sinners of mankind, and His Mediatorial intercession and reign.

6. The Justification of the Sinner by Faith alone.

7. The work of the Holy Spirit in the Conversion and Sanctification of the Sinner.

8. The Immortality of the Soul, the Resurrection of the Body, the Judgment of the World by our Lord Jesus Christ, with eternal blessedness of the righteous and the eternal punishment of the wicked.

9. The Divine Institution of the Christian Ministry, and the obligation and perpetuity of the ordinances of Baptism and the Lord's Supper.

5. Charles Hodge's statement may be found in *Biblical Repertory and Theological Review* 8 (1836): 430.

6. A. James Reichley, *Religion in American Public Life* (Washington, D.C.: The Brookings Institution, 1985), 180-81; 191-93. Reichley is quick to point out, however, that "evangelicals differed among themselves on the proper relationship between religion and politics" (181), a fact that will be clearly seen in following chapters.

7. Note Arno C. Gaebelein, *Half A Century: The Autobiography of a Servant* (New York: Publication Office of *Our Hope*, 1930), 68. Compare "How the Hope of Israel Work Became Undenominational," *Our Hope* 4 (July 1897): 3-5. When Gaebelein protested Cadman's attack on the Bible, he was told by high evangelical officials of the Methodist Church not to be hasty for "sooner or later we must fall in line with these results of scholarly Biblical Criticism." While many of his conservative friends stayed in the denomination, Arno C. Gaebelein immediately severed his connections. He became a leader in the fundamentalist movement within evangelicalism. Cf. David A. Rausch, *Arno C. Gaebelein, 1861-1945* (Lewiston, N.Y.: Edwin Mellen Press, 1983).

8. Shailer Mathews, *The Faith of Modernism* (New York: The Macmillan Company, 1924), 34-35.

9. L. Gaussen, *Theopneustia*, trans. David Scott (rev. ed., Chicago: The Bible Institute Colportage Association, n.d.), 351; 355.

10. Ibid., ii.

11. Charles Hodge, *Systematic Theology*, vol. 1 (London: Thomas Nelson and Sons, 1875), 151.

12. D.L. Moody, *Heaven* (Chicago: Bible Institute Colportage Association, 1880), 7-8.

13. D.L. Moody, *Pleasure and Profit in Bible Study* (Chicago: Bible Institute Colportage Association, 1895), 21. Moody began in his section, "Clipping The Bible," by saying: "There is another class. It is quite fashionable for people to say, 'Yes, I believe the Bible, but not the supernatural. I believe everything that corresponds with this reason of mine.' They go on reading the Bible with a pen-knife, cutting out this and that." As will be seen later, Moody's aversion to rationalism brought him into direct conflict with the rational Judaism of Rabbi Isaac Mayer Wise.

14. Note Nathaniel West, "History of the Pre-Millennial Doctrine," *Premillennial Essays of the Prophetic Conference Held in the Church of the Holy Trinity, New York City* (New York: F.H. Revell, 1879), 315.

15. Nathaniel West, *The Thousand Years in Both Testaments* (New York: Fleming H. Revell, 1889), vi.

16. See George C. Needham, "Reasons for Holding the Prophetic Conference," *Prophetic Studies of the International Prophetic Conference, Chicago, November, 1886* (Chicago: Fleming H. Revell, 1886), 215.

17. E.F. Stroeter, "Christ's Second Coming Premillennial," *Prophetic Studies*, 17-18.

18. Nathaniel West, "Prophecy and Israel," *Prophetic Studies*, 122-25.

19. Henry M. Parsons, "Judgments and Rewards," *Prophetic Studies*, 81. For earlier quote, note W.J. Erdman, "Fullness of the Gentiles," *Prophetic Studies*, 56-57.

20. William R. Nicholson, "The Gathering of Israel," *Premillennial Essays*, 237.

21. Ibid., 234, 239. Bishop Nicholson insisted that he found himself "in the midst of an embarrassment of riches" when it came to proving from the Bible that the Jewish people would be restored to Palestine" (223). He noted that the "gathering of Israel" would be accomplished in two installments. Before the Messiah returned, many of the Jewish people would "be gathered back in their unconverted state." They would rebuild the Temple and reestablish Temple services. The Messiah, Jesus Christ, would return, Bishop Nicholson claimed, and then the rest of the Jewish people would accept their Lord and be restored to the land as well. He preached that the Holy Land would be restored to its former beauty and universal peace and harmony would bless the world (cf. 228, 231, 235).

22. E.F. Stroeter, "The Second Coming of Christ in Relation to Israel," *Addresses on the Second Coming of the Lord Delivered at the Prophetic Conference, Allegheny, Pa. December 3-6, 1895* (Pittsburgh: W.W. Waters, n.d.), 148, 150. Notice Stroeter's use of the term "elder brother" for the Orthodox Jew.

23. Ibid., 138-39. Dr. Stroeter, as many fundamentalist-evangelicals, could not escape such feelings of obligation. He continued:

> But here he is, the imperishable, ubiquitous, irrepressible Jew, the most conspicuous and emphatic figure of all history. The Jew, without a king or a government of his own, has seen the mightiest empires rise and has attended their funeral. An exile from his own land, he has witnessed every civilized country of the Old World change ownership over and over. No nation has ever prospered in his land, the land that flowed with milk and honey while he dwelt there; he has prospered in every land, under every clime. He receives no hearty welcome, no legislative favors, no social advantages anywhere, hardly justice; but in the race for wealth, for success and for honors in art and science and literature he leads everywhere. He has been branded with infamy, loaded with unutterable contempt; behold him, the cringing, crouching, unresisting object of pity!

24. E.F. Stroeter, "Editorial Correspondence," *Our Hope* 4 (December 1897): 183-84. Sixteen of these letters were published in *Our Hope* from December 1897 to June 1897.

25. *Our Hope* 4 reprinted an abridged edition of his letter. Note "Rabbi Mendes On Zionism" (September 1897): 98-102. *Our Hope* was edited by

Dr. Ernst Stroeter from 1894 to 1897 with the help of Dr. Arno C. Gaebelein. Gaebelein then edited the fundamentalist-evangelical periodical until his death in 1945. Stroeter stayed in Europe to fight anti-Semitism there.

26. Note *Catholic World* 25 (1877): 367. Ernest Sandeen mentioned in *The Roots of Fundamentalism* (Chicago: The University of Chicago Press, 1970) that an English reviewer (of premillennial thought) for the *Christian Observer* "seemed very much like Alice in Wonderland—stumbling around in an unfamiliar landscape, rather astounded at what he was finding and often quite cross" at the concept of the restoration of the Jews to Palestine (p. 23). Note p. 93 for Dr. Sandeen's synopsis of the *Princeton Review* and *Christian Intelligencer*.

27. C.I. Scofield, "The Israel of God," *Our Hope* 8 (April 1902): 574. The following quote is on p. 577.

28. For early drafts of the NAE doctrinal statement and the process involved, note James DeForest Murch, *Cooperation without Compromise: A History of the National Association of Evangelicals* (Grand Rapids, Mich.: Wm. B. Eerdmans Publishing Company, 1956), 62-71. Compare the actual constitution in the report, *Evangelical Action: A Report of the Organization of the National Association of Evangelicals for United Action* (Boston: United Action Press, 1942), 102-3. This 160-page report was compiled and edited by the Executive Committee. The NAE doctrinal statement that members had to sign stated:

> It shall be required that those holding membership shall subscribe to the following doctrines:
>
> (1) That we believe the Bible to be the inspired, the only infallible, authoritative word of God.
>
> (2) That we believe that there is only one God, eternally existent in three persons; Father, Son and Holy Spirit.
>
> (3) That we believe in the deity of Christ, in His virgin birth, in His sinless life, in His miracles, in His vicarious and atoning death, in His ascension to the right hand of the Father and in His personal return in power and glory.
>
> (4) That because of the exceeding sinfulness of human nature we believe in the absolute necessity of regeneration by the Holy Spirit for salvation.
>
> (5) That we believe in the resurrection of both the saved and the lost; they that are saved unto the resurrection of life and they that are lost unto the resurrection of damnation.
>
> (6) That we believe in the spiritual unity of believers in Christ.

29. "New York News," *The Israelite* 21 (October 24, 1873): 5.

30. Isaac Mayer Wise, "What the Religion of America Will Be," *The Israelite* 21 (November 14, 1873): 4. Cf. "The Free Religious Association: Opening of the Session—Addresses by Oliver Johnson, Charles Storrs, the

Rev. O.B. Frothingham," *The Israelite* 21 (October 31, 1873): 4-5; "Free Religion (concluded)," *The Israelite* 21 (November 7, 1873): 4-5.

31. Isaac Mayer Wise, "The Religion of Future Generations: Part II," *The Israelite* 21 (December 5, 1873): 4. Cf. Part I of this article in the November 28, 1873 issue, page 4.

32. Ibid., Part I of this article.

33. For example, in an excerpt in *The Israelite* 21 (July 11, 1873): 4, the following appeared:

> The Supreme Court of Ohio has decided that this is a secular state, and the public schools are secular institutions.

> The School Board of Cincinnati two years ago, prohibited the use of the Bible in public schools. An injunction was served on them and the matter was brought up before the Superior Court of Cincinnati. This court decided against the action of the School Board. An appeal was taken, and now the Supreme Court sustained the School Board. Either the reading of the Bible is a religious worship, then it can not be imposed upon the public schools; or the Bible is looked upon as a mere text-book in the school, then the Board has a right to prescribe which book should, and which should not be used in the school. This settles the question for Ohio, and makes the common schools actually free schools. So Ohio is a secular State.

On the Jewish fears of evangelical dominance, cf. "Profane Passah Thoughts," *The Israelite* 22 (March 27, 1874): 4, which stated:

> The attempts in our country, in behalf of the cross, to undermine and upset liberty, are frequent and violent....the Church must oppose the progress of freedom as it does the progress of science, although most men are better than their religion. Therefore the repeated attempt to change the Constitution of the United States into an instrument of evangelical sectarianism, to the exclusion of all citizens who love freedom above church discipline, and prefer blunt honesty to oiled hypocrisy....Therefore, and for many other reasons, liberty is not safe yet in this country, and it will never be here or anywhere else as long as the symbol of the cross stands above the symbol of freedom.

34. Isaac Mayer Wise, "Lecture I: 'Jesus the Pharisee,'" *The Israelite* 21 (July 11, 1873): 5.

35. Ibid., Part II (July 18, 1873): 5. Wise lectured and wrote:

> In all this, however, there is no Christianity. Jesus was not the author of Christianity. He became the cause of its origin, as we shall see in the two next lectures. He was a Pharisee, a patriot, an ardent enthusiast, whose aspiration was to save his people, to redeem Israel from the bondage of invaders and corruptionists. Politics, ethics, and religion being then an indevisable unit, and in a true sense of the terms, they always will be, he was a religious, moral, and political character in one person.

36. The second lecture series begins on July 25, 1873, p. 4-5.

37. See Isaac Mayer Wise, "Paul and the Mystics," *The Israelite* 21 (August 22, 1873): 4-5. This Lecture III series began August 15, 1873 and ended September 5, 1873.

38. Ibid., conclusion of Lecture III (September 5, 1873): 5.

39. "Washington Letter," *The American Israelite* 26 (November 19, 1875): 5.

40. "Philadelphia Letter," *The American Israelite* 26 (December 10, 1875): 5.

41. Note "A Hoax and a Disclaimer," *The American Israelite* 26 (March 25, 1876): 7.

42. "New York Letter," *The American Israelite* 26 (April 7, 1876): 7.

43. "Correspondence," *The Israelite* 21 (July 4, 1873): 6.

44. "Another Converted Rabbi," *The Israelite* 21 (August 8, 1873): 6.

45. Note *The American Israelite* 26 (May 12, 1876): 5.

46. Editorial Notes, *The American Israelite* 30 (March 7, 1884): 7.

47. For a discussion of Joseph Rabinowitz, his relationship to Hebrew Christianity and missionary enterprises, and his connections with the growing fundamentalist-evangelical movement, see David A. Rausch, *Messianic Judaism: Its History, Theology, and Polity* (Lewiston, N.Y.: The Edwin Mellen Press, 1982), 92-98.

Chapter 3. Perspectives

1. Note Barry A. Kosmin, Paul Ritterbasnd, and Jeffrey Scheckner, "Jewish Population in the United States, 1986," *American Jewish Year Book: 1987* (New York: The American Jewish Committee, 1987), 164-91, for relevant statistical data, comparisons with 1930 population statistics, and recent trends.

2. A Curriculum for the Afternoon Jewish School (New York: United Synagogue Commission on Jewish Education, 1978), 557.

3. Judith H. Banki, "What and How Jews Teach About Evangelicals and Christianity," in A. James Rudin and Marvin R. Wilson, eds., *A Time To Speak: The Evangelical-Jewish Encounter* (Grand Rapids: William B. Eerdmans, 1987), 91-102.

4. The results were published in David A. Rausch, "What and How Evangelicals Teach about Jews and Judaism," in *A Time To Speak*, 76-89.

5. Paul E. Pierson, *Themes From Acts* (Ventura, Calif.: Gospel Light Regal Books, 1982), 29-30.

6. Ibid., 32-33.

7. Bill Myers, *Dr. Luke Examines Jesus: Want Your Life Changed?* (Wheaton, Ill.: Scripture Press Victor Books, 1981), 126.

8. "Betrayed and Tried," *Junior Teacher: The Church Is My Family*, Unit I, Lesson 2, Living Word Curriculum (Ventura, Calif.: Gospel Light, 1988), 9.

9. "Jesus' Death and Resurrection," *4s and 5s Teacher: Teach Me About Jesus and His Friends*, Unit II, Lesson 6, Living Word Curriculum (Ventura, Calif.: Gospel Light, 1983), 37.

10. "Jesus Dies and Lives Again," *4s and 5s Teaching Guide*, Unit I, Lesson 5, The Bible-in-Life Sunday School Curriculum (Wheaton, Ill.: Scripture Press Publications, 1988), 27.

11. "He Saves and Keeps Me," *Juniors Now: In-Class Student Bible Study Guide*, Unit I, Lesson 1, The Bible-for-Today Sunday School Curriculum (Wheaton, Ill.: Scripture Press Publications, 1988), 4.

12. Ibid., Unit II, Lesson 1, 14.

13. "Rejected," *High School Teaching Guide*, Unit I, Lesson 3, (Wheaton, Ill.: Scripture Press Publications, 1988), 18.

14. "Bible Study Three: On My Own, Matthew 9:36-16:20," *Youth Illustrated* 54 (March 20, 1988), 23.

15. "Jesus Is Alive," *Nursery: Teacher's Guide*, Unit VII, Lesson 5, Bible-in-Life Curriculum (Elgin, Ill.: David C. Cook, 1988), 34.

16. "Jesus Helps Us Forgive One Another," *Kindergarten: Teacher's Guide*, Unit III, Lesson 9, Bible-in-Life Curriculum (Elgin, Ill.: David C. Cook, 1988), 51.

17. "What About Hypocrisy?" *Senior High: Teacher Guide*, Unit 32, Lesson 9, Bible-in-Life Curriculum (Elgin, Ill.: David C. Cook, 1988), 54.

18. Ibid., Lesson 5, 34. Compare *Junior High: Teacher's Guide*, pages 32-33, for a discussion and chart of Jesus' relation to Jonah's three days and three nights in the belly of a big fish (from Matthew 12:38-41).

19. "Trial and Crucifixion," *Adult: Teacher's Guide*, Unit I, Lesson 4, Bible-in-Life Curriculum (Elgin, Ill.: David C. Cook, 1988), 30-31. The following quotes are from pages 32-33.

20. Ibid., "God's New Covenant," Unit II, Lesson 10, 72.

21. "Jesus Is Alive!" *Nursery: 2s and 3s Teacher's Manual*, Unit II, Lesson 5 (Cincinnati: Standard Publishing Co.), 33. See page 8 for previous quotation.

22. "Jesus Heals a Man Who Is Blind," *Beginner Teacher: 4's and 5's*, Unit I, Lesson 3 (Cincinnati: Standard Publishing Co., 1988), 17.

23. "Paul Begins to Tell About Jesus," *Beginner Teacher: 4s and 5s*, Unit II, Lesson 6 (Cincinnati: Standard Publishing Co., 1988), 33.

24. "Paul Tells a Crowd About Jesus," *Beginner Teacher: 4s and 5s*, Unit II, Lesson 11 (Cincinnati: Standard Publishing Co., 1988), 60. The "Lesson Background," page 59 states in part: "Talk about basing judgment on circumstantial evidence! That's exactly what the Asian Jews did in the Jerusalem temple in this account!.... The Asian Jews stirred up a hysterical

mob by the words they shouted in verse 28. The charges were similar to the charges brought against Stephen in Acts 6:11-13. The temple in Jerusalem had a large Court of Gentiles. Here proselytes, or Gentile converts to Judaism, could come to worship God. But inside this area, closer to the very holy heart of the temple, there were areas where only Jews were allowed to go. In fact, signs were posted that warned the death penalty—a penalty upheld by the Roman government...the mob dragged Paul out of the Court of Israel into the Court of the Gentiles."

25. "Jesus Took the Blame for Me," *Middler Teacher: Grades 3-4*, Unit I, Lesson 5 (Cincinnati: Standard Publishing Co., 1988), 27.

26. "Victory!" *Junior Teacher: Grades 5-6*, Unit II, Lesson 5 (Cincinnati: Standard Publishing Co., 1988), 37; cf. 34. On page 38, the child playing Joseph of Arimathea states: "To be honest, I was so upset that Pilate would give in to those trumped-up charges and crucify an innocent man that I didn't think about what might happen to me. All I could think about was that they had crucified my Lord."

27. "Victory!" *Middler Teacher: Grades 3-4* (Cincinnati: Standard Publishing Co., 1988), 30.

28. Stuart E. Rosenberg, *The Christian Problem: A Jewish Problem* (New York: Hippocrene Books, 1986), 11.

29. Joshua O. Haberman, "The Bible Belt is America's Safety Belt," *Policy Review* (Fall 1987): 40.

30. Jack R. Fischel, "The Fundamentalist Perception of Jews," *Midstream* (December 1982): 30.

31. Ibid., 31.

32. Joshua O. Haberman, "Fundamentalists and Jews," *Midstream* (November 1983): 46.

33. Ibid., Rael Jean Isaac, 46.

34. Nathan Perlmutter, "Jews and Fundamentalists," *Reconstructionist* (December 1985): 20-23.

35. Ibid., 23.

36. Letter from Russell T. Hitt to Rabbi Marc H. Tanenbaum, November 23, 1963. Hitt wrote: "I hope our paths cross again soon and often."

37. Letter from Russell T. Hitt to Rabbi Marc H. Tanenbaum, August 9, 1966. Hitt noted: "Also I want you to know it would be a great privilege to bring our families together. We both are busy but we'll fit in with your plans in New York. I'd love to entertain you and your wife in our home in Merion. No doubt AJC business brings you this way often."

38. "Dialogue, Love and Witness," *Eternity* 18 (August 1967): 6-7.

39. G. Douglas Young, "Lessons We Can Learn from Judaism," *Eternity* 18 (August 1967): 22.

40. Belden Menkus, "Our Subtle Anti-Semitism," *Eternity* 18 (August 1967): 23-24. Menkus tried to alert evangelicals to differences between Orthodox, Conservative, and Reform Jews.

41. Note the hundred pages of edited conversations with Frank E. Gaebelein in David A. Rausch, *Arno C. Gaebelein, 1861-1945* (Lewiston, N.Y.: Edwin Mellen Press, 1983). Frank E. Gaebelein's letter appeared in the October, 1967 issue of *Eternity*, page 4.

42. Michael Wyschogrod, "Judaism and Evangelical Christianity," in Marc H. Tanenbaum, Marvin R. Wilson, and A. James Rudin, eds., *Evangelicals and Jews in Conversation on Scripture, Theology, and History* (Grand Rapids: Baker Book House, 1978), 42-43. Professor Wyschogrod stated earlier:

> The Jewish observer of the Christian scene, particularly of the evangelical Christian scene, finds it difficult to understand why the legislation of the Pentateuch plays such a relatively small part in the evangelical consciousness. These commandments are there in the Pentateuch, in black and white, for everyone to read. Why does Christianity, including evangelical Christianity, not pay more attention to the Mosaic law? The Jewish observer is, of course, aware that the Christian attitude to the law is conditioned by the New Testament. But it is precisely here the Jewish-Christian dialogue is necessary. Jesus and the apostles were Jews. The New Testament is a book that comes out of the Jewish world and largely presupposes the rabbinic universe of discourse without which much of it is easily misunderstood (p. 42).

43. Ibid., 47-48.

44. Refer to Marc H. Tanenbaum, Marvin R. Wilson, and A James Rudin, eds., *Evangelicals and Jews in an Age of Pluralism* (Grand Rapids: Baker Book House, 1984); and A. James Rudin and Marvin R. Wilson, *A Time To Speak: The Evangelical-Jewish Encounter* (Grand Rapids: William B. Eerdmans, 1987). This latter volume was published in conjunction with Dwight A. Pryor's Center for Judaic-Christian Studies in Austin, Texas (now located in Dayton, Ohio).

45. Asher Finkel, "Scriptural Interpretation: A Historical Perspective," *Evangelicals and Jews in Conversation*, 150.

46. Edwin M. Yamauchi, "Concord, Conflict, and Community: Jewish and Evangelical Views of Scripture," *Evangelicals and Jews in Conversation*, 184-85. The former quote appears on page 183.

47. Kenneth S. Kantzer, "Six Hard Questions for Evangelicals and Jews," *Evangelicals and Jews in an Age of Pluralism*, 260. Kantzer's same questions and points appear in his lengthy editorial, "Concerning Evangelicals and Jews," *Christianity Today* 26 (April 24, 1981): 12-15, for the evangelical periodical's more than 300,000 readers to comprehend.

48. These ten points are reproduced in Rudin and Wilson, eds., *A Time To Speak*, xi-xii. Compare "Judeo-Christian Values and Social Justice," *Eternity* 36 (September 1985): 57-59.

49. Ibid., ix.

50. William Sanford LaSor, "An Evangelical and the Interfaith Movement," *Judaism* 27 (Summer 1978): 337. LaSor's article is followed by Martin E. Marty, "Interfaith at Fifty—It Has Worked!"

51. See James D. Davis, "Rabbi Seeks to Pull Jews, Christians Closer Together," *Fort Lauderdale News, Palm Beach Sentinel,* December 12, 1986. Rabbi Eckstein also stated during the interview: "Some fellow Jews suspect us of selling out to Christians. Some Christians think we just want them to stop evangelizing. So our continuing challenge is to stay credible in both communities. Compare Yechiel Eckstein, *What Christians Should Know About Jews and Judaism* (Waco, Tex.: Word Books, 1984).

Chapter 4. Theologies in Conflict

1. For example, there has been great debate within the World Council of Churches. Note Harvey T. Hoekstra, *The World Council of Churches and the Demise of Evangelism* (Wheaton, Ill.: Tyndale House Publishers, 1979), where the debate over evangelism is discussed. On page 184 he explains that even "within the WCC staff," some support an aggressive evangelistic enterprise.

2. See Tetsunao Yamamori, *God's New Envoys: A Bold Strategy for Penetrating "Closed Countries"* (Portland, Oreg.: Multnomah Press, 1987). Cf. *To Reach The Unreached: A Report to the Lausanne Committee for World Evangelization by the Strategy Working Group* (Monrovia, Calif.: World Vision International, 1978). Yamamori begins his book by stating: "When the twenty-first century begins, an estimated *83 percent* of the world's non-Christian population will reside in countries closed to traditional missionary approaches. This book proposes new strategies for reaching these approximately 3.5 billion 'unreachable' people. It also proposes 'a challenging new vocation for those called to the missions field'" (p. 15).

3. William W. Wells, *Welcome To The Family: An Introduction to Evangelical Christianity* (Downers Grove, Ill.: Inter-Varsity Press, 1979), 9-10.

4. Ibid., 170.

5. Ibid., 176.

6. Ibid., 177.

7. *High School Teaching Guide* (March-May), Unit I, Lesson 5 (Wheaton, Ill.: Scripture Press Publications, 1988, 28.

8. *Adult Teaching Guide: Isaiah* (March-May), Lesson 11 (Wheaton, Ill.: Scripture Press Publications, 1988, 112.

9. Note E. Luther Copeland, *World Mission, World Survival: The Challenge and Urgency of Global Missions Today* (Nashville: Broadman Press, 1985), 27. Copeland is Senior Professor of Christian Missions at Southern

Baptist Theological Seminary. He warns evangelicals, however, that Christians represent a smaller percentage of the global population than they did in 1900; that western and communist countries have declined in Christian percentages while the Third World has expanded; that the distribution of Christians worldwide is quite uneven; and that about 13 percent of all Christians live in absolute poverty in developing countries. These "qualifying factors" of the success of modern missionary enterprises are coupled to the fact that "1.3 billion persons on this globe are inaccessible to foreign missionary presence, and over three billion are beyond the reach of uninhibited foreign missionary efforts" (p. 29).

10. "Dialogue, Love and Witness," *Eternity* 18 (August 1967): 7.

11. "Somehow, Let's Get Together," *Christianity Today* 11 (June 9, 1967): 912-14.

12. Donald G. Bloesch, "Key '73: Pathway to Renewal?" *The Christian Century* 90 (January 3, 1973): 11.

13. John E. Skoglund, "Key '73 and Modern Man," *Foundations* 16 (January-March 1973): 3.

14. Jitsuo Morikawa, "Key '73—An Incongruous Surprise," *Foundations* 16 (April-June 1973): 104. Cf. editor Skoglund's "Key '73 and Theology" editorial, pages 102-3, where he notes the crucial themes that emerged from the conference in relation to the evangelistic lifestyle.

15. Arthur F. Glasser, "What Key '73 Is All About," *Christianity Today* 17 (January 19, 1973): 13. For Harold Lindsell's comments, see "Editor's Note," 3.

16. Solomon S. Bernards, "Key '73—A Jewish View," *The Christian Century* 90 (January 3, 1973): 12.

17. Ibid., 12-13.

18. Ibid., 14. Rabbi Bernards ended his article with quotations. He wrote:

In closing, let me quote two notable Jewish scholars...Professor Abraham Joshua Heschel once observed: "If we [Jews] dedicate our lives to the preservation of Judaism, how can we take seriously a friendship that is conditioned ultimately on the hope and expectation that the Jew will disappear? How would a Christian feel if we Jews were engaged in an effort to bring about the liquidation of Christianity?" Martin Buber declared: "The gates of God are open to all. The Christian need not go via Judaism, nor the Jew via Christianity in order to enter into God.

19. Carl F.H. Henry, "Jews Find the Messiah," *Christianity Today* 17 (April 13, 1973): 28-29.

20. "Statement on Key '73," *Journal of Ecumenical Studies* 10 (Spring 1973): 389-90. The stated goals of the Key '73 program which they could not condone were quoted as follows in a footnote below their statement:

According to the Key '73 Congregational Resource Book, "plans call for a gigantic offensive in which every person in North America will be challenged with the claims of Jesus Christ" (p. 11). It envisions "every unchurched family in North America being visited by someone who comes with loving concern to share his faith in Christ. Every individual...is to be contacted. These calls will be a person-to-person sharing with some 165 million people. Key '73 will also include an effort to place the Christian Scriptures in every North American household" (p. 12). On page 79, specific mention is made of a program of "Sharing Messiah with Jewish People," using a training manual prepared by Peace for Israel, Inc.

21. Carl F.H. Henry, *Confessions of a Theologian: An Autobiography* (Waco, Tex.: Word Books, 1986), 345. Henry noted of the achievements of Key '73: "In many communities Key '73 motivated Christians simultaneously if not cooperatively to creative ways of bearing a common witness. It roused interest in what other churches in other cities were doing."

22. "The Groovy Christians of Rye, N.Y.," *Life* 70 (May 14, 1971): 78ff.

23. Billy Graham, *The Jesus Generation* (Grand Rapids: Zondervan Publishing House, 1971), 15. Cf. "Jesus Revolution," *Time* 97 (June 21, 1971): 56-63; "Jesus People," *Newsweek* 77 (March 22, 1971): 97; and "Street Christians: 'Jesus as the Ultimate Trip," *Time* 96 (August 3, 1970): 31-32.

24. Article II of the Constitution and By-Laws of the HCAA had three points:

1. To encourage and strengthen Hebrew Christians and to deepen their faith in the Lord Jesus Christ.

2. To propagate more widely the gospel of our Lord and Saviour, Jesus Christ, by strengthening existing Jewish Missions, and fostering all other agencies to that end.

3. To provide for the evangelical Christian churches of America an authoritative and reliable channel how best to serve the cause of Jewish evangelization.

25. For an extended treatment of fundamentalist-evangelical attitudes during this period, see David A. Rausch, *Zionism Within Early American Fundamentalism, 1878-1918* (Lewiston, N.Y.: Edwin Mellen Press, 1980). Chapter 7 includes an extensive evaluation of *The Fundamentals* and Hebrew Christians involved in the movement. Cf. A.E. Thompson, *A Century of Jewish Missions* (New York: Fleming H. Revell, 1901) and Elias Newman, "Looking Back Twenty-Five Years," *The Hebrew Christian Alliance Quarterly*, 25 (Summer 1940): 24.

26. "Messianic Judaism," *The Hebrew Christian Alliance Quarterly* 1 (July and October 1917): 85-86. Although those calling themselves "Messianic Jews" in the 1970s were unaware that they had not originated a new name, the name and the concept dates back at least to the nineteenth century.

27. Ibid., 87. 1 Corinthians 12:31 states: "But eagerly desire the greater gifts. And now I will show you the most excellent way." The apostle Paul then launches into chapter 13, his central chapter on "love."

28. In addition to being a minister in the Protestant Episcopal Church, Mark John Levy was the founder of the Christian Jew's Patriotic Alliance in the latter nineteenth century and had succeeded in bringing the subject of Messianic Judaism before the British Hebrew Christian Alliance in the 1890s. They "tabled" his resolution. During the same period in South Africa, Philip Cohen's Jewish Messianic Movement published the journal, *The Messianic Jew*. Cf. *Journal of the General Convention of the Protestant Episcopal Church, 1916*: 86, 128, 142, and 148.

29. Note Hugh Schonfield's letter under "Greetings From Friends," *The Hebrew Christian Alliance Quarterly* 25 (Summer 1940): 28. The letter was dated May 16, 1940, and was sent from London, England. Schonfield had high hopes that the founding of the International Hebrew Christian Alliance (IHCA) in 1925 would pull together the Jewish Christian consciousness around the world. He wrote in *The History of Jewish Christianity* (Oxford: Kemp Hall Press, Ltd., 1936) that "one of the immediate results of its constitution was that many secret Jewish believers in Jesus, including a number of rabbis, began to communicate with the executive (of the IHCA)." Schonfield confirmed to Rev. Daniel Juster, the Spiritual Leader of Beth Messiah Congregation in Rockville, Maryland, in the latter 1970s, that he had indeed been "badly burned" by the alliance and was "very bitter" over his experience after the publication of his book in 1936. He began to rethink his spiritual experience and "came to new conclusions." He indicated to the Messianic Jewish leader, Dan Juster, that Juster's faith in Messianic Judaism was "naive" and that Juster would have to someday "grow up," just as Hugh Schonfield had done. Hugh J. Schonfield died in 1988.

30. Note "Unwelcome Immigrants," *Time* 99 (March 26, 1973): 111. Cf. "New Name: The Messianic Jewish Alliance of America," *The American Messianic Jewish Quarterly* 60 (Summer 1975): 4, 6. Opposition to Messianic Judaism from a Hebrew Christian missionary organization may be seen in William E. Currie's two month series, "Messianic Judaism is Old Hat," *AMF Monthly* 80 (November and December 1975). On October 18, 1975, the Fellowship of Christian Testimonies to the Jews concluded: "BE IT RESOLVED, therefore, that the FCTJ stand apart from and in opposition to Messianic Judaism as its evolving today."

31. James C. Hefley, *The New Jews* (Wheaton, Ill.: Tyndale House Publishers, 1974), 128.

32. The doctrinal statement that undergirded the founding of Rosen's organization declared:

We believe in the Divine Inspiration, infallibility and authority of the Old and New Testament.

We believe in the Triune God and the deity of the Lord Jesus Christ, the only begotten Son of God.

We believe in His sacrificial atonement at Calvary, His bodily resurrection from the dead and His premillennial second coming.

We believe that the New Birth by faith and obedience to Christ places each believer in the Body of Christ of which the local congregation is an expression. We believe that it is necessary for the Christian to be separated from the worldly system of sin and to resist the person of Satan.

Finally, we believe in the lost condition of every human being, whether Jew or gentile, who does not accept salvation by faith in Jesus Christ, and therefore in the necessity of presenting the gospel to the Jews.

33. The Messianic synagogues in the United States and Canada number approximately 100, and they are heavily charismatic Protestant in orientation. The Hebrew Christian movement initially consisted of anti-Pentecostal fundamentalist-evangelicals, but both groups have had to learn to work together in what they view as the "cause of missions to the Jews." It is estimated that as many Christians convert to Judaism in a year as Jews convert to Christianity. The phenomenon of Messianic Jews who embrace Judaism totally as a religious system is not large, but growing. In the mean time, Rosen wrote to his Christian supporters in November 1984: "We need your prayers and help, not because we are bleeding, but because we are succeeding! I can't remember a time in my 27-year career as a missionary-evangelist when the Jewish people were more open to the gospel, or a time when conversions were more frequent. Even the increase of opposition is evidence that we are succeeding. But our very success has created our biggest problem. Because our message has been so well-received and because our particular approach has been so effective, we are stretched to the very limit of what even enthusiastic people can handle."

34. Donald A. McGavran, *Momentous Decisions in Missions Today* (Grand Rapids: Baker Book House, 1984). One evangelical magazine responded to an author who had questioned Rosen's approach to missions with the comment, "Moishe has been a good friend over the years." The mild criticism of Rosen was deleted from the article. Articles by Messianic Jews, however, were also rewritten in evangelical periodicals. In addition, *Eternity* magazine found the Messianic Jewish movement as portrayed in one scholar's article "too positive," declaring that the magazine had "historically opposed" Jewish Christian congregations. *Eternity*, however, did not oppose Rosen's Jews for Jesus. *Christianity Today* totally rewrote Daniel Juster's "Messianic Judaism; An Update" to such a degree that an editor's name had to be added to the Messianic Jewish leader's original. Juster's piece was felt to be "too controversial." Nevertheless, Moishe Rosen as a Hebrew Christian remains untainted by such editorial procedures and appears to have a more or less free reign in influencing evangelical editors, professors, and mission experts.

35. Ibid., 132. In this section, McGavran illustrates how national churches in Israel talked Rosen out of sending missionaries to Israel (only for a while, because Rosen later sent missionaries). McGavran declares that Israel was thus deprived of "far more" effective evangelists to Jews in that country.

36. Marc H. Tanenbaum, "No, They Have Forsaken the Faith," *Christianity Today* 26 (April 24, 1981): 25. Cf. John Fischer, "Messianic Jews Are Still Jews," 25; also Daniel C. Juster and Daniel W. Pawley, "A Messianic Jew Pleads His Case," 22-24 in the same issue. See Alan L. Mittleman, "Reflections on a Jewish Theology of Puralism" in *This World: A Journal of Religion and Public Life* 19 (Fall 1987): 5-13.

37. See "Torah Dispute: 2 Sides Speak Out, 1 Silent," *Los Angeles Times: Metro News Section* (March 1, 1980): 1; and "Messianic Jews Stir JDL Wrath," *Valley News* (March 24, 1980): 1. Cf. "Torah Stolen In A Religious Dispute," *Herald Examiner* (March 2, 1980): 8, and "2 JDL Members Held In Theft of Sacred Scroll," *Valley News* (February 29, 1980): 11. William Gralnick in "Report From Atlanta," *Present Tense* 6 (Summer 1979): 15, compared the Ku Klux Klan to the JDL. "What the Klan wants to do for its lower-middle class, rural, white Protestants," Gralnick concluded, "is what the Jewish Defense League did for its supporters—make them feel that somebody is fighting, really fighting, for them." In this regard, note Herbert Richardson's (ed.) *New Religions & Mental Health* (New York: Edwin Mellen Press, 1980), for a discussion by numerous scholars on the legal and psychological dangers of anti-cult hysteria.

38. David Berger and Michael Wyschogrod, *Jews and "Jewish Christianity"* (New York: Ktav Publishing House, 1978), 14.

39. Ibid., 66. *The Chosen People*, periodical of the American Board of Missions to the Jews (ABMJ), indicates that these diverse efforts of the Jewish community are having an effect. Their June, 1987 issue is dedicated to "The Anti-Missionaries." The cover declares: "All's fair in the Anti-Missionary war for the Jewish soul, a well-organized, well-funded operation. Their goal? To completely shut down the preaching of the Gospel to the Jewish people." An overview of the New York Task Force and their tactics, as well as other antimissionary agencies, is summarized; and an article about Susan, a young Jewish Christian of five years, tells of the pressure exerted upon her to go back to Judaism. Another article in the issue, "Tried By Fire" (11-12), tells of Jason and Sandra Cohen, Jewish converts to Christianity who were won back to Judaism by the efforts of Baruch, a neighbor's son and fervent antimissionary. This issue of The Chosen People even publishes "The Path Back to Judaism" (16-18) from antimissionary literature and written by a Hebrew Christian who traveled back to his Jewish faith and roots. While the periodical laments his decision to return to Judaism, it does print his article (with their response). ABMJ has changed its name to Chosen People Ministries, and near the end of this

issue gives its readers a chance to contribute to its Hebrew Christian missionary enterprise. The blank reads: "Enclosed is my gift of $_____; use it to cut through the untruth in the Jewish community and preach the gospel. If only one Jewish person hears the gospel as the result of this gift, it will be enough."

40. Rev. Herbert Links concluded his paper, "But What About the Jews?" with these words:

> My predecessor Reverend Daniel Finestone, also a Presbyterian minister, was once asked by a friend why he had chosen the name "The Christian Approach to the Jews." He replied, "Is there any other approach?"

> As a Presbyterian minister and a "completed" Jew, I earnestly pray that the subtle undermining thrust of this document is radically altered or soundly defeated and that a strong unequivocal statement will emerge affirming our responsibility as Christians to share the Lord Jesus as the Messiah with all—especially with those for whom He came—the lost sheep of Israel. I hope we will arise and implore our denomination to move in this direction.

41. "From the President," *The Chosen People* 93 (June 1987): 2. Harold A. Sevener's expanded words are noteworthy:

> In this issue of *The Chosen People*, you will read about the most serious problem facing us today: the well-organized antimissionary efforts of the Jewish community.

> Their tactics range from one-to-one friendships with Jewish believers to using the legal system to harass missionaries. They seek to cause a rift between evangelical churches and mission agencies such as ours. They hold seminars to train people how to counteract the "missionary message." And they have considerable effect.

> This is what is taking place within the Jewish community. We have had increasing numbers of Jewish people receive Jesus as Messiah and Savior. We have seen numerous Messianic congregations established. Because of this positive reaction to the gospel, there are those within the Jewish community who have now organized antimissionary groups to try and stop the proclamation of the gospel to the Jewish people.

> We are in a conflict for the souls of men. We are sowing the seed faithfully by the spirit of God, and through our missionary workers, the seed is being watered and cultivated. Yet the enemy is always present, ready to snatch that seed of faith. Never before in the history of Jewish missions has there been such an organized assault by the Jewish community on missionaries and Jewish evangelism.

> We need your prayers and your support to win this battle!

One year later, in June 1988, Michael Rydelnik of Chosen Peoples Ministries (the former ABMJ), Long Island, and Susan Pearlman of Jews for Jesus, were brought together by the Christianity Today Institute with

Jewish representatives A. James Rudin of the AJC and Yechiel Eckstein of the Holyland Fellowship of Christians and Jews to discuss evangelism of the Jewish people. Tension reigned from the beginning to the end of their argument. Their debate appears in an October 1988 issue of *Christianity Today* magazine.

42. Leighton Ford, "A Letter to Richard," in Marc H. Tanenbaum, Marvin R. Wilson, and A. James Rudin, eds., *Evangelicals and Jews in Conversation on Scripture, Theology, and History* (Grand Rapids: Baker Book House, 1978), 299-300. Both Jewish and evangelical editors felt that the letter conveyed such sensitivity and forthright expression that it was included in the volume of papers of the first national conference.

43. Ibid., 310.

44. William Sanford LaSor, "An Evangelical and the Interfaith Movement," *Judaism* 27 (Summer 1978): 339. This special issue was on "Interfaith at Fifty: An Evaluation of the Movement by Catholics, Protestants and Jews." LaSor was chosen as the evangelical representative.

45. Note "Readers Response," *Worldview* (July-August 1978): 46.

46. Vernon C. Grounds, "The Problem of Proselytization: An Evangelical Perspective," in Marc H. Tanenbaum, Marvin R. Wilson, and A. James Rudin, eds., *Evangelicals and Jews in an Age of Pluralism* (Grand Rapids: Baker Book House, 1984), 223. Cf. his "The Delicate Diplomacy of Jewish-Christian Dialogue," *Christianity Today* 26 (April 24, 1981): 26-29.

47. Blu Greenberg, "Mission, Witness and Proselytism," in *Evangelicals and Jews in an Age of Pluralism*, 236-37. The former statement is on page 230.

48. Rabbi Yechiel Eckstein, *What Christians Should Know About Jews and Judaism* (Waco, Tex.: Word Books, 1984), 320-21.

Chapter 5. Political Agendas

1. See George Gallup, Jr., and Jim Castelli, *The People's Religion: American Faith in the 90's* (New York: Macmillan, 1989), 261-65 for this quote (page 265) and the quotes above. The concluding section is entitled, "The Future Religious Makeup of the United States." These authors also summarize, in the final sentences of the book that in the 1990s "faith will hold steady, the institutional church will be not quite so firm, and the population will be more pluralistic than it is today. And Americans will continue to be unique, with an unmatched combination of high levels of education and high levels of religious belief and activity."

2. Ibid., 215-18.

3. Note Joshua O. Haberman, "Exploding Myths About Evangelicals," *National Jewish Coalition Bulletin* (June 1986): 1, 5.

4. Note Gallup and Castelli, *People's Religion,* 209. Cf. *Nationwide At-titudes Survey, September 1986: A Confidential Report Presented to Anti-Defamation League of B'nai B'rith* by Tarrence, Hill, Newport & Ryan, p. 156.

5. For a detailed analysis, see David A. Rausch, *Zionism Within Early American Fundamentalism* (New York: Edwin Mellen Press, 1980), especial-ly chapter 8, "The Gelling of Fundamentalism and the National Restora-tion of the Jew."

6. "Israel Becomes a Nation Again," *Our Hope* 55 (July 1948): 26-27. This excerpt also states: "Ten days later (as we write), it is evident that this small state has been launched in stormy waters. Regular military units of the Arab states are attacking on many sides, crying out: 'We are ready to die for Allah!' while well-equipped Jewish forces, called 'Haganah,' are defending their strongholds with steadfast zeal and this word on their lips: 'We are ready on every front!'"

7. See "Dr. Poling Answers Your Questions," *Christian Herald,* 70 (Oc-tober, 1947), p. 4.

8. "Gabriel Courier Interprets the News," *Christian Herald* 71 (Novem-ber 1948): 13.

9. For more detail on these events and others, see Carl Hermann Voss and David A. Rausch, "American Christians and Israel, 1948-1988," *American Jewish Archives* 40 (April 1988): 41-81.

10. Wilbur M. Smith, *World Crises and the Prophetic Scriptures* (Chicago: Moody Bible Institute, 1950), 171. Cf. his article a decade later, "Jerusalem in Prophecy," *Moody Monthly* 61 (October 1960): 39-40.

11. Rev. James L. Kelso's "interpretive appraisal of the Arab-Jewish conflict" follows the special news report "Jerusalem: A Third Temple?" *Christianity Today* 11 (July 21, 1967): 34. The quotations from Kelso are on pages 35-36.

12. Note "Perspectives on Arab-Israeli Tensions," *Christianity Today* 12 (June 7, 1968): 6-8. Dr. Kelso's statement is on page 7, while Dr. William Culbertson's views are on pages 6 and 8.

13. Bert De Vries, "*His Land* and History," *The Reformed Journal* 21 (April 1971): 10-11. The advertisement quotes are found on page 6.

14. Bert De Vries, "*His Land* and Prophecy," *The Reformed Journal* 21 (November 1971): 11, 13.

15. Bert De Vries, "The Palestinian Issue," *The Reformed Journal* 25 (April 1975): 10-11.

16. See Richard V. Pierard, "Cacophony on Capitol Hill: Evangelical Voices in Politics," in Stephen D. Johnson and Joseph B. Tamney, eds., *The Political Role of Religion in the United States* (Boulder, Co.: Westview Press, Inc., 1986), 83ff.

17. See Mark O. Hatfield, *Conflict and Conscience* (Waco, Tex.: Word Books, 1971). Cf. Robert Eells and Bartell Nyberg, *Lonely Walk: The Life of Senator Mark Hatfield* (Chappaqua, N.Y.: Christian Herald Books, 1979).

18. Robert Wuthnow, "The Political Rebirth of American Evangelicals," in Robert C. Liebman and Robert Wuthnow, eds., *The New Christian Right* (New York: Aldine Publishing Company, 1983), 172.

19. "Meet the Press," Sunday, October 12, 1980, National Broadcasting Co., Inc. Cf. Richard V. Pierard, "Reagan and the Evangelicals," in Marla J. Selvidge, ed., *Fundamentalism Today: What Makes It So Attractive?* (Elgin, Ill.: Brethren Press, 1984), 47-61.

20. Wuthnow, "Political Rebirth," 174. Refer to his data on pages 167-73.

21. See William G. McLoughlin, "The Illusions and Dangers of the New Christian Right," (128-29) and Stanley J. Grenz, "*Listen America!* A Theological and Ethical Assessment," (196) *Foundations* 25 (April-June 1982). This entire issue is devoted to a symposium on the New Christian Right. Cf. Michael Johnston, "The 'New Christian Right' in American Politics," *The Political Quarterly* 53 (1982); William Willoughby, *Does America Need the Moral Majority?* (Plainfield, N.J.: Haven Books, 1981), 1. Refer to pages 143ff. for Willoughby's comments on attacks on the Moral Majority by Jewish leaders mentioned below.

22. Rousas John Rushdoony, *The Institutes of Biblical Law* (Nutley, N.J.: The Craig Press, 1973), 236.

23. Greg L. Bahnsen, *Theonomy in Christian Ethics* (Nutley, N.J.: The Craig Press, 1977), 445-46.

24. "The Execution of Rebellious Children," *Calvin Speaks* 1 (July and August 1980).

25. See Meredith G. Kline, "Comments on an Old-New Error," *The Westminster Theological Journal* 41 (Fall 1978): 172-89. This is a book review essay on Greg L. Bahnsen's *Theonomy in Christian Ethics* (1977), which the Christian Reconstructionists had awaited breathlessly. They were devastated by Dr. Kline's sharp rebuke.

26. Murray Friedman, *The Utopian Dilemma: American Judaism and Public Policy* (Bryn Mawr, Pa.: Seth Press, 1985), 47. Cf. Seymour Martin Lipset and Earl Raab, "The American Jews, the 1984 Elections, and Beyond," in *The New Jewish Politics*, 33-40.

27. Ibid., 63-64.

28. Ibid., 97.

29. Herbert L. Solomon, "The Republican Party and the Jews," *Judaism* 37 (Summer 1988), 281.

30. See "Notes and News: Will the First Jew in the White House Be a Woman?" *Moment* 12 (September 1987): 12-13.

31. See "The Elections and the Jews," *The Jerusalem Post International Edition* (August 27, 1988): 11-12.

32. Peter Mull, "Profile: Neoconservatives Wage a War of Ideas," an interview with Midge Decter, *Eternity* 39 (October 1988): 41.

INDEX